A Thousand Steps to Parliament

A Thousand Steps to Parliament

Constructing Electable Women in Mongolia

MANDUHAI BUYANDELGER

The University of Chicago Press
Chicago and London

The University of Chicago Press, Chicago 60637
The University of Chicago Press, Ltd., London
© 2022 by The University of Chicago
Published 2022
Printed in the United States of America

31 30 29 28 27 26 25 24 23 22   1 2 3 4 5

ISBN-13: 978-0-226-81872-6 (cloth)
ISBN-13: 978-0-226-81874-0 (paper)
ISBN-13: 978-0-226-81873-3 (e-book)
DOI: https://doi.org/10.7208/chicago/9780226818733.001.0001

Library of Congress Cataloging-in-Publication Data

Names: Buyandelger, Manduhai, author.
Title: A thousand steps to parliament : constructing electable women in
    Mongolia / Manduhai Buyandelger.
Other titles: Constructing electable women in Mongolia
Description: Chicago ; London : The University of Chicago Press, 2022. |
    Includes bibliographical references and index.
Identifiers: LCCN 2022003329 | ISBN 9780226818726 (cloth) |
    ISBN 9780226818740 (paperback) | ISBN 9780226818733 (ebook)
Subjects: LCSH: Women politicians—Mongolia. | Women political candidates—
    Mongolia. | Political campaigns—Mongolia. | Women—Political activity—
    Mongolia. | Neoliberalism—Political aspects—Mongolia. | Mongolia—
    Politics and government—1992-
Classification: LCC HQ1236.5.M657 B89 2022 | DDC 305.409517—dc23/eng/20220214
LC record available at https://lccn.loc.gov/2022003329

♾ This paper meets the requirements of ANSI/NISO Z39.48-1992 (Permanence of Paper).

To my daughter, Eevee; to my mother, Mengetiin Buyandelger;
and to the daring and capable women of Mongolia

Contents

Abbreviations

CMTU—Confederation of Mongolian Trade Unions
DP—Democratic Party
GEC—General Election Commission
GO—Governmental Organization
LYP—League of Young Pioneers
MCC—Millennium Challenge Compact
MPP—Mongolian People's Party
MPRP—Mongolian People's Revolutionary Party
MWC—Mongolian Women's Committee
NGO—Nongovernmental Organization
PRC—People's Republic of China
RYL—Revolutionary Youth League
UN—United Nations
UNDP—United Nations Development Fund
USSR—Union of Soviet Socialist Republics

Note on Translation and Transliteration

All translations from Mongolian and Russian are mine unless the quotes derive from Mongolian or Russian sources that have already been translated into English. In transliterating Mongolian or Russian into English, I mostly used the MNS 5217:2012 standard. In it, the transliteration of the Mongolian Cyrillic Ө is Ö and the transliteration of the Mongolian Cyrillic Y is Ü and У is U. I combined MNS 5217:2012 standard with the ISO international standard in transliterating the Mongolian Cyrillic X. I used H for female words (as in HÜN) but used KH for male words (as in KHAR). However, I used the established format for published authors, such as MUNKH as opposed to MÖNH, which would comply with the systems I chose. Therefore, there will be inconsistencies in my citations in the uses of certain names. The current system of name presentation by the General Authority for State Registration of Mongolia follows the international passport format, with the last names following the first without a possessive form. While such a style is practical for international bureaucratic systematization, I adhered to the Mongolian way of presenting names: the patronym comes first, with a possessive suffix (-yn or -iin) followed by a given name.

Hillary Clinton in Mongolia

On July 9, 2012, United States Secretary of State Hillary Clinton visited Mongolia (fig. P.1). The *New York Times* reported that Clinton, along with the Obama administration, had come to view Mongolia "as a model of how democracy can be born from authoritarianism," an assessment that functioned as an indirect critique of neighboring China and nearby Singapore, countries whose leaders had argued that democratic values were possible to realize only in the West (Perlez 2012). So, rather than mention the arrest of a former president of the country prior to her arrival, which might have spoiled the image of an emerging Mongolian democracy, Clinton praised the nine women who had just been elected to Parliament—three times as many as in the previous election in 2008 and the largest number of women to win seats since the country began holding democratic elections in 1990.[1] Clinton's visit also coincided with the International Women's Leadership Forum in Mongolia, at which Clinton continued her celebration of the women who had become members of Parliament.

This book tells the story of what preceded, prepared, and often complicated candidates's successes and how their experiences inform the interdependence of gender and politics in Mongolia. Scrutiny of women's experiences in politics in a democratizing Mongolia suggests that their roads to Parliament were filled with turbulence; legal, financial, and political hurdles were set against them at every turn. Women politicians had to deal with their parties' explicit preferences for male candidates, the high financial cost of campaigns, and the Parliament's repeal of a gender quota right before the 2008 election.

The book is an anthropological exploration of women's day-to-day efforts to navigate electoral politics, to shape *electable* selves, to gather and deploy

FIGURE P.1. US Secretary of State Hillary Clinton meets with Mongolian President Tsakhiagiin Elbegdorj at the president's yurt in Ulaanbaatar, 2008. Brendan Smialowski via Getty Images.

resources, and to devise new strategies for success. It shows that at the time of Mongolia's move toward democratization and neoliberalism, women candidates had to create new selves, thereby participating in the transformation of the politics of gender in Mongolia and in the perception of women among the populace. Central to my analysis is the concept of *electionization*. I use this term to capture the sprawling nature of political campaigns, the penetration of electoral politics into everyday life, and the ways that social structures built for election campaigns have often overtaken what are usually state and community roles in governing and maintaining the country. Mongolia has become increasingly dependent on elections for basic infrastructural, bureaucratic, and organizational functions; electionization has become a fragmented, surrogate form of governing.

At the same time, as I illustrate, the populace has appropriated elections as a mechanism for dealing with the instabilities of neoliberalism and thus has transformed elections into something much greater than their intended purpose. Although I have been researching and learning about women candidates and elections from 2006 to 2020, the focus of this book is on the 2008 and 2012 elections with a follow-up on the 2016 election. The 2008 election included some of the most visibly aggressive campaigning, a sudden repeal of a 30 percent women candidate quota, and unexpected postelection violence, all of which illuminate the entanglement of gender, politics, and global capitalism. With a 20 percent quota and new design, the 2012 election had a better outcome for women. Although the quota was handy for women in the 2016 election, the efforts to improve on the achievements lost its traction. My ethnography unpacks the contexts, histories, and experiences of female candidates during the 2008 and 2012 parliamentary elections.

This anthropological account offers Mongolia as an example of how democratic elections and neoliberal projects often unfold quite differently than normative models might assume. Instead of ushering in an era of efficient and lean government, for instance, as predicted by proponents of neoliberalism, elections can reproduce a hefty form of governing based on the discretion of individual incumbents who reproduce the state that extends into a much bigger ad hoc formation than expected. Mongolia's postsocialist political formation is complex and unwieldy, as the country had embraced neoliberal "shocks" in the 1990s while also reanimating, sometimes without intending to do so, the previous socialist practices of seventy years (1921–90) and is now operating as a kind of syncretic democracy. Mongolia embraced democratization in the 1990s, not only as a method of organizing its political life but also as a new attribute of its national identity: one meant to set it apart from earlier Soviet patronage (as well as from Mongolia's other major neighbor, China) and open doors to greater representation in the international arena. Although Mongolia did not eradicate its former "communist" party (the Mongolian People's Revolutionary Party or MPRP) at the end of socialism, as did countries in East-Central Europe, for Mongolia being "democratic" has been, in addition to being a political imperative, a strong social, cultural, and economic aspiration.[2]

With democratization in the 1990s, Mongolia had a vibrant development of free press, a market economy, and a civil society and, within a decade, became a fairly democratic society. By the late 2000s, with the promise of resources associated with the mining industry in sight, the political powers began curbing some of these institutions and expressions of discontent. For instance, the state suppression of postelection riots in 2008, allegations of torture and other human rights abuses, and the death of five citizens during the riots, illustrate that democracy is fragile. Much of the Mongolian populace has been concerned about excessive corruption, governmental surveillance, abuses of power, and politicians' lack of competence and ethics.

The economic "boom" of 2009–14, which was mostly due to foreign investments in mining and the expected future revenues from that sector, brought hopes for prosperity for the middle class and entrepreneurial inspiration. However, it soon turned into an economic downfall, with the middle and lower classes scrambling to eke out shrunken livelihoods. Because the neoliberal changes were initiated mostly by the heads of Democratic Party (DP), many people have come to conflate democracy with neoliberalization, thus causing a disenchantment with democracy. There has been a rise in populism, nationalism, misogyny, and increases in electoral financing, which remains obscure. As of 2021, the Mongolian People's Party (MPP), in leadership since 2016, has gained further leverage as a way of managing the COVID-19 pandemic.[3]

Given these precarious developments in the recent past, how does democratization—both in its ideal form and in reality—inform gender politics and women's positions in Mongolia? The new era of openness, international travel, and free market opportunity has been generally beneficial to many women (as well as to many men). However, as Mongolia has enthusiastically shed its socialist past, it has also jettisoned many programs and quotas that state socialism had implemented to support women's socioeconomic and political advancement. In the days of high socialism, it had been important for socialist states to showcase women's advancement in the international arena. According to the "evolutionary" development scheme adhered to by the state, women's positions were often interpreted as one of the barometers of the country's modernity and its place in that evolutionary story. The Mongolian state invested in women because the issue was important to its more powerful allies, who evaluated Mongolia's leaders and then endorsed subsidies, loans, and friendships.

After the collapse of socialism, however, such endorsements were no longer at issue, and state leadership had no outside incentive to advance women in political leadership.[4] Echoing male-centered capitalist interests, the state's attention to women's advancements weakened even further. Thus, amenities such as subsidized daycare centers and political measures such as a gender quota for women in leadership were abandoned during early democratization in the 1990s—at least until the repercussions of such abandonment led to catastrophic outcomes and women began to demand them more forcefully in the 2000s.[5] In Mongolia, as in most former Eastern Bloc nations as well as in many other former socialist countries, the representation of women in the national parliament dropped from 25–30 percent under socialism to just 3–8 percent during democratization (1992–2004).[6] However, in 2012, due to the adoption of the 20 percent candidate quota, for the first time during the new democratic neoliberal era, nine women (almost 12 percent) gained legislative seats. In the spirit of the socialist era's showcasing of modern and progressive achievements, Mongolia's leaders supported the staging of the International Women's Forum during the visit by then US Secretary of State Hillary Clinton (see fig. I.1 in the Introduction).

Thanks to the legacy of the socialist state's push to educate women in all professions and at all levels, women constitute a greater proportion than men of the university-educated, and they often occupy important professional positions where their expertise is indispensable. However, while women are welcome in principle and by law, the practical processes and paths toward making it into national leadership are fraught with difficulties. Many obstacles turn out to be gender-specific, although they are not always visible as such from the outside. Some obstacles do not become apparent to women candidates until they are already in the midst of running for seats and campaigning. Many factors contribute to such difficulties, including that women, having been economically marginalized during privatization in the 1990s, do not command as much access to wealth as do men.

In commercialized and almost exclusively candidate-sponsored elections (fundamentally different from the fund-raising model in the United States), wealth is the prime factor. Just to give one example, according to the statistics provided by the Voter Education Center, between 1992 and 2012, the political parties increased their campaign expenditure on a single candidate by 2,295-fold (Oyuntuya 2013a). Many female candidates rely less exclusively on money but draw instead on other resources, such as their accomplishments (for example, diplomas from prestigious institutions like Stanford and Yale), the righteousness of their ideas, their reputations, and their networks, especially networks that reach into international terrain. They strive to shape themselves into *electable* selves who are perfect, polished, and irrefutable: *intellectful* or "full of intellect" (*oyunlag*), charismatic, and beautiful. Globally mediated images of women in power, such as Hillary Clinton, Angela Merkel, and even Margaret Thatcher for the older generation, along with international workshops on the empowerment of women influence the dominant Mongolian understanding of charisma and the appropriate personae for politicians. Therefore, it may not come as a surprise that some of the ethnographic descriptions I offer in this book on Mongolian female candidates can apply to women in politics anywhere. Their identities as cosmopolitan, upper class, educated, and sophisticated are just as important as their properly Mongolian identities—that is, identities related to their birthplace, language, marital status, and concern for Mongolia's future. Even as they speak Mongolian and outline their leadership plans for Mongolia, they also showcase identities that bring them closer to global leadership. This task is intriguing given the often exoticized image of Mongolia in the global imaginary of places.

In my previous book, *Tragic Spirits* (Buyandelger 2013), an ethnography of shamanic practices among the Buryat in Mongolia, I argued that shamanism was modernity's unacknowledged coeval; the spiritual was woven into the very fabric of Mongolian political life. In writing *A Thousand Steps*, on the experiences of female candidates in Mongolia's democratic elections, I needed to bring together the images of Mongolia as traditional and distant with Mongolia as populated with female politicians sporting power suits, giving speeches in the international arena, conversing with Hillary Clinton, and attending Harvard and Yale.

Indeed, it is a rather bizarre task to situate women in politics in a space that they already inhabit and have shaped and informed for decades, even if under different political regimes. I see my task here as offering an extreme form of anthropological defamiliarization. When I was growing up in Mongolia in the 1970s and 1980s, the country seemed to embody the United Nations' Decade of Women through international meetings, representations of women as educated and modern, and the promotion of women in social and political spheres. The activities that surfaced during the UN Decade of Women were preceded and then followed by various women-promoting measures as well. My mother, Mengetiin Buyandelger, was one of the first television journalists at the Mongolian National Broadcasting station (established in 1963, it was the country's only station, called Mongol Televiz). I grew up surrounded by men and women in suits and career dresses, who, I now see, occupied impressive positions: journalists, editors, directors, engineers, culture specialists, researchers, and heads of all kinds of organizations and departments. Our next-door neighbor was one of Mongolia's first camerawomen; my mother, starting in 1966, was one of the first Mongolians to carry Nikon's first SLR camera. The main journalist from the Mongolian Women's Committee, the late Ishkhandyn Erdenechimeg, was a family friend. Here, perhaps, might be one beginning of the story I tell in this book. Whenever Erdenechimeg visited, she brought the lingering aroma of Miss Dior and real coffee beans; neither had been available in Mongolian shops in the 1980s. This was a sign of international connection, and a very gendered one. Around that time, too, our upstairs neighbor, Yündengiin Erdenetuya, became chairperson of Mongol Televiz—one of the highest posts in the nation. I grew up among career women of this sort.

I naively assumed that gender equality, at least in the limited way in which state socialism had begun to implement it, would continue and improve during democratization. Instead, the new democratic system turned out to require its own kind of battle, offer its own opportunities, and have its own rules. It demanded new kinds of women and men. By attending to the everyday politics of elections and to the nuances of the campaigns of female candidates, this book describes some of the local and global dynamics that have led such voices as the *New York Times* to bemoan the "excruciatingly slow process . . . [of] securing a greater presence . . . [for] women in parliament" worldwide (Sengupta 2015). I seek to answer a question posed by the Inter-Parliamentary Union: Has the whole world hit some sort of "glass ceiling"? *A Thousand Steps to Parliament* is a map of some women's travels, both promising and difficult, toward political positions of their own.

During the years of researching and writing this book, Hillary Clinton lost to Donald Trump in the 2016 election, a result that shook the world and unleashed misogyny and sexism. Recently, when a former Mongolian MP, Ms. Tsedevdambyn Oyungerel, announced her candidacy for the 2021 presidential election, the social media feed exploded with sexist insults and defamation of Oyungerel. Explosions of violence against women and women's careers being disproportionately affected during COVID-19 along with other troubling news prove that a need to attend to gender issues at a structural level remains active.

Electable Selves: *"Every Woman for Herself!"*

Decision Events

"I think I have a very good chance of winning a parliamentary seat. I have a track record of managing winning electoral campaigns for my male colleagues," Legtsegiin Ariuna, an aspiring Mongolian parliamentary candidate, said to me.[1]

> Once, I managed a campaign on a shoestring against a much more powerful opponent. I had my team get up very early on Election Day. By the time the city woke up, my team had decorated all the neighborhoods with balloons and portraits of our candidate. We tied balloons to the gates of the voting center and hung posters with a message to vote for our candidate. It was spectacular! We took over on that last day by a small margin and that was because of me. I know how to run an election campaign and I know how to win. Everyone for whom I worked won a seat. It is now my turn to run.

As I sat on a gold and beige upholstered sofa in Ariuna's stylish new condo in downtown Ulaanbaatar, I asked her why she hadn't run as a candidate herself in Mongolia's previous elections. Why would 2008—the country's sixth democratic election since the end of state socialism in 1990—be her first time? "Because before we, women, did not feel fully comfortable doing so. But now, with the sanctioned quota system in place, requiring that at least 30 percent of each political party's candidates be women," she told me, "we feel both confident and legitimate."

"But you were running the campaigns and you knew how things worked. Wasn't it appropriate that you ran?" I pressed for more explanation. Ariuna was also one of the trustees of the Union of Democratic Women (UDW), the women's coalition of the Democratic Party (DP), which afforded her an insider's influence to become elected as a candidate. "No," she confided, while serving me homemade vegetable soup in a fine china set.

It does not work like that. It feels daunting to stand right next to your male party colleagues, claim the same space, and compete against them. In the last election, it was obvious that the men would win anyway. There was very little chance for women. You see, the legitimation of the quota not only gives us the confidence to run, but it also implies that there is at least some chance of winning a seat, that there is some acknowledgment by men that we are colleagues of equal status. Without the quota, there was almost no chance. So women did not bother running.

Despite numerous odds stacked against them—limited funds, marginalization within politics, and overall misogyny—many women in political parties were nevertheless excited about the upcoming election of 2008. And the reason behind all of this was the quota for women candidates, to which Ariuna referred and which, after years of lobbying, had been approved by the Mongolian Parliament, the State Great Hural, in 2006. It was with this legislation that women felt that they finally could realize their long-term intentions to compete for parliamentary seats.[2] Even though the women candidates were aware of the possibility that the election results could be manipulated, they were counting on the fact that the quota afforded them a political space of their own that was relatively free of such intervention.[3] In the summer of 2006, I met many women who had already been structuring their lives around their upcoming competition in the election: securing campaign financing, freeing their schedules, allocating their family responsibilities to other members, preparing their electoral programs, and critically assessing their looks, achievements, and competence for candidacy.

The quota became an impetus for many additional women to finally decide to run for parliamentary seats during the 2008 election, even though a small number of women had been elected to office in previous elections since democratization.[4] In Sherry Ortner's words, the quota was a chance to change the "institutional base of the society . . . to support and reinforce the changed cultural view" (1974, 87). Many women had hoped that with the quota, outright expressions of misogyny—especially public ridicule and denigration of women based on gender—would be subdued, and that women would be taken seriously on their own terms. The quota legitimated women's candidacy on a par with men and even animated the content of the country's first constitution, which stated these rights as early as 1924.[5] Within political parties, women finally felt validated after having been relegated to behind-the-scenes managerial, secretarial, and support work.[6] With the quota in place, women felt they did not have to resort to unofficial, ad hoc, cunning tactics in order to make up for their so-called deficiencies as women and for the lack of sufficient funds to compete against powerful male incumbents.

Many women hoped the quota would help them to compete based on their preparedness (*beltgegdsen*) and would compensate for some of the skyrocketing campaign costs. "The great thing about the quota is that the heads of the political parties are now in search of prepared (*beltgegdsen*) women to run for seats," said Natsagiin Dulamsuren, CEO of one of the new television stations who was also preparing to run for a seat. Although it was unclear exactly what being a prepared candidate meant, and each candidate interpreted preparedness in her own way, in general it was expected that a candidate would possess impressive looks, outstanding achievements and recognition, charisma, wealth, and other magnetic capabilities to get elected. *Beltgegdsen* also connotes an electable or an irrefutable candidate. I adopt *electable* as opposed to the more literal and general *prepared* because it is better suited in a context of electoral campaigns and reflects the aspirations of the women and the expectations of voters and colleagues in political circles.

By the summer of 2007, however, in the midst of preparations for the following year's election, rumors had begun to circulate about the aspirant women's lack of preparedness, and the dearth of capable women for candidacy. I started to hear that much rivalry had arisen within women's sections of the political parties over the nomination of candidates for the 30 percent quota. In the meantime, the rumors about women candidates' unpreparedness led them to further intensify their campaign preparation, as they were yet to compete to be included in the quota.

Then, in late December 2007, Parliament repealed the quota that was launched just two years prior. The timing for the repeal was chosen strategically. It was during the last session to make amendments to the 2008 election law. With no more sessions to come, the repeal of the quota could not be reversed. The women's collective lobby group launched an intense campaign to reinstate the quota and even managed to make the president issue a veto against Parliament's revocation of it.[7] Parliament approved the president's veto, but the next day many MPs found ways to vote against it.[8] Parliament then continued to ignore petitions from women's organizations and gave no solid explanation besides a rumor about a lack of prepared women.[9]

The issues about women's lack of preparedness and their internal rivalries, as I learned later, had little relevance to repealing the 30 percent candidate quota. Instead, most of Parliament was aiming to get elected as a consolidated whole (*büren büreldhüüneeree*) although it consisted of different factions (*frakts*) or interest groups of the two dominant parties, the DP and Mongolian People's Revolutionary Party (MPRP). The select leadership of the two parties were aiming to approve a mining agreement known as *Oyu Tolgoin geree* with international investment groups. After much squabbling, the government proposed 51 percent on Mongolian state equity stakes, which was scorned by the foreign mining enterprises such as Ivanhoe and Rio Tinto and other Western investors. The American lobbyists pressured the US administration to pressure the Mongolian government to eliminate corruption and even stop the Millennium Challenge Account (Bulag 2009). Various members of the public remained wary and skeptical toward the foreign investment and government.[10] In a climate of public skepticism toward foreign investment and political leadership, Parliament was motivated to keep newcomers at bay, especially the most outspoken champions of the environment, human rights, and several women candidates who were requesting the changes to the mining laws.[11]

In retrospect, some people inside the political parties dubbed the 2008 election "a mining lobby election." Chapter 2 discusses the ways in which politicians used that election to take the populace's resistance to foreign investment and skepticism toward the political leadership and turn them into compliance through a promise of a future mining share to each citizen. In this context, the 30 percent women candidate quota would have enabled the election of some women who would have challenged the decisions to approve the mining agreement.

My original intention to study the impact of the quota had transformed into a study of the circumstances and strategies of women candidates following the *repeal* of the quota. For individual women, the quota repeal was a "decision event," which are occasions when the "multiple strands of personhood achieve unity and singularity," for example, during "the overturning of accustomed patterns of intelligibility and the advent of a radically new idea" (Humphrey 2008, 357). Women were now "on their own" and without any official arrangements with which to counter the populace's patriarchal values, male-centered politics, and exorbitantly expensive campaigns. As Oyungerel, a candidate back then, said: "The repeal of the quota became a motivation for women to sharpen their campaigning skills, which was a sort of a silver lining. We also half-jokingly told each other: '*Ami amia hicheegeeree!*'" The last phrase translates as "look after yourself on your own" or "every woman for herself!" Oyungerel's words mark the beginning of the new neoliberal era of politics. In 2008, campaigning became more of an individual responsibility than was true in previous elections. In the longer run, however, it consisted of individual as well as collective actions and group mobilization.

A Thousand Steps

This book is a study of women candidates' experiences, strategies, and circumstances in running for seats in three consecutive elections—2008, 2012, and 2016—and is situated against a backdrop of Mongolians' adoption of free democratic voting. Its goal is not to evaluate electoral outcomes (for example, which electoral designs or campaigning strategies worked the best or worst and why) or to make strategy suggestions for women seeking election to national parliaments.[12] As a sociocultural anthropologist, I am interested, rather, in the day-to-day experiences of female parliamentary candidates leading up to and during elections. I reveal some of the less visible obstacles women encounter as they run for seats, and I describe their long-term efforts to shape themselves as *electable* candidates. (My research does not extend to their work once elected as members of Parliament.)

Contrary to the Mongolian women's expectation that Western-style democratization would improve gender equality, the new system has favored male-centered politics and traditional patriarchal arrangements. During state socialism, the representation of women in Parliament hovered at around 25–30 percent, but after socialism that number plummeted to 6–8 percent. This was partly because the state socialist decrees that promoted women into leadership were quietly jettisoned during the dismantling of the old regime in the 1990s. The fight for similar legislation during democratization, the candidate quota, as I described in the previous section, yielded insufficient results.

Therefore, the women candidates who campaigned during the 2008 election are of particular interest. They competed for seats at a time of rapid transformation of elections with no quota in place, with minimal help from their political parties, and in constituencies that were up to three times larger than the previous ones. The loss of the quota marked a notable setback in the transformation in the culture that feminists and (some) female politicians had been trying to undertake. Instead of competing in their legally designated space, women were now seen to be "impinging" on male space and thus invalidating their efforts even before they began. There was a demonstrated indifference to the presence of women on the part of the political parties (except for one smaller party, the Civil Will Party, headed by Sanjaasurengiin Oyun). In the 2008 election, the competition for seats became a personal pursuit among women with whatever private resources they could muster rather than the legal, official, and respectable road to Parliament they had paved but lost. This lack of official routes for women to run for seats has led them to engage in a variety of strategies against the backdrop of male-centered politics.

The quota repeal in 2007 resulted in a setback for women's competition for parliamentary seats in the 2008 election, but in the long run it also sparked the beginning of a renewed feminist call for reform. Feminists in political parties, in governmental organizations (GOs) and nongovernmental

organizations (NGOs), as well as individual artists and activists, all began explicitly addressing the lack of women in politics. They participated in various
capacities in three large-scale lobbies that took place in the interval between
the 2008 and 2012 elections. There were consistent lobbies for laws on gender
equality, laws against domestic violence, and calls to remake the 2012 election
law more favorable to women. As an outcome, many more people enhanced
their critique of the media representation of women, as well as the public
perception of women in politics (Undarya 2009, 2018). Some hopes emerged
for a positive turn.

One of the changes was, for instance, Parliament's approval of a 20 percent candidate quota for female candidates right before the 2012 election. It
is important to note that at least in the DP's case, as relayed to me by Oyungerel, the leadership approved the quota based on public opinion research
regarding the perceived electability of female candidates.[13] The report of that
study, "Women's Participation in Political Leadership" (in two parts in 2011
and 2012), claimed that between 55.7 and 62.1 percent of voters were open
to supporting female candidates. This survey research helped convince the
leadership of the political parties to endorse the 20 percent quota for the 2012
election.[14] This quota remained active and helped thirteen women to win
seats in subsequent elections in 2016 and 2020.

That survey and the report were part of an effort to gain passage of the
long-overdue law on gender equality, the work on which was renewed and
expedited after 2008 and passed in 2011. The head of the National Committee
on Gender Equality at that time, Baasankhuugiin Enksaikhan, who oversaw
the work behind the gender equality law, told me about the comprehensive
"gender mainstreaming" work that informed that report. Enksaikhan had
personally lobbied individual male MPs, "knocking on their office doors in
the Parliament building and requesting their understanding." She shepherded
the law through the Ministry of Justice and even found ways to convince
some of the opposition to take a neutral stance or excuse themselves from
voting. As she told me about the mobilization of all the entities interested in
women and gender, workshops held on gender issues for media personnel,
periodic competitions for the best women-supporting and gender-equality-
promoting TV programs and journalism, and advocacy among men's NGO
groups, I formed an image of large numbers of women and some men taking countless steps along a path leading to a more gender-equal parliament.
Importantly, this comprehensive lobbying to pass the law on gender equality
impacted not only the populace's acceptance of women politicians but also
continued to motivate women candidates pursuing their dreams for political
office despite the difficulties.

FIGURE I.1. Hillary Clinton (ninth from right) with Mongolian female politicians and government officials and President Tsakhia Elbegdorj (eighth from right) during her visit on July 9, 2012, which also coincided with the International Women's Leadership Forum in Ulaanbaatar, Mongolia. Photo courtesy of Tenzing Paljor.

The title of this book, *A Thousand Steps to Parliament*, describes the long road of the female candidates I shadowed, as well as the endless steps that other women have taken in order to improve women's opportunities for leadership. Eleven female candidates won seats in the 2012 parliamentary election, a fact that, as I noted in the Preface, drew the attention of US Secretary of State Hillary Clinton, who flew to Mongolia to congratulate President Elbegdorj on this accomplishment (fig. I.1). This book is an anthropological account of the histories, experiences, and cultural strategies of female candidates running for parliamentary seats. I consider the everyday, institutional, cultural, and gender politics leading up to the event that Clinton celebrated, as well its aftermath.

Electable Selves

To craft *electable selves*, women candidates strive to rescript their gendered performance through techniques of self-polishing. Such techniques are influenced by national and transnational politics and the global circulation of institutions, images, and practices: a circuit into which their own efforts also feed back. *Electable selves* is also an abstraction of these new political subjects who are constantly remaking themselves so as to reach an irrefutable status based on their capabilities rather than on the money they can pour into their campaigns. Although the female candidates I studied have deliberately steered their resources toward and structured their lives around elections, while also learning new skills to pursue a political candidacy, they are not exclusively the products of electoral campaigning.

Efforts to become electable sometimes go in tandem with a general effort to gain "gender proficiency, [which] entails the ongoing, everyday public negotiation of moral proscriptions for being good at being a man or a woman" within a particular cultural setting (Paxson 2004, 12). In Mongolia, a woman who successfully pursued a life and career outside of politics could become an electable candidate by coincidence. For the most part, however, a pursuit of formal politics enhances a certain *habitus*—"a system of internalized structures, schemes of perception, conception, and action common to all members of the same group" (Bourdieu 1977, 86). It also encourages a mastery of particular skills and prompts an activation and assertion of certain qualities that do not always coincide with gender proficiency, especially since the qualities both for electability and for gender proficiency are ambiguous and are constantly negotiated. In tracing the evolvements of electable selves, I found it helpful to draw on literature in anthropology and history that deals, broadly, with theories of subject formation, gender and politics, and neoliberalism.

To begin, we must understand the contemporary moment by considering the *legacies* of women's political engagement during state socialism. Dispelling a dominant assumption that Mongolian women only became politically active with the advent of democratization and the influential arrival of liberal feminism in the 1990s, chapter 1 delivers a historical analysis of how the state socialist Mongolian Women's Committee shaped women as political subjects, instilling in them mass mobilization and advocacy skills and normalizing their place in politics. I offer a point of view that differs from most anthropological studies of women and socialism (Andors 1983; Stacey 1983; Gal and Kligman 2000; Kligman 1998; Valdur 2020; Verdery 1996), which analyze the impact of socialist state policies on women and gender by assessing major economic, social, and cultural transformations of the period and the socialist state's biopolitical focus on sex and reproduction.

Instead, I emphasize women as political agents as they actively fought for maintaining the Women's Committee when the male-dominated leadership repeatedly demoted the organization. The women did not retreat from the political realm but managed to negotiate their positions and were able to influence the welfare state. The multigenerational battle to preserve and maintain women's organizations expanded into a sprawling and ongoing project throughout the socialist era. By revealing this account, I also counter some of the Western liberal feminists' dismissal of the socialist women's organizations as mere arms of the state and their members as not "real" feminists (see, for example, Reuschemeyer and Wolchik 2009). Following Kristen Ghodsee (2019), Saba Mahmood (2005), and Joan Scott (2009), I show how agency operates within relationships of power both outside and inside liberal settings.

The most distinct outcome of the socialist women's work with and within the state was the normalization of women in politics, which influenced women in the democratic era.

Many women born between the 1950s and 1980s have transported a set of *habitus* that became a basis for political and other leadership pursuits for younger generations. For instance, being able to engage with diverse people, deliver speeches and presentations, being pleasant (*ayataihan*), and generally socially active (*niigmiin idevhtei*) as a community member is a basis for conducting oneself in public in Mongolia. I call this ability a *fluency in being public*, in order to convey not only a person's sense of feeling comfortable in public but also a sense of being fulfilled by the engagement. A Mongolian term, *nüür hagarsan*, which literally translates as "with a face that is out" (as opposed to "in" or "closed") describes a person who has achieved an ability to conduct oneself in public. It is used as the opposite of being shy and inhibited and usually marks reaching a threshold of culturally and socially appropriate conduct in public for a young adult. Although *nüür hagarsan* certainly characterizes the women candidates I discuss in the book, it does not grasp the women candidates' mastery and ease in interacting with a variety of people and their leadership skills. Being fluent in being public is more suitable for this discussion than *nüür hagarsan*, as it conveys action, subjectivity, experience, and naturalness of their conduct even if they might have rehearsed their parts.

For the most part, though, overall qualities that individuals develop by being members of active sociality were once supported by the state as part of a socialist upbringing that asserted the primacy of the social over the private realm. At an individual level, however, such political connotations were not significant. Rather, for girls and women, such a habitus afforded a diverse range of social and political engagements that otherwise would have been limited in a male-dominated society. Thus, when at the end of socialism, the formal structures, rules, and directives for women's support in leadership were jettisoned, the impact of these structures, such as the normalization of women in politics, remained.

For instance, Serjee was born in early 1980 and combines earlier socialist style campaigning strategies she learned from her older *sisters* in her political party with her newly trained liberal feminist sensibilities and methods of self-representation and empowerment. I follow Serjee's precampaigning activities within her political party through Michel de Certeau's (1984) lens of looking at the relationship between space, types of actions, and power. By doing so, I elucidate in chapter 4 how women's agentive tactics in a male-dominated, structurally determined space are just as important as their actions in their own spaces in shaping electable selves.

In addition to mass mobilization, assembling support groups, and using the official structures of politics, many women candidates for Parliament in the contemporary moment have turned to individualized campaigning strategies that contribute to what I describe as *electionization*, the near-total takeover of the life of the country by electoral campaigns.[15] In their effort to counterbalance the massive campaign efforts of men, aspirant women also engage in various activities of perfecting themselves into electable candidates who cannot be refuted. Collectively, I call their many ongoing strategies—of *charging their brains* (*tolgoigoo tsenegleh*), framing themselves as *intellectful* (*oyunlag*), and shaping new kinds of beautiful, feminine looks—techniques of *self-polishing*.

In pursuing all-around self-polishing and by constantly remaking their best capabilities, electable selves also echo neoliberal selves who are characterized by a drive for continual self-improvement and self-reinvention to meet the capricious demands of the market and are expected to remain flexible owing to the system's perpetual uncertainty and rapid transformation (Freeman 2014; Ong 2006; Rose 1999). However, the relationship of many women candidates with the dominant system differs from that of their neoliberal selves. Instead of playing along with the demands of ever-expanding campaigns—electionization—by competitively sponsoring theirs, many of these women strive to transcend the commercialization by framing themselves as *oyunlag* (intellectful) and by emphasizing their professional and educational achievements and high moral standards. The notion of *oyunlag*, by definition, downplays a focus on money and material pursuit, instead putting forward qualities that suggest authority on knowledge and truth. By activating the notion of *oyunlag* as their primary characteristic, electable selves are distanced from the values of the market and capitalism and work instead toward changing them. Their campaigns are anchored in creative activities and, especially, resources from *intellectful* activities and cultural capital.

Yet, these women are in a complex situation that requires tactical nuance. Elections in today's Mongolia have become spaces for inventing and negotiating additional gendered—and classed—attributes. Looks now matter even more and require styles that communicate multiple messages to various audiences from a certain kind of femininity, class belonging, and nationalism. Voters scrutinize candidates as embodiments of campaign promises and for signs of prosperity, modernity, and confidence with which they envision their own future. Fast-changing fashion makes women candidates especially vulnerable to criticism and dismissal, compared to men, who are automatically associated with politics.

In this context, female candidates strive to achieve a particular femininity that sets them apart from beauty queens and trophy wives, one that commands attention and respect. The boundaries that these women create through their looks and dispositions are not just vertical, like invisible walls, but also horizontal ones to elevate themselves. Their upward breaking away is more about creating new femininity. Those aspirations are about both the degree (for example, how much makeup) and kind (for example, dress or suit) of items used on the body. But it is also about the bodies that they shape and display. The self-polishing activities of female candidates are not only for attracting voters but are also responses to their male colleagues, who mostly view them as "stepping stones" (*gishgüür*) for their own advancements.

The performance of candidates on the campaign stage extends to their presentation in visual media, from television programs to social media and posters of all kinds. Campaign images are especially vital sites for negotiating representations of gender and politics; as such they are influential "technologies of gender" (de Lauretis 1987). Joan Scott argues that neither gender nor politics is a stable entity, but the "instability of each looks into the other for certainty"; because of this instability, there is a tendency to emphasize the naturalness of the sexes as a way of securing certainty (2019, 25). I offer an ethnographic parallel to Scott's psychoanalytic explanation and bring in how a notion of culture contributes to a rearticulation of gender. By expanding to analyze the content, hierarchy of placements and circulations, and stories of image-making, I show how the media infrastructure influences women's participation.

My examination of how gender has been remade, particularly for women, and in the domain of political participation as seen through the lens of elections, is also a contribution to the anthropology of gender as well as the anthropology of postsocialism—as object and analytic, and as an epistemological probe for analyzing societies after socialism.[16] Earlier feminist anthropologists contributed to an understanding of women's roles and power in family and domestic spheres (for example, Wolf 1960; Stack 1983). Then anthropologists deconstructed the division between public and private (Gal and Kligman 2000), arguing that this obscures those spheres of women's agency and action that lay beyond the public and that the division itself also reproduces power differentials (Brenner 1998; Leshkowich 2014; Ong and Peletz 1995). These anthropologists have shown how the "public" is implicated in the "private" and vice versa. In the anthropology of elections, for instance, Katherine Bowie (2008) examines Thai women's powerful influence on elections through their kin networks, showing how women's influences extend beyond what is considered domestic and thus blur the line between public and private.

This book offers an analysis of women's experiences in a sphere that is known as formal politics. Although I argue that electionization entails the formal campaigning penetrating the private spaces and domestic realms,

I discuss the domestic lives, intimate relationships, and family politics only when they are relevant to the campaigning experiences and strategies of my interlocutors. I chose to do so because the women I studied viewed themselves as autonomous in regard to deciding on their career choices and lifestyles and were convinced that they were not defined by men. They had different marital statuses, parenting situations, and domestic arrangements. Regardless of their situation, they structured their relationships and strived to arrange their domestic lives so that they could pursue their political goals. For example, Oyungerel divorced her (second) husband because he prohibited her from pursuing politics or any career that would make her popular in public. She subsequently married an American man who supported her career. A woman I call Serjee steadfastly pursued politics from a young age and then chose an international husband who was her "devoted fan" and helped her to cultivate herself as a politician. Since most Mongolian families tend to be "extended," from a Western perspective, with close relatives nearby and aiding domestic and childcare activities, women with younger children were able to participate in politics.

In thinking about women competing in formal politics, I found conceptual links with the works of anthropologists studying women's entry into traditionally male occupations, such as the London Stock Exchange (McDowell 1997) and Wall Street (Fisher 2012). Building on these works, this book shows how female candidates' thousand steps are entrenched in and transform the dominant models of gender and femininity. They help to dispel an earlier view that women of high status speak only in a male idiom, one that does not advance women as women (Ardener 1975). Melissa S. Fisher (2012) and Linda McDowell (1997) show that while working in largely male-dominated spheres, far from becoming more masculine (in the finance world, quintessential male behaviors are associated with taking risks and thinking about gains), women learned to perform "a classed feminine identity" that involved presenting a particular look, being thoughtful, and presenting risk-averse qualities. As Fisher (2012) argues, instead of becoming a part of the men's world, these women began to make spaces for other women. Although based on women's experiences on Western societies, Fisher (2012) and McDowell (1997) are helpful for understanding the women candidates in Mongolian parliamentary races because of the similarity in official male-centered spaces, which I explore in my next section.

Electionization

In order to recognize electable selves as subjects of a particular sociopolitical development, we must note that democratic *elections* in Mongolia have

FIGURE I.2. Voters gathered to meet their new candidates for election. Ulaanbaatar, 2008. Photo by the author.

evolved into something much bigger than and different from the "original" corresponding institutions in Euro-American settings. Elections and their attendant campaigns have expanded into structuring forces that shape the very characteristics of capitalism, gendered subjects, subjectivities, and almost every aspect of everyday life in Mongolia. I argue that *elections* as time-grounded *events* have transformed into *electionization*—ongoing *processes* that shape the society at large.

Electionization describes a condition in which electoral campaigns have penetrated all spheres of life, blurring the boundaries between public and private, formal politics and informal everyday interactions, and have redirected economic and social resources. Much of the electorate now encounters elections as more than a mechanism for choosing leadership and experiences them, in addition, as a social safety net and as opportunities to mitigate the uncertainties of neoliberalism. People from all walks of life, not just the candidates, become integrated into elections—its gig economies, social assemblages, resource circulation, and associated industries of media, entertainment, and research and consulting, to name a few (fig. I.2).

Consider the fact that Mongolia also stages presidential and local elections every four years in addition to the parliamentary elections. Between 1990 and 2020, the country had twenty-four elections, all of which used similar configurations for campaigning, resource channels, workers, and professionals.

As such, Mongolia has become increasingly dependent on elections for basic organizational functions as the institutions built for elections have become the main agents of institutionalization. Electoral campaigns have thus become surrogate forms of governing even beyond the campaign period and, instead, continue for most of the four years in between elections. Candidates fill in the governing roles by channeling resources and sponsoring welfare services and emergency measures to gain voters' recognition.[17]

Consequently, competing in elections entails sponsoring *electionization*, which means running a part of a constituency like an incumbent but using one's own funds. The financial challenge for campaigning in electionization is particularly burdensome for newcomers and for women, as about 70 to 88 percent of campaign expenditures in 2012, for instance, came from a candidate's personal funds (Oyuntuya 2013a) and electoral financing, unlike in other democracies, remains largely a personal affair. As discussed above, most women candidates strive to shape themselves into *electable* candidates as tools to overcome the demands of these kinds of commercialized election campaigns. They participate by putting forth the most valuable assets they have—the perfected versions of themselves: beautiful, *oyunlag* (intellectful), and charismatic selves that they groom from inside and outside for years in preparation for election. They also work to change politics and resist the campaigns but remain their subjects, albeit resisting ones.

Electionization in Mongolia is a consequence of several transformations. In the 1990s, the country's democratic elections also used the tiered administrative structures from the former socialist system. This made the adoption of elections efficient and fully embedded them in communal life. Neoliberalization—which entailed shrinking the welfare state and structural adjustment policies, known as "shock therapy," and included liberalization of trade and prices and shutting down state enterprises—led to massive impoverishment. Political parties, NGOs, and local administration began acting on behalf of the welfare state by presenting donations and gifts to combat poverty and economic downturns. Various assemblages emerged around elections based on kinship, locality, and interests. The rules, firewalls, and official practices that would contain elections as events, rather than as processes, however, were still in the process of being implemented. Mongolia adopted Western-style institutions, but not necessarily some of the Western notions, such as the autonomous liberal individual, the division between private and public, and a polity as a formation that is based on the rule of law. By contrast, much of day-to-day life in Mongolia, including some parts of formal institutions, depends on kinship, bartering, and other informal ways of caretaking and securing opportunities.

Hence, elections are most potent in their less visible spillover into everyday life beyond formal events, institutions, and practices. Indeed, as campaigns and other election-related practices have become ubiquitous and taken over other institutions, Mongolians have been structuring their lives and social relations around elections and seeking opportunities through them. Therefore, elections are not institution-bound events, after which society goes back to everyday operations; instead, they now overhaul social life and continue to influence the everyday after the "event." Thus, there are multiple outcomes of electoral campaigns (that is, infrastructures, networks, institutions, markets, relationships, and subjects and subjectivities) which often acquire lives of their own. Mongolians' appropriation of elections in order to deal with the uncertainties of neoliberalism makes elections more significant than a mechanism of selecting the country's next legislative body.

Therefore, this book contributes to the study of the current epoch by pointing out the impact of neoliberalism on politics beyond the market and economic consequences. It illustrates the consequences of the free market's takeover of elections, especially electoral campaigns, in the absence of the strong protection of democratic institutions. With the term electionization, I also expand the research on neoliberalism from its dominant focus on economics to include politics in a more substantive way. I show this through examples of electoral campaigns filtering, steering, and shaping many aspects of the "free" market economy as well as campaigns serving as a national stage for securing the people's consent in making decisions about large national enterprises, such as mining. The commercialization of elections affects everyday practices and social relations, new social and cultural practices, and the related development of new gendered subjects and subjectivities.

Feminisms and "Women in Politics"

This book shows how Mongolian women are now being formed by, and formative of, the symbolic meanings, networks, and techniques of elections as a sociocultural force. I expand on existing anthropological studies of voters and their agency (Banerjee 2007; Bowie 2008; Miles 1988) to show that candidates, too, have been reconstituted by a variety of internal and external circumstances and influences. Female candidates' subjectivities are influenced by feminisms, historical and contemporary, domestic as well as transnational. Even if many of the female candidates I met did not consider themselves feminists, their subjectivities were still influenced by aspects of socialist, postcolonial, and liberal feminisms. These subjectivities provide an opportunity to bring together the history of feminisms and to write a newer feminist history not only in a postsocialist mode but also in a post–Cold War, newly transnational mode.

"Feminism" does not have a Mongolian-language equivalent, and when it is used it is rendered in English. Although the word/concept is not used widely in everyday life, when it is, it refers to individuals who are working toward improving women's rights as well as to individuals, usually women, who are seeking (mostly) political power. Democratization brought feminism as a discourse, identity marker, and political consciousness to Mongolia. This articulation and understanding is new in the sense that during socialism the word feminism became often associated with the bourgeois West and was rarely used.[18] However, a state socialist feminism (which was in many ways the opposite of a Western liberal one) was widely and consistently practiced, albeit without being referred to as such.

I demonstrate here that the programs that were originated by the state socialist women's organization known as the Mongolian Women's Committee (MWC) and its predecessor organizations (discussed in chapter 1) shaped everyday politics of gender nationwide and, although taken for granted, were the most influential arrangements that shaped women candidates' political ambitions in the democratic period. Women's organizing has transformed swiftly since the end of state socialism—from centralized to pluralistic—and continues to expand and diversify. The MWC, significantly shrunken in its outreach, renovated itself for its new role as a champion for women's well-being and employment during the harsh period of capitalist transformation. Distinctly, new liberal and/or transnational feminists emerged to create their own NGOs, often with the help of international funding and feminist organizations. Initially, they distanced themselves from the views and members of the former MWC.

Within this transformation and expansion of the larger feminist landscape in democratizing Mongolia in the 1990s, a new phrase, "women in politics," stood out and quickly became widespread. Yet I was surprised to learn that in Mongolian popular rhetoric (and also in some of the topical scholarly literature) terms such as "feminism" or the "women's rights movement" rarely appeared together with discussions of "women in politics" or "women in leadership" (favored phrases in Mongolia) and vice versa (see, for example, Lawless and Fox 2010). I soon noticed that the terms "feminism" and "women in politics" and their synonyms flag distinct topics, projects, and associations not only in Mongolia but elsewhere as well.

"Women in politics" is used mostly within international programs that are aimed at research and capacity-building and in GOs and NGOs that provide training and support for women aspiring to leadership positions.[19] It appears that at least one origin of the term "women's empowerment" or "women in leadership" is related to the United Nations' International Research and Training Institute for the Advancement of Women (UN-INSTRAW), which was established in 1979 at the recommendation of the first World Conference on the International Women's Year in 1975 in Mexico. For the second conference in 1980, the conference report emphasizes that the Institute urges all specialized agencies "to assist the Institute in carrying out training and information research programs on the needs of women" (United Nations 1980, 100). The third conference report states that governments and NGOs should support programs that are designed to improve circumstances for women in decision-making and managerial positions (United Nations 1980, 87). Finally, in the declaration that came out of the fourth World Conference of Women in Beijing in 1995, we encounter phrases such as "women's empowerment" and "access to power" as well as the following objective: "Increase women's capacity to participate in decision-making and leadership" (3 and 83).[20] Following the Beijing 1995 conference, the Beijing +5 meeting in 2000 and the Beijing +10 meeting in 2005 discussed a need for stronger, more precise language and coined the term "women in decision-making" (Krook and True 2012).[21]

Since the Beijing 1995 meeting, the United Nations (UN) has been sponsoring numerous programs administered together with local NGOs and GOs for capacity-building, empowering women, and gender mainstreaming. It also launched the Millennium Development Program, which provides grant funding to nations that meet goals of gender parity. A goal tailored specifically for Mongolia is to increase the participation of women in politics and decision-making.[22] UN programs on empowering women in Mongolia work with organized entities, the state, NGOs, and political parties, and thus tend to enforce (willingly or not) the tenets of those most organized women's movements (if not state-based). The language of these organizations and programs uses phrases such as women in leadership, women's empowerment, and capacity-building but rarely mentions the word "feminism."

Indeed, the connotation of the term "feminism" varies worldwide, depending on the historical and political circumstances of the practices and movements associated with it. For the purposes of clarity, let me use US feminism as a foil for comparison. For instance, the term "feminism" in the US context is different from its meaning in Mongolia, owing to the political circumstances during the time of its application. Among the scholarly and lay public in the United States, the word "feminism" evokes not so much state and international organizations as movements outside and, in some cases, against the state and top-down entities more generally (see Jaggar 1994 and Weston 2002). Importantly, these outside movements have sometimes been able to influence Congress and other governing bodies by lobbying. Many US feminists, however, do not always consider the women who are pursuing official power within political parties as central to feminist movement politics as such, because their primary loyalty is not to feminism but to their parties and other goals. Kristen Ghodsee (2014) critiques such Western feminists for discrediting the feminists in the former communist/state socialist regimes such as in East-Central Europe and for imposing a Western-centric understanding of feminism. This separation of true feminists from others might be useful and acceptable in the United States, where movements from the outside historically have been efficacious.

By contrast, as political scientist Monique Leyenaar (2004, 22) has noted, in Sweden and Denmark, the large number of women in politics has followed from their involvement in feminist movements of the 1960s and 1970s. They have framed their projects both inside and outside the state, working to revitalize their presence not only as feminists but also as political party members. In many countries, however, movements existing outside of official institutions have often not achieved as much influence as their members would like. Hence, for instance, in former socialist countries like Mongolia, women had to gain power within the state in order to leverage their feminist projects.

In postsocialist democratizing Mongolia, "feminism," operating from outside and in opposition to the existing structure, and "women in leadership," working inside party systems, are not divided the way they may be in other places, as is true in much of the US context. Many women in politics have also been members of civil society.[23] Yet, the new feminists in the postsocialist period in Mongolia combine ideas derived from feminist movements in the United States and Europe, from First- to Third-Wave feminism, and some values from discourses on "women-in-politics." As such, the new Mongolian feminism has many grassroots features: it operates from the ground up, is inclusive, collaborates with gay and lesbian groups, remains independent of the state and political parties, and addresses issues of human rights, sexual harassment, and domestic violence—none of which were concerns during socialism. The "women in politics" discourse in Mongolia, meanwhile, tends to address matters such as the legal and institutional representation of women, parliamentary quotas, women's training for political offices, and breaking the glass ceiling. Besides women who belong to political parties, different women participate in this discourse, including feminists outside of the state.

While there are tensions and disagreements among the various actors of these groups, there is also a great deal of cooperation. Indeed, civil society has influenced the circumstances for female candidacy and supported women in politics, whereas women in Parliament have been crucial in passing legislation on gender equality and domestic violence drafted by members of civil society. Thus, in the Mongolian context, female candidates do not fall into an exclusive category of "women in politics" that pertains only to upper-class elites but are related to the larger feminist movement in the democratic era, which, in turn, is influenced by the legacy of socialist organizing and mobilization.[24]

My ethnographic and historical research in Mongolia contributes to feminist anthropology by highlighting how the same terminologies come to vary in meanings owing to specific social conditions and cultural differences, as well as differing assumptions about those terminologies. Saba Mahmood's (2005) critique of Western feminists, whom she argues often conflate agency with freedom (her case is women's engagements in the Islamic revival in Egypt), is also applicable in the Mongolian context. We need not demand that all women have canonical liberal agency and "free will" in order to speak of their practices as being in the service of women's needs and desires. Working within the state does not make them mere vessels for false consciousness. Scholars in political science, sociology, and other disciplines have been examining the low representation of women in national politics throughout the world. They have been discussing, for instance, the effect of formal and institutional strategies such as quotas, pipelines, education, electoral designs, and globally circulating campaign management strategies pertaining to the advancement of women.[25] Anthropology contributes to this inquiry by showing the cultural, social, and local specificities that give shape to these strategies and their outcomes. Ethnographic research is especially crucial in a place like Mongolia where institutions, laws, and processes are still evolving, unlike in established democracies, where institutions have been channeled into more-or-less predictable trajectories and tendencies.

Ethnographic research in political anthropology shows that Western notions may take on entirely different meanings when imported to a new place (Nugent and Vincent 2009; Paley 2002 and 2008). For instance, the concept of democracy in Mongolia, at least initially, has been understood as a freedom to pursue new opportunities rather than as a set of institutions and values like those in the West (Sabloff 2013). In a more specific context of women's advancement in politics in Mongolia, for instance, a notion of "pipeline"—a path from a local-level nomination all the way to a parliamentary candidacy—is not as reliable as one might expect because of unstable politics. Thus, being in a pipeline might be less consequential than trying to generate more opportunities in unpredictable domains. Even more culturally specific, a candidate's lengthy time in a pipeline, especially one starting from a low-level position, might work to the disadvantage of her reputation. In cases in which women have started out as assistants to male politicians and then moved to higher positions, people tended to suspect that the woman, even after achieving the higher post, remained in the shadow of a powerful figure and thus did not attribute her power and authority to her credit as they did to other women of comparable standing. Even higher education for women does not lead to political empowerment in a straightforward way.[26] In electoral campaigns, textbook-style strategies tend to become routinized against individually crafted and locally specific tactics. I argue that because, in the Mongolian context, female candidates have managed to find their own ways of campaigning against both misogynistic culture and commercialized elections, they make legible new kinds of feminist interventions both inside and outside the state.

On Research

The research for this book unfolded over three different phases: preliminary research during nonelection time in the summers of 2005–7; participant observation during the 2008 and 2012 elections; and follow-up research on the 2016 election. (However, this book also draws on my earlier engagement with Mongolia as I had conducted my first research during the period from 1996 to 2004.) Each phase stands as its own portion of the research while also influencing the other parts. The importance of studying women candidates resides in the fact that they are no longer limited to token numbers but now represent sizable numbers, such that they "form parts of encompassing culture" (Herzfeld 2000, 228).

During my preliminary research over the three summers of 2005–7, I attended meetings organized by the Mongolian government, NGOs, and international organizations. Many female candidates were NGO leaders or affiliated with the NGO world. Their affiliation proved useful for their electoral candidacy not only because civil society provided another body of support but also because the political parties saw the women candidates' reputation in civil society as a useful currency. However, due to the international funding agencies' requirement for NGO members to be free of political affiliation, the NGO affiliation often alienated the women candidates from their political parties. I discuss how women candidates strive to remedy such a disadvantageous position.[27]

It was also during this period that I learned how the implementation of the 30 percent women candidate quota had intensified the latters' "self-polishing"—individualized activities to perfect one's physical looks and intellectual capacities. Although most women candidates were already engaged in self-perfecting as a necessary part of pursuing recognition in their chosen fields, the elections led them to reach for new thresholds in transforming themselves much beyond what they imagined before. For many candidates and aspirants, "campaigning" extended well beyond the formal stump speech, the fleet of media appearances, and the scheduled meetings with voters during the official campaigning period. That "campaigning" lasted all four years between elections and fed into the condition of electionization. By shadowing several female candidates for six months preceding the 2008 and 2012 elections, I attended campaigns daily and began to discern the details of how elections function as cultural and political assemblages not just for producing candidates but also for producing gender.

My second, and main, phase of research took place during the two consecutive parliamentary elections: six months of participant observation in 2008 and six months of participant observation in 2012. I carried out the bulk of the research in the capital city of Ulaanbaatar, with several trips to various provinces, where I shadowed the women candidates during their campaigns as well as conducted interviews with voters both singly and in focus-group settings. At the beginning of my research on the 2008 election I juggled several campaigns and attended select events from each of several candidates. As the campaigns evolved, however, I had to focus exclusively on one candidate. That is, I shadowed one candidate's full-time campaign regardless of her plans and schedules, even if that meant that I would miss events in other candidates' campaigns.

Focusing on one candidate's campaign was not enough. The simultaneity of electoral campaigns posed another challenge to ethnographic research. Even a campaign of just one candidate had multiple components that ran simultaneously, and it was easy to miss something crucial or remain unaware of the rest of the campaign while I followed a candidate herself. After becoming well acquainted with more than twenty female candidates, I devised a tiered system of research and trained four full-time research assistants to work as volunteers for candidates in their campaigns. I also had one research assistant collect and record materials from broadcast media, campaign advertisements, and major newspaper coverage. Let me explain this three-tiered approach.

Level One involved focused participant observation with a number of key candidates in various parts of the country and at varying stages of their campaign. Among these women, Radnaagiin Burmaa, a candidate from the DP, was the primary interlocutor I shadowed on a daily basis for several weeks leading up to and during the official campaign in May and June 2008, from 9:00 a.m. and often to after midnight or until 3:00 a.m. for most of the period.[28] (Before shadowing Burmaa in April and May, I had shadowed Saldangiin Odontuya.) My research assistant, Nerguigiin Baasanhuu, conducted participant observation on the everyday functioning of Burmaa's campaign office and volunteered as an assistant to the campaign manager. Together with other volunteers, she distributed the candidate's media to the constituency, prepared meals and delivered them to the advocates, organized meetings, and collected information.

Level Two of my research involved three research assistants whom I trained and who worked as assistants to three additional female candidates' campaigns: Jurmediin Zanaa, an independent candidate; Chimediin Bazar, a journalist and candidate from the Civil Will Party; and Sanjaasurengiin Oyun, an incumbent and the head of the Civil Will Party. My research assistants accompanied the candidates daily, attending campaign meetings and fund-raising events, working as staff members by distributing candidate materials, and operating as observers during voting and counting. I met with all my research assistants weekly in an informal discussion group and they compiled reports of their observations at the end of the elections.

For *Level Three* in my tiered research approach, I mostly conducted interviews and made short visits as opposed to full-fledged participant observation. I extensively interviewed several female candidates from various political parties, including some well-known women in politics (Tsedevdambyn Oyungerel, Chimediin Bazar, Manjaagiin Ichinnorov, Shagdaryn Battsetseg, Tögsjargalyn Gandi, Natsagiin Udval). My methods in learning about these women's experiences were eclectic compared to my full-time shadowing of women candidates in levels one and two. While I have not included every candidate's whole story in this book, each candidate added to its thematic and analytical aspects in her own way, whether she confirmed a feature that is relatively consistent among female candidates or added something unique.

My interlocutors also included media personnel, researchers working for survey, polling, and media-monitoring companies, administrative staff in constituencies, and independent consultants known as *piarshik* from PR (public relations). Many of the consultants preferred to remain anonymous. I also interviewed voters extensively. Some interviews were in groups, including more than twenty focus-group interviews, while others were individual interviews. Most of the time I combined the two styles. In addition to usual fieldwork material such as interviews, notes, and material items, I have collected extensive television footage on elections.

If during 2008 I concentrated on the "outside" performative aspects of the campaigns, during the 2012 parliamentary election I delved into the "inside," often hidden, politics of elections and political life in Mongolia at large. I studied the making of the electoral laws, forces behind main events and transformations, and the nuanced mechanisms of elections. I traced the internal politics of political parties and interviewed influential political actors. Overall, from 2005 to 2012, I observed the outcomes of many changes in legislation and electoral rules, the women's movement, and female candidates' transformations. My method in this book depends greatly on detailed tracking of the lives of women who are at once exemplary, broadly representative, and unique.

In 2017, I did follow-up research on the 2016 election. The updates that I obtained reconfirmed that the elections remained as an all-encompassing driving force for the economic, social, and cultural lives of almost everyone I met, including people who were not associated with political parties or electoral campaigns. Nevertheless, many people were structuring their lives and planning changes (sometimes as drastic as migrating to another country or changing their jobs and professions) based on the outcome of the 2016 election and in anticipation of the next one in 2020. Astonishingly, some of the most well-established men and women—the people I would associate with relative independence from mercurial electoral politics—could not contain their emotions as they told me about the election. Many burst into tears because they had lost their livelihoods or were humiliated by other party members because they were not members of the winning party. They role-played various scenarios from the 2016 election, commenting critically on events, and passionately relaying their feelings, experiences, and thoughts on them. Elections have turned into electionization and now rule the country and shape subjects and subjectivities.

I studied select members of the two major political parties, the DP and MPRP, which split into Mongolian People's Party (MPP) and MPRP in 2010, as well as those of several smaller parties, especially the Civil Will Party.[29] The DP was developed from a coalition of numerous smaller parties that emerged following the end of socialism in 1990. Its main principles are, according to its webpage, freedom of expression and individual conviction, and building a society that is based on democracy, a market economy, and human rights.[30] The MPRP (or MPP from 2010) defines its main principles as social democratic and its values as national independence, freedom, integrity, safety, and peace.[31] The two parties' formal self-descriptions are not dissimilar and neither contrast with or contradict each other.

In practice, however, the members of these two parties tend to position themselves against each other in regard to their values and dispositions. In particular, the DP members I met have commented on the MPP's hierarchical structure and the closed and formal nature of its meetings, and praised their own meetings as open to all members and took pride in their party's internal democracy (*dotood ardchilal*). In contrast, the MPRP/MPP members commented on DP's structure as somewhat chaotic and less organized. In my personal experience I found the DP members more open and casual. Many MPP members were eager to help as well, although initially they appeared reserved and formal.

In addition, different kinds of archival work were rewarding in their own ways. I was able to locate a good deal of material on the quota battle, including some from the parliamentary archives. Socialist era decrees on promoting women, the issues of the periodical *Mongolian Women*, and memoirs and biographies, especially a three-volume collection of letters, reminiscences, and interviews by Gerelsuren and Erdenechimeg (2014) were crucial for brushing the official history published during socialism against the grain. I treated these sources, especially the official history books, not just as sources, but also as products of a particular regime of power that enabled certain languages while disabling others. Such reading permitted me to discern, in the obscure language of the party-state, women's agencies and works that might otherwise be effaced or erased. By doing so, I was trying to identify what Ann Stoler calls "the pliable coordinates of what constituted . . . common sense" in excluding the agencies of the Mongolian people from state publications (2009, 3). Writing a history of women's experiences under the socialist state was a bit like assembling an incomplete jigsaw puzzle. It meant comparing official events and dates against oral histories and memoirs. It involved locating women's agency in the past and tracing a kind of "feminism" during state socialism, which I argue should be understood as part of a larger project of nation-building and formation of the welfare state in a domestic realm as well as a part of the transnational world of feminist movements in the international sphere. I consider the archival and historical work I have done to be not only a source of data but also a contribution to Mongolian women's history. With this historical research I also argue that the socialist era political upbringing of women has been crucial for contemporary women's participation in democratic elections. The women have been conditioned for political offices before they were influenced by liberal feminism. They continue to update themselves in a new system that presents them with little support but many obstacles.

Two Unique Elections

The two elections, in 2008 and 2012, differed in design and, subsequently, in their outcomes. Mongolia has had a seventy-six-seat Parliament since 1992. Most elections were based on seventy-six single-seat constituencies and votes were cast according to a majoritarian system, which means candidates get elected by receiving the most votes. All Mongolian citizens who are eighteen and older have a right to vote.

The 2008 election was one of the most challenging for women candidates. First, in addition to the quota repeal, the revised election law had transformed the seventy-six single-mandate constituencies into twenty-six constituencies with multiple (two to four) mandates. The enlarged constituencies required more money for campaigning. Owing to the limitations in campaigning in person, the 2008 election candidates heavily utilized media to expand their outreach, which further escalated the costs.[32] Second, the campaign period was also shortened to three weeks (previous election cycles had varying but longer periods), which prevented newcomers from sufficiently introducing themselves to the voters.[33] Incumbents, on the other hand, were already receiving free screen time by default as MPs. Third, because the enlarged constituencies had multiple mandates, officially, the competition took place among different party members as well as among members of the same party. However, according to some female candidates, the actual competition was not as clearly party-based. Male candidates, even those from competing parties, found ways to strike alliances in the process of campaigning (if not before) and win seats among themselves while often excluding female candidates of their own parties.

In retrospect, the election of 2008 was the most pronounced gatekeeper that secured much of the power of the then-ruling groups and thus especially enabled them to move forward in 2009 with the mining agreement that was furnished during their incumbency (Chaney and Stanway 2010). Unlike any previous elections, this one was followed by a postelection demonstration on July 1, 2008, which quickly turned into riots and the government's violent suppression of such. This was the first time the country had experienced a violent riot and also the government's first use of ammunition to combat agitation since the 1930s. I discuss this in chapter 5 in the light of how the riots and abuses were seen by political actors.

The electoral system in 2012 was different from that in 2008. Some legal and cultural improvements were made in terms of women's participation. For instance, the constituencies were restored to their previous numbers, from twenty-six larger constituencies to seventy-six smaller ones. This meant that the candidates had better opportunities to reach out to voters in person as opposed to relying mostly on the media. The election law was also revised by Parliament on December 14, 2011, to switch from a majoritarian to a mixed-member proportional vote, which helped women to get elected not only directly by voters but also through their party lists.[34]

Mongolian lawmakers have disparate opinions about which of the two electoral voting systems better suits Mongolia. The majoritarian vote (employed in the 2008 election and in most others) polarizes political parties (and voters) and it is the most cumbersome for women candidates to compete in. A mixed-member proportional voting system is better for women and new candidates, and it was employed in 2012. However, it creates fractions within the parties by mixing up different party members and undermines the centralized power of individual political parties. After much debate among legislators and political parties, the law of the 2016 election switched back from a mixed-member proportional voting system to a majoritarian one. This change denied an opportunity for women to get elected through their party lists.

Chapter Outline

CHAPTER 1: LEGACIES

The first chapter dispels the widespread assumption that Mongolian women became politically active only with the advent of democratization and the uptake of liberal feminism in the 1990s. By exploring how generations of women during socialism worked to get the male leadership to recognize women's roles in the nation and to promote women-friendly policies, I trace the development of women as active political subjects. These socialist legacies have been crucial for women's campaigning during the democratic period.

CHAPTER 2: ELECTIONIZATION

Elections in Mongolia differ greatly from their counterparts in Western countries. I explore the ways in which parliamentary elections have been transformed from time-bound events to a perpetual structuring force—electionization. Elections now govern everyday life, shape subjects and subjectivities, and continue as a sociopolitical formation in flux. The populace has appropriated electoral campaigns as new opportunities and safety nets that help mitigate the instabilities brought about by neoliberalism. Sponsoring electoral campaigns, therefore, means participating in ad hoc governing, which presents new obstacles for women candidates as financing remains murky and largely a private affair.

CHAPTER 3: SURFACES

Chapter 3 sheds light on the depth of the relationship between gender and politics. I take the reader to the campaigns on the streets of the city of Ulaanbaatar and to the television studios. It theorizes the motives behind the explosion of portrait posters and how the gendered world of campaigns is recreated through visibility and invisibility. Drawing on Joan Scott's (2019) insight that anxiety about leadership instability in democracy recreates gender inequality, the chapter illustrates how such inequalities get reified through the notion of culture. Gender inequality persists despite women's active embodiment of valuable cultural traits, such as education and skills, as male politicians capitalize on essentialized and "primordial" notions of masculinity.

CHAPTER 4: BACKSTAGE

I take the reader to the backstage of elections, focusing on the precampaigning that informs the official campaigning on stage. I follow a candidate who creates her campaign base by making exchangeable nonmonetary capital that allows her to enter into political negotiations with her superiors. By complicating Michel de Certeau's (1984) concept of strategy versus tactics, I provide a lens with which to view what I call affective and architectural ways of navigating the rigid and oppressive hierarchy of the male-dominated establishment.

CHAPTER 5: *INTELLECTFUL*

This chapter explores how, through being *intellectful*, women candidates attempt to imagine politics differently. Their envisioning sometimes challenges the social forms of electionization but is also shaped by it. In contrast to chapter 4, where women campaign from within the party, here the women's strategies arise both from within and outside of their political affiliations. Although held in high esteem as a concept, being *intellectful* has subtle and paradoxical limits in the context of campaigns that substitute for some functions of governing, charity, and the private sector. And while political groups covet these women and use them for their advancement, they also tend to keep these women at a distance, lest their extraordinary skills undermine the groups' own power.

CHAPTER 6: SELF-POLISHING

I explore how "self-polishing"—a set of practices geared toward making perfect electable candidates—generates particular kinds of postsocialist subjectivities for female candidates, subjectivities informed by contesting and complementing global, national, and local forces associated with new gender identities. Through self-styling—largely through enhancing their looks via wardrobe updates, voice training, and beautification techniques—these women strive to command the attention of voters, a distinction that sets them apart from other kinds of famous women. In contrast, inner cultivation, also a part of self-polishing, is meant to bring them closer to voters by displaying their caring and down-to-earth lifestyle-improving skills. I have structured the chapter around individual women candidates who engage in these strategies of self-polishing against the conflicting views of electability held by voters and the political leadership.

CONCLUSION: THE GLASS CEILING AS A LOOKING GLASS

The Conclusion distills the main findings of the study in the sphere of gender transformation, political systems, the structures of democratic elections, and their overlaps. It emphasizes the obstacles for women in politics and their impact on the society at large and asserts that the very practices and processes of campaigning and gaining power have become socially legible and broadly influential "technologies of gender," to borrow Teresa de Lauretis's (1987) formulation. The Conclusion reminds us how the new cultural and social practices in the context of electionization can become a form of domination.

Thus, *A Thousand Steps to Parliament* examines the making of electable women candidates as they come head-to-head with commercialized campaigns and male-centered politics in a new neoliberal era of politics and free democratic elections. Their efforts are geared toward transforming external circumstances through quotas, passing legislation, and educating voters, as well as toward improving internal conditions such as the state of their own bodies, minds, and identities as particular feminine subjects. By treating their bodies and minds as infinite, pliable, and renewable, these women employ some of the neoliberal practices of self-polishing in order to achieve new feminine identities with which to contest the commercialized elections. The thousand steps of these women in Mongolia point us toward the paths to representation that are being taken by women around the world, and are yet to be trod in many other national legislatures. Their efforts reveal that individual transformations are insufficient and that there is an urgent need to deal with neoliberalism encroaching on democracy and women's achievements at national and global levels.

Legacies: Gender and Feminist Politics under State Socialism

Fluent in Public

In March 1925 the chairwoman of the Women's Section (a part of the Mongolian government's Propaganda Department), Sukhbaataryn Yanjimaa, gave a scathing presentation at the MPRP's Central Committee meeting. The goal of the national women's organization, she argued, was to disseminate a new ideology of the socialist state and also to educate women and to release them from backwardness. To achieve these aims, the organization should be its own entity and not a part of the Propaganda Department. Yanjimaa requested resources for the Women's Section and approval to expand its outreach (Gerelsuren and Erdenechimeg 2014, vol.1). Making convincing presentations was one of Yanjimaa's numerous activities as a revolutionary, feminist, and a politician who became the acting president of Mongolia in 1953–54.

This presentation marks many beginnings for the development of women's political subjectivities, and for transformation of gender at large, for generations to come. As a result, the Women's Section (a part of the Propaganda Department) was expanded into the autonomous "Women's Department" with its own budget and administrative personnel (Gerelsuren and Erdenechimeg 2014, vol.1; Nordby 1988, 98; Shirendev 1969, 16). The meeting issued a decree to start a periodical, *Women's Thoughts* (Batchuluun 1982; Gerelsuren and Erdenechimeg 2014, vol.1:8), and allocated a budget to invite a mentor from the Women's Section in the Soviet Union. In 1925, a member of the Comintern, Vera Tarantayeva, arrived in Mongolia as an advisor to the country's Women's Section. The Central Committee also approved a budget for schools, cultural events, and other educational activities for women (Gerelsuren and Erdenechimeg 2014, vol.1).

Yanjimaa argued for these resources, as her goal was the "emancipation" of women by including them in newly emerging "public" domains: schools, work units, social gatherings, and political organizations. Her ambitions went beyond those of the state, which was preoccupied with ideological control of women against the menaces of Buddhism and imperialism but had little interest in empowering women.

This chapter illustrates how, by incorporating women with the new political sphere, Yanjimaa and subsequent leaders of the women's organization shaped women as public persons and political subjects, normalized women's presence in the society, and fought for women's space in political arena. These leaders' actions and goals have been transmitted to succeeding generations. Learning about the actions of earlier women leaders helped me understand many of the characteristics of the contemporary women political candidates, especially a set of habitus I call "fluency in being public"—the multitude of ways of engaging with a diverse group of people and communicating one's social and political stances through one's words, symbols, body language, and other culturally specific means.

Since the nation's democratization in the 1990s, women's "capacity-building" workshops and centers for women in politics—all from abroad—have proliferated in Mongolia. Many of these workshops were organized by new political parties in Mongolia, initiated by UNIFEM (United Nations Development Fund for Women) and other international organizations, especially, by Western-funded NGOs. These actors as well as many Mongolians viewed women's interests in running for office and their preparedness as outcomes of these workshops. These workshops were certainly helpful in helping women to improve their professional appearance, speaking ability, and conduct, especially in the capitalist media-saturated world where candidates must rigorously compete for the attention of voters.

However, as I spent time with female candidates while they mobilized followers, gave speeches from podiums, mingled with each other, and persuaded voters—I saw that they were not just the products of capacity-building workshops, candidate training, and campaigning in the style of Hillary Clinton. They were carrying over some of the embodied practices of being in public—the legacy of socialist political upbringing to some degree—to the new political system. Many of these women grew up as leaders: class captains, youth leaders, winners of talent shows, and in general, having above-average social participation (*niigmiin idevh saitai*). Having worked for the campaigns of their male colleagues, many possessed fluid expertise in successful campaigning in the light of the country's unstable political milieu. Many international workshops were useful for learning about formal textbook layouts of campaigning but helped little with the current Mongolian situation given the political and cultural differences that did not accommodate the rules that worked elsewhere.

A workshop in the summer of 2007 is a good example. An American, Sara Simmons, who had been a Deputy Director of Strategy for California Governor Arnold Schwarzenegger's 2006–7 election campaign and a Director of Strategy for John McCain's 2007–8 presidential campaign, came to disseminate campaigning strategies for female candidates in Mongolia. After many women aspirants dutifully attended the long hours of Simmons's lectures, I overheard them say that although the workshop was very interesting, it was not applicable to the Mongolian situation. "She just does not know our situation," some women said, nodding to each other in a knowing fashion.

Simmons was all about sticking to a campaign plan. She focused on time management with a shared calendar, set division of labor among the staff, firm budget allocation—all basically dedicated to relentlessly and orderly bulldozing through the campaign period. Simmons's plan was devised for a stable politics with established and time-tested laws. But things worked differently in Mongolia because the laws and their implementations were still being worked out. There were many gaps and ambiguities to navigate. Unlike societies based on the rule of law, in Mongolia, laws compete and contest with customary structures of kinship, locality, and face-to-face encounters, even though the electoral laws and mechanisms in place try to diminish the influences of the latter. Most of the women attending Sara Simmons's workshop were aware that in such an unstable political environment, an individual's prowess, charisma, and skill at "being fluent in public" had potential to influence the system. In contrast, following the rules did not always lead to success.

Despite the enthusiasm of the women in pursuing political offices and the overall advancement of women in society, Mongolia at large has been male-dominated both during socialism and democratization, albeit in different ways. During socialism, leadership positions were regularly occupied by men, even though the state supported women in education and the workforce as a part of governing in a form of biopolitics. Starting in the mid-1950s, the politburo took note of a lack of women in leadership despite their skills and expertise and issued decrees to appoint women to higher positions, with the Mongolian Women's Committee (MWC) overseeing all operations. The MWC's presence served as an inspiration for women and a symbolic security point that kept the overt expressions of misogyny at bay. With democratization, despite women's high hopes, the new system ended up being just as male-dominated and in some respects even more so than state socialism. The decrees on promoting women from the socialist state were jettisoned quietly in the 1990s, and reinstating the quota in the new democratic era proved to be highly problematic. With each step the country has taken toward neoliberal capitalism, gendered inequalities have increased at almost all levels in everyday life, including income and wealth disparity.[1] Electoral campaigns, which, unlike in other places, remain clandestinely and privately funded, favored more men—who had already benefited more from capitalism in building wealth—than women. Such changes had consolidated politics in the realm of men and further marginalized women.

There was no shortage of ambitious women aspiring to run for office despite the many obstacles associated with male-centered politics.[2] Women's socialization, especially during socialism, was conducive to women's aspirations to participate in society and even compete for leadership positions. In fact, some aspirants and candidates specified to me that running for seats—*ner devshih*, a Mongolian phrase for the term that literally means to elevate one's name—was something they felt compelled to do because they liked being recognized in public. They felt excited receiving nominations in a large auditorium, giving public speeches, directing their followers and supporters, and meeting voters, among other things. A sense of being validated, included, and capable, the gendered discriminations notwithstanding, is one of the key political subjectivities of women who seek political seats.

In terms of what constitutes subjectivity, I found Sherry Ortner's definition of subjectivity, which emphasizes the dialectical aspect of the term, most suitable for the purposes of this study. Subjectivity is the "state of mind of real actors embedded in the social world, and . . . cultural formations that (at least partially) express, shape, and constitute those states of mind" (Ortner 2005, 46). The Mongolian examples also illuminate Ortner's argument about "subjectivity as the basis of 'agency,' a necessary part of understanding how people (try to) act on the world even as they are acted upon" (2005, 34). I trace the working of subjectivity into agency through concrete examples of actions of the women's organization from within state socialism.

A female candidate on the stage is a continually refined buildup of various struggles and subjectivities as well as institutional and societal transformations. It is necessary to ask: What were the historical and contemporary circumstances of these women's political ambitions and their fluency in being public? What were the socializations, ideologies, and experiences of these women that helped them to withstand misogyny and disregard the looming sexism in their surroundings? How did they subscribe to the rhetoric of gender/sex equality? These questions are important because these women candidates come from different backgrounds, from very well-off to relatively humble, and thus they did not become candidates exclusively due to the privileges that would have come as a part of their backgrounds. But many of these women came of age during late socialism or experienced socialism's legacies during earlier democratization in the 1990s. Many women had the chance to embrace the rhetoric of equality or its legacies, gain fluency in being public, and experience some of the effects of women-promoting policies. These skills and aspirations have proven handy during democratization and neoliberal capitalism.

Undisclosed Agents

By exploring the legacies of socialist-era women leaders, I argue throughout this chapter that contemporary women candidates' political subjectivities stem from women's multigenerational efforts to advocate for themselves and find space within the patriarchal socialist state, which, in turn, has been influenced by women's political actions and aspirations. More specifically, I argue that the legacies of the long-term mobilizations of Mongolian women to carve out a space within state socialism and influence male-dominated politics had a crucial impact on their political subjectivities that continues to affect how they perform as political subjects in a new postsocialist context.[3] The Mongolian Women's Committee (MWC 1924–90) led the socialist feminist undertaking.[4] I contend that the MWC's efforts to institute structures and legislation, as well as its ideological work of advocating women's professional advancement, led subsequent generations of women to aspire to leadership positions. This socialist legacy of women as active political subjects has been an important, although overlooked, platform for fashioning the new women politicians of the democratic era since 1990.[5]

With the above argument, I dispel two assumptions about Mongolian women and gender politics held mostly by Western liberal feminists and international organizations. The first assumption is that Mongolian women became politically active only with the advent of democratization and the introduction of liberal feminism in the 1990s, having been inactive under state socialism (1924–90). The second assumption is that women's organizations during socialism were only the handmaidens of the state and did not produce any tangible outcomes for women. This chapter demonstrates, contrary to these two assumptions, that the work of the MWC during state socialism was crucial in shaping the political subjectivities of women and making them a socially and politically engaged group. Women's political motivations endured even when the official rules and structures of promoting women, which included the national legislature and leadership in all institutions requiring 30 percent representation by women, were jettisoned with the end of

state socialism in 1990. Despite a lasting impact, the achievements of socialist women's organizations tend to be seen as empty propaganda or simply
as things of the past, not only by some Western feminists but also by many
younger-generation Mongolians, as with the advent of democratization the
latter were overtaken by a dream of building a new and better society free
from former socialist influences. Some assumed that democracy as a formation is inherently a more gender-equal formation than the socialist one. In
other words, the socialist women's achievements have been looked down
upon internationally and even domestically.

Kristen Ghodsee (2019), an ethnographer of Eastern Europe, also notes
that Western liberal feminists disparage socialist women's organizations as an
arm of the state and do not see the women as real feminists because they
argue that feminism can exist only outside of the state (see Funk and Mueller 1993 as an example of such an approach). Anthropologist Saba Mahmood
(2005) explains that the disdain of Western liberal feminists' toward similar successes by women operating outside of the liberal setting stems from
a theoretical misunderstanding—conflating agency with resistance. In her
ethnographic work, she shows that Egyptian women are agentive while
participating in the Islamic mosque movement. She relocates agency from
the Western democratic setting that assumes a space outside of the existing
power relations into a context of power relations in which women may gain
a place. If Ghodsee (2019) and Mahmood (2004) situate agency in undemo-
cratic settings, Joan Scott looks at agency in a Western democratic setting.
She argues that having agency does not imply that individuals exercise free
will (1991, 793); rather, subjects' "agency is created through situations and statuses conferred on them." According to Scott, power relations, then, are a
precondition for both becoming a subject and acquiring agency. "Becoming a
subject," Scott (2009, 47) explains, "meant being placed in certain positions in
relationships of power (men and women, teachers and students, workers and
employers . . .) and through that positioning acquiring agency—agency . . . as
an attribution of traits and responsibilities upon which subjects are expected
to act."

These authors' insights help us to understand the skewed conceptual
lenses through which many in the Euro-American West view places like Mongolia. At the end of the Cold War in the 1990s, Mongolian women were pre-
sumed to have few if any political rights and to understand little about their
status as citizens and gendered beings. Several Mongolians who worked for
international women's NGOs in Mongolia since the end of socialism have
noted to me in conversation that international staff, usually with little knowledge about the country, assumed ignorance on the part of the "natives" and

tended to attribute the insights and achievements of Mongolians to their own outside training and influence. A bias against socialism, Orientalism, a sense of superiority in an age-old colonialist fashion, and ignorance about different feminisms continue to feed misconceptions about and disregard for the outcomes of socialist gender politics by some academics and specialists from the Euro-American West.

Anthropologists Susan Gal and Gail Kligman (2000) shed additional light on the Westerners' bias against socialist feminisms. They note that "observers— from both East and West—have made infamous the gap between image and practice in state socialism, between what was said, what was done, and what was experienced" (2000, 6). The gap seems jarring because in capitalist societies the gap between discourse and practice has not disappeared, but the development of the public sphere, the plurality of voices, and capitalist mass media tend to obscure this fact. In contrast, during socialism, the disjuncture seems stark because of the absence of plural voices that would, in a capitalist society, fill up the space between expectation and reality (2000, 6).

I see the gap between rhetoric and reality as a conceptual space for women's aspirations toward equality. This might be idealistic on my part. However, even in the context of the Western—and therefore less fervent—world, feminist historian Joan Scott (1996) argues that abstract principles about the equality of the sexes or about the promotion of women were not meant to be a reflection of real life but represented much more than that. An abstract principle needs "to stand outside specific political contexts, as a universal principle, so that it can be invoked as a check on specific abuses of power. The tension between [a particular historically circumscribed condition] and an enduring universal ideal cannot be resolved; it is what gives the concept its ethical and practical force" (Scott 1996, 165). Abstract principles create "the ethical space between an ideal of the autonomous pursuit of understanding and the specific historical, institutional, and political realities that limit such pursuits" (1996, 177).

Scott's argument is also applicable to the conditions in Mongolia, as the abstract principles had created the ethical space that gave women the opportunities to negotiate with the male leaders of MPRP for a more expansive understanding of women's needs and positions, to come up with policies to realize those ideals, and to find inventive ways to overcome the obstacles that came from the state itself. The state's procedures for promoting women were embedded in its ideological and practical concerns. In order to keep the population under its influence, the socialist state had to include them in its policies and prove to them that they were better off than they would have been in most other places. This also meant that women's achievements and positions were mostly contingent upon the structures, resources, and value systems the state provided.

The abstract principles of the equality of sexes survived the collapse of socialism. During democratization, the importance of women in the nation's new development, and their capacity to lead modernization projects, boosted their confidence and ambition. The women influenced democratization especially by building one of the most important new sectors: the civil society. This was reminiscent of the ways in which women initiated new jobs that overlapped with the state policies while at the same time proposing policies to serve the needs of other women. Contrary to Mongolians' own desire to eschew much of the socialist history in order to build a new society, and contrary, too, to the neoliberal assumption that the end of socialism and transition to democratization marked a decisive break from the past, democratization has, in fact, been rooted in the legacies of state socialism (Buyandelgeriyn 2008). Revealing the Western denial of agencies and achievements that the Mongolian women had accumulated before democratization (or attributing them largely to liberal feminism) is necessary for continuing to decolonize anthropology and women's studies.

Both the state and the abstract principles tend to be overlooked and sometimes disparaged by Western liberal feminists. However, they may have forgotten about one of the most important measures the US government undertook as an official commitment to equality in the 1960s: "In 1961, at the behest of Esther Peterson, head of the Women's Bureau in the Department of Labor, President Kennedy established a Commission on the Status of Women" (Scott 1981, 28). Fifty state commissions were created in 1963. Further, in resistance to the defeat of a resolution against sex discrimination and in a climate of officially endorsed equality, a more radical feminist movement emerged (1981, 28). This movement was obviously different from that in socialist/communist states in that it flourished in multiple directions as different strands took on lives of their own. Nevertheless, as in Mongolia, the success of the feminist movement in the 1960s in the United States is owed to its forgotten official endorsement by the government and to the role of the abstract principles under which the government acted.[6]

Furthermore, Kristen Ghodsee's (2019) study of the socialist women's movement further demonstrates that the establishment of a Commission on the Status of Women in the United States was a response to a much more organized and assertive international feminist movement led by the national women's organizations of socialist countries. The socialist women's organizations argued against delineating women's issues separately from the state, economy, colonialism, class, and race. Because socialist feminism was much more radical than liberal feminism, and women saw their role as working with men together on all other issues, the United States found it too menacing. Hence the president's office stepped in in order to advance the women's commission in the United States to prevent the spread of socialist ideologies there (Ghodsee 2019). This history of the reinforcement of feminism in the United States due to the influence of the socialist feminist movement yet again highlights Scott's (2009, 47) notion of a subject as stemming from being a part of the relationships of power from which these subjects acquire agency. Liberal feminists and their followers tend to attribute their achievements solely to their own struggles outside the state while forgetting its enabling influence. Conversely, when it comes to socialist women, they see the power of the state but little of the agencies of the women. It is hard to blame them entirely if we recognize that they are also the subjects of different types of power—capitalism, patriarchy, and Cold War politics, among others.

In what follows, in the process of maintaining and expanding the MWC and its predecessor organizations in the face of male state leaders, women emerge as agents in the society and in politics. Mongolia is a distinct example of how women continued their engagement in the political sphere against the leadership's pressures to withdraw from politics after winning the socialist revolution and dealing with subsequent crises. Unlike in many places, where women's conditions backslide following a more elevated status during mobilizations for revolutions and wars, Mongolian women were able to maintain their role in political and social life following such events.[7] The MWC did so by continually reinventing their identity based on the changing goals of the nation, by taking responsibilities in various spheres of national development, and mobilizing women in its initiatives. Being a part of the transnational network of socialist women's organizations added to the development of political agency of women and influencing national and international politics.

Women in Presocialist Mongolia (Pre-1921)

Exotic warrior princesses, autonomous queens (Weatherford 2011; Sarantuya 2012; Shuudertsetseg 2011), de facto rulers, and free noble women with rights to property (Humphrey 1993) dominate the scholarly and popular representation of Mongolian women.[8] Little known during socialism's rule within Mongolia, such images, and sometimes actual historical figures, became known to the Mongolians themselves during late socialism and the democratization of the country. In contrast, for much of its socialist past, the state rendered presocialist women as victims of exploitation of the feudal system and as an uneducated and backward class that lived at the bottom of a premodern establishment.[9] Some foreign accounts published during that period were, at least in part, responses to these propagandistic—although not entirely untrue—representations from the socialist period. For instance, William B. Ballis and Robert A. Rupen (1956) argue that even in presocialist Mongolia, women had important decision-making and economic roles in their households. Throughout the country they rode horses and in some places both married and unmarried women had relative sexual freedom, and their parents usually welcomed their unmarried daughter's children. Women's resourcefulness, however, as Ballis and Rupen (1956, 236) note, is not an indication of their equal status.

There is little research on ordinary women during the presocialist period, especially when Mongolia was a tributary state of the Qing Dynasty (China) (1691–1911). Buddhism (Lamaism) has been a dominant religion and treated women as inferior to men (Bawden 1968). The scant mentions of women in archival documents from the Qing period tend to be legal complaints about women or instructions on their punishments (Kaplonski 2014). The circumstances of women did not improve during the brief period of Mongolia's autonomy following the end of the Qing Dynasty in 1911 and before the socialist revolution in 1921. They were mentioned in the legal code only as subjects of prohibition and regulations in order to ensure someone else's rights (Kaplonski 2014, 80). For instance, to ensure the proper behavior of lamas, women and girls were prohibited from living in the monastery-city or capital, Niislel Khuree (2014, 80).[10]

Women lived everywhere else, including in "*Naimaa khot*" (a "trade town"), a densely populated, bustling center near the prohibited monastery-city with international entertainments and services, including some American (Tsolmon 1995) but mostly Chinese and Russian businesses. The town provided something akin to a public space where the elites, artists, and merchants—including women—gathered for meals and tea to discuss politics, read poetry, and watch performances. This was, however, a small portion of the Mongolian population, which was otherwise mostly nomadic and, at the turn of the twentieth century, numbered fewer than a million people.

Outside these centers, in the sparsely populated nomadic countryside, social gatherings took place in marketplaces and monastery compounds (there were over 750 such compounds throughout the country before their destruction in the 1930s) during local festivals and ritual gatherings (Kaplonski 2014). Although women were free to attend most of these events, it is hard to speculate on the extent to which herder women who watched after livestock and cared for young and old family members could attend these services, even if they were free to travel.

While a generalization, it is mostly true that much of Mongolia, for most of the period from the thirteenth through the nineteenth centuries, was patriarchal as well as patrilineal, and patrilocal. Marriages were exogamous and were usually arranged by parents when the children were young, although sometimes parents considered their children's romantic interests. Yet most marriages were known as *bogtloh* ("marriage-by-capture," either literal or symbolic). Monogamy was the norm among the general populace, while noble and aristocratic men were free to, and sometimes expected to, be in polygamous marriages. In the nomadic areas, people tended to follow gender-organizing rules through their management of living space, division of labor, and bodily movements.[11] Women were mostly responsible for the household matters, and men tended to the matters related to trade, travel, seasonal relocations, and social networking.

Women's domestic influence varied according to region, the economic status of their families, and their relationships with their natal families. On average, most women exercised influence, if not power, through their children, especially sons, and their natal kin, and by controlling the household economy. Overall, during the prerevolutionary period, there were complex forms of agency and subjectivities as women negotiated Lamaism, patriarchy, marriage, and kinship relations.

A Department of One's Own (1924–32)

The socialist revolution in 1921 gradually brought Mongolia under the influence of the Soviets and Mongolia became the second socialist country after the Soviet Union. The new government in Mongolia made immediate efforts to involve women in the revolution, enrolling them in formal education, and beginning a program of political instruction. The government planned to win over the population from the Buddhist influence that had dominated the country's spiritual and socioeconomic life for the previous three hundred years (Kaplonski 2014, 79–80).

Behind what is seen as the government's support of women, however, there were also a few very active women who were part of the feminist movement that was taking shape in Europe, Russia, and parts of Asia. They became members of the Mongolian People's Revolutionary Party (MPRP) in 1924, attended the second meeting of the Third International in 1921, and met and consulted with Clara Zetkin, who was the Head of the Comintern's Section for Women.[12] The Mongolian women leaders also corresponded with G. D. Kasparova, a Soviet feminist who worked at the Comintern and who informed them about international changes (Gerelsuren and Erdenechimeg 2014, vol. 1:5).

The first version of a national women's organization, known as the *Emeg-teichuudiin Tasag*, or Women's Section, was formed on March 19, 1924. It was formed in the Central Committee of the MPRP as a part of the Propaganda Department. As Judith Nordby notes, "it was to be responsible for the political enrollment and education of women, the promotion of literacy and general education for women, and women and children's health and welfare" (1988, 97).

In a few months, the country's first Constitution (1924) announced equal rights for men and women (Part One, Article 11), on November 26, 1924, and gave both men and women the right to vote and to be elected to all governing institutions, including the then parliament (Part Two, Chapter 4, Article 34) (*The Constitutions of Mongolia* 2009). The establishment of the Women's Section and the declaration of equal constitutional rights were two achievements that gave women legal and political rights to influence the state from within its structural and ideological limits.

The Women's Section's first set of goals in 1924, besides literacy and political education for women, included the promotion of women into the Party, labor force, public service, and the military; organizing female factory workers into unions; eradicating prostitution; and educating women about health and hygiene, infant care, and nutrition, and about household economy. The MPRP's focus on the political uplift of women was in part influenced by trends emanating from Russia. The Bolsheviks had organized a Women's Section of the Communist Party well before the Revolution in 1917 in order to persuade women to take their side and not to support the counterrevolutionaries (Wood 1997, 30).

Similar to their Soviet counterparts, the Mongolian Women's Section wanted to be more than the propaganda outlet of the state. It aimed to improve women's conditions in the country as well as to take part in international events. "International Women's Day has been celebrated since 1924 and delegates were also sent to Moscow. In 1927, three female members of the Party visited the Soviet Union to take part in the International Women's Day celebration, [and] . . . visited factory facilities for women such as canteens and nurseries" (Nordby 1988, 99). Upon their return, they pressured the MPRP to embed women's issues within the Party agenda. In a similar fashion, the Women's Section came up with plans for improving women's conditions—not the other way around—and it sought approval, funds, and resources from the MPRP, thus expanding the welfare function of the state to women.

The relationship between the MPRP and the Women's Section was not always smooth, due to the contestation in regard to identity and the role of the organization. For instance, the first head of the Women's Section, Damdinii Pagamdulam (1924–25), was a feminist educated in Western Europe who openly spoke about eradicating marriage-by-capture, prostitution, and enrolling women as members of the Party. She was banished within a year of the start of her leadership.[13] The next head of the Women's Section, Sukhbaataryin Yanjimaa (1925–27), introduced earlier, was no less radical. But as a widow of the revolutionary commander Damdinii Sukhbaatar, she was not easily removed from her position.

As mentioned at the beginning of this chapter, Yanjimaa transformed the Women's Section—a part of the Propaganda Department—into the Women's Department with its own budget and personnel in 1925. Even then, the changes that Yanjimaa and other women envisioned were new and difficult to implement, and the organization's staff was small. In the beginning, women were slow to join the Party: there were only twenty-four female party members in 1924, but by 1928 there were more than one thousand female members (Nordby 1988, 97–99) out of approximately 11,400 total party members (in 1927) (1988, 185). The number of women in the temporary schools organized throughout the country increased from twenty in 1924 to almost 2,000 in 1931. Even when women joined the Party, however, they had to deal with "indifference to their presence since it took the men some time to get used to the idea that women could be literate, educated and contribute to the public life" (Nordby 1988, 98). Many women were caught between more traditional demands of remaining in domestic occupations and the new socialist government's propaganda that urged them to join the MPRP and the Revolutionary Youth League and to participate in social activities.[14]

Nevertheless, Yanjimaa (and other leaders) inspired women and shaped their political subjectivities. For instance, Jargalyn Sosor remembered her first attendance at a public meeting back in 1925, when she was ten years old, which she recounted in her 1974 interview for *Women's Thoughts* magazine and which is republished in Gerelsuren and Erdenechimeg (2014, vol. 3:17). At the meeting, Yanjimaa got up on a wooden stage and said in a clear voice:

> So, comrades . . . for centuries, we, women have been the slaves to men and servants to the house. Thanks to the Revolution and the People's Party, we are now free, like men. It is now time to pursue literacy.

Inspired by Yanjimaa, Sosor enrolled in a women's school at her Province center in 1931. There, she met two women in charge of overseeing women's matters at the local branch of the MPRP. In 1938, Sosor became a coordinator at the MPRP section in her Province and then a vice president of the women's organization. At that time, the Central Committee of the MPRP passed a resolution to elect women's representatives in each provincial district. Sosor's task was to elect these representatives from the most distant areas in order to "release them from backwardness" (Gerelsuren and Erdenechimeg 2014, vol. 3:17). According to Sosor, already by 1930, the state's policies had begun to shape women by making them into not only recipients of its services and followers of its directions but also active participants (2014, vol. 3:17). Sosor's enthusiasm resonates with the content of the media of that time. In 1931, in the women's periodical titled *Working Women* (previously *Women's Thoughts*), a woman named Dar'zav wrote an article titled "Women Should Become National Leaders." Already back then she argued that women should constitute 20 percent of leadership and 50 percent of the administration in all organizations (*Working Women* 1931, vol. 21, no. 1: 3–5, as cited in Batchuluun 1982, 99).

The amount of work that the Women's Department set to carry out was astonishing. By working closely with the MPRP and the Revolutionary Youth League (RYL), it established branches all over the country within administrative units (of provinces and districts) as well as in state farms and collectives, in factories, and in other enterprises. Through women's annual congresses (open to both members and nonmembers), the Women's Department disseminated information about its goals and instructions for organizing literacy campaigns and schools (Nordby 1988, 98). The list of the Women's Department's proposed plan from 1925 included the following:

> Make many women literate
> Recruit into the MPRP, the RYL, Confederation of Mongolian Trade Unions (CMTU)[15] (*Mongolyn Üildverchnii Evlelüüdiin Kholboo*), and Membership of Collectives, and have women run in all kinds of elections
> Supervise regional branches of the Women's Department
> Devise plans for further work
> Elect and send delegates [presumably to regional branches]
> Organize meetings [presumably regional]
> Organize meetings among managers/heads
> Organize all work related to women's interests, and child-related work
> Establish hospitals, birthing homes, and infant and child-care centers
> Use media for propaganda among women
> Send women to schools [might be professional schools beyond basic literacy]
> Recruit women to work in factories
> Organize literacy schools
> Establish (in collaboration with other organizations) an orphanage
> (Gerelsuren and Erdenechimeg 2014, vol. 1:8).

The groups' leaders worked especially closely with ordinary women at the local level. The instruction brochures for these leaders required them to read and explain articles in the periodicals to local women, make presentations, teach literacy, help women to enroll in more advanced schools, make posters, establish sewing and knitting groups, and involve the most active women in their organizational work (Gerelsuren and Erdenechimeg 2014, vol. 1:9). While the Women's Department operated as part of the state, it also fought for ways for the state to benefit women. Almost all the state leadership was male and little attention was paid to women's issues. It was the Women's Department that advocated for women's rights and, importantly, for including women in the structures of the state and its policies. It was critical that the Women's Department had capitalized on the state's attempt to incorporate the populace into its ideological domain by encouraging women to become active in a newly emerging political sphere from the early days of state socialism. It was the necessary beginning of the development of women's political subjectivities, especially in the form of being public persons, which would last beyond state socialism.

Restrategizing: From Propaganda to Workforce (1932–59)

Despite the achievements of the Women's Department (or perhaps because of their success), the MPRP demoted it back to a Women's Section of the Propaganda Department in 1932 (Gerelsuren and Erdenechimeg 2014, vol. 1:12). Among the reasons for downgrading, the MPRP might have emulated the Bolsheviks in the Soviet Union who critiqued feminism as a bourgeois movement (Wood 1997, 30). Moreover, the Women's Section in Moscow was liquidated in 1930 because the Communist Party declared that women of the Soviet Union had achieved political and civilian proficiency and thus no longer needed such an organization (1997, 212).

The MPRP had little interest in ensuring women's rights and the equality of the sexes, especially since women were no longer a priority or a threat to the revolutionary government. As Chris Kaplonski (2014, 83) writes, despite promises to build nurseries and other facilities that would allow women to work and participate fully in political life, by 1940 there were only six kindergartens in the entire country. The Women's Department also could have been demoted as part of the overall loosening of the leftist (prosocialist) politics in response to the 1932 civil war—an organized resistance to expedited collectivization, confiscation of property, and suppression of religion.[16] The state had to backpedal and no longer needed the Women's Department for its propaganda. All these changes suggest that women's issues were not the concern of the MPRP unless they were aligned with other—in the view of the male leadership, more important—interests of the Party.

Notably, the Women's Section responded to its demotion by proposing initiatives to reach the goals of the MPRP (Gerelsuren and Erdenechimeg

2014). In the 1930s, the Mongolian state was launching Soviet-style industrialization but experiencing a severe labor shortage. In contrast to these memories relayed by the women interviewed by Gerelsuren and Erdenechimeg (2014), the official history textbooks published during socialism (Bira 1984; Lhamsuren 1985) do not mention the labor shortage or women's contributions. Instead, they note an expansion in industrial development (Bira 1984, 431–38) and the increase in the number of skilled workers from 3,000 in 1934 to 10,000 in 1939 (Lhamsuren 1985, 196). We learn from Gerelsuren and Erdenechimeg (2014) how the post-1932 Women's Section redirected its efforts from the political education of women to training and integrating them into the workforce. Industrialization required skilled workers and trained professionals.[17] A large part of the mostly nomadic pastoralist population of about 800,000 people needed to become an industrial working class.

The labor shortage must have been further exacerbated by ongoing violence. The new government eliminated the rightists (procapitalist) in 1929. Then, in 1932, the rapid leftist attempt to expedite the socialist reconstruction culminated in civil war. This was accompanied by the purging of the Buddhist clergy, aristocrats, intelligentsia, ethnic minorities, and anticommunists in the late 1930s (Kaplonski 2014). As a result, almost 40,000 people were eliminated (5 percent of the total population) (Atwood 2004, 68). In some settlements (the ethnic Buryats, for instance), men were persecuted almost in their entirety, and thus women had to work on the state and collective farms (Buyandelger 2013). Despite the widespread desolation from decades of violence, the state continued to expand its construction and development projects (see Shirendev 1969). It promoted women into the labor force in order to increase productivity rather than to empower them.

In 1938, the state promoted the Women's Section back into the Women's Department, reviving all of its thirteen provincial branches (Gerelsuren and Erdenechimeg 2014). The RYL, CMTU, and other branches of the party were also expanded and strengthened (Shirendev 1969, 359–60). The demand for labor created an opportunity for the Women's Department to expand its outreach and to come up with new projects, such as the following:

> Train women [vocationally]
> Help with job placement in factories and other enterprises
> Provide social welfare for working women
> Ensure the involvement of women in the implementation of state policies
> Organize cultural and social events during free time
> Organize evening literacy workshops and hire teachers from among
>   school graduates (Gerelsuren and Erdenechimeg 2014, vol. 1:11).

The number of women in paid employment, which included workers in industry and also in bureaucratic institutions, increased from just seven in 1923 to 2,697 in 1940 (Gerelsuren and Erdenechimeg 2014, vol. 1:11). Through its activities for involving women in the labor force, the Women's Department reframed itself as a valuable apparatus of the state. It presented its works and aspirations as fulfilling the demands of the nation.

Many feminists in the West argue that women's increased participation in the workforce in totalitarian countries was a form of oppression, as it was not based on women's own choices (for more on this discussion, see Gal and Kligman 2000). From this perspective, the Women's Department involving women in the workforce could be seen as antifeminist.[18] However, in a totalitarian regime with endemic state violence, any deviation would be purged. This was the case, as we saw above, for the first head of the Women's Section, Pagamdulam, who advocated for radical rights of women, only to be banished from her post, and then spent her remaining years hiding from persecution (Nima 2009). Six different women then took turns carrying out the work of the Women's Department between 1925 and 1932. Such a quick turnover, if nothing else, suggests a turbulent period for the organization.

Thus, contrary to Western feminists' claim that women's organizations during socialism were the mere handmaidens of the state, I argue that the women's organization in Mongolia were shaped by its efforts to deal with the male-dominated leadership. It is the struggle to maintain the organization as a platform for women's actions against the leadership's disregard for it that created a legacy for later generations of women politicians and normalized the presence of women in politics. While the Women's Department encouraged women to step into the workforce, it also forced the state to acknowledge these women's value, reward them, and provide support. This was important, for, through its involvement, the Women's Department ensured that the extraction of women's labor that the state was intent upon would benefit not only the state but also women themselves. Furthermore, by making itself useful through initiating jobs on its own and with the approval of the state, the Women's Department revived itself from demotion. Its initiatives were within the framework and expectations of the state, but at the same time, by doing projects that it initiated itself, the Women's Department also shaped the politics of gender and state socialism more broadly.

During World War II, the Women's Department organized activities to support the Soviet army with food, clothing, cash, livestock, horses, and medicine.[19] A herder woman named Tsegmid, who traveled from the southernmost Dundgovi Province in Mongolia to the front line of Sverdlovsk [Yekaterineburg] in the USSR at the age of eighteen, reported the following:[20]

A minister's car arrived to pick me up from the Province. After arriving in the city [Ulaanbaatar] as a group we rode in a car to Naushk [border town], and then by train to Moscow for nine days. Once in Moscow, we were divided into smaller groups and each went to a different front line. I went to the battlefield in Sverdlovsk with the chairman of the Central Committee Surenjav. I was almost a child and had little understanding about my way around. We went directly to the battlefield. We were distributing our gifts right on the battlefield. Planes were flying above us and we heard the canon firing. It was scary. Altogether we had 217 wagons [trains] of goods. (Gerelsuren and Erdenechimeg 2014, vol. 1).

The losses during World War II continued to exacerbate the human capital crisis.[21] The Soviet Union, ravaged from the war, needed products from animal husbandry. It imposed a development scheme that consisted of five-year plans. Mongolia's first five-year plan for 1948–52 was highly unrealistic: livestock was to increase 50 percent. The goal in livestock increase generated a need for the development of other industries, such as pastureland management, infrastructure, veterinarian and emergency services, and livestock breeding (Shirendev 1969, 524). The country needed to expand transportation, build roads, integrate new technologies, and develop communication through radio and telephone stations, and later (in the 1960s) a television station. New towns and settlements were built around state and collective farms and around industrial complexes. Both men and women were recruited to become workers, engineers, technicians, accountants, journalists, scientists, doctors, nurses, teachers, performers, architects, and other professionals to populate these new settlements. If, in 1946, 26 percent of the workers were women, in 1952 they constituted 40 percent (Ballis and Rupen 1956, 389).[22] It is no surprise then that the state promoted women to the workforce and to relatively high-ranking positions in all professions, including traditionally male-dominated fields like heavy machinery, transportation, mining, and the hard sciences.

Regardless of the state's primary intention to build the country's workforce, many women became empowered through their employment both economically and socially by building formal and informal support networks through their work units, the CMTU, and the women's organization.[23] Women leaders learned to fight for their advancement and make themselves indispensable by aligning their goals with the concerns of the state and by providing initiatives for advancing those goals. This struggle was one of the general foundations of the development of women's political subjectivities. This section illustrates how, in the 1930s, when the state no longer needed the ideological work of the Women's Department and had demoted it, women leaders refashioned the organization's program to create a much-needed workforce for the nation's growing industrialization and during WWII. In the process, the Women's Department and its sprawling nationwide branches involved local women to advocate, initiate, lead, and mobilize others.

The Power of Transnational Feminism (1959–70)

In 1947, the politburo of the MPRP eliminated all positions and branches of the Women's Department throughout the country. It appears that with women firmly in the workforce and with WWII over, the Women's Department was no longer needed for the MPRP on the scale that it was during the time of national crises and hardship. It declared that the women's organization should be not a political organization but a cultural and educational one, and its funding was not to be supplied by the MPRP but sourced from local administrations and enterprises. Thus, the Women's Department was subsumed under the CMTU in 1950 and reestablished its 5,125 branches throughout the country only to be moved to the Peace and Friendship Agency a year later and have all those branches liquidated yet again (Siilegmaa 2004). As part of the Peace and Friendship Agency, the organization was renamed the Mongolian Women's Committee (MWC) in 1958. Its responsibilities were now reduced: it no longer had the right to work with women in Mongolia but dealt only with matters related to international relations. Based on these demotions and reroutings of the women's organization, it appears the MPRP decided that the nation no longer needed a women's organization as a political and social body. Instead, it was a complimentary face for the country's international representation.

In response, the leaders of the MWC looked to their international networks to reestablish the organization within the nation. The MWC's expanded international relations appear to be partly due to the emergence of other socialist countries beyond the Soviet Union and the founding of the Women's International Democratic Federation (WIDF) in 1945 in Paris.[24] The MWC's predecessor organization, the Women's Department, joined the WIDF in 1946, and Mongolian delegations participated in the WIDF's second (1948) through sixth (1969) congresses, and, starting in the 1970s, had permanent members on the WIDF staff. The MWC continued to participate in many subsequent conferences until the late 1980s.[25] Through these participations and networking the MWC was informed about events in other countries. This international connection became key for reestablishing the MWC in the country.

The new head of the MWC, Tserenpiliin Siilegmaa, as narrated in Gerelsuren and Erdenechimeg (2014) and Siilegmaa (2004), decided to treat the 1959 celebration of International Women's Day in Malmö, Sweden, as an opportunity to revive the demoted women's organization in Mongolia. She made a proposal to the Central Committee of the MPRP to declare March 8 a national day of celebration of women. When this was approved, the MWC sent letters to all its previous branches throughout the country, calling on women to participate in the celebration. Almost every organization, school, administrative unit, and industrial and agricultural enterprise did so by organizing concerts, contests, meetings, and gatherings. Slogans, posters, pamphlets, brochures, and themed publications were produced throughout the country. The major theaters and cultural centers (for example, the Opera and Dance Theater, the Palace of Young Pioneers) staged special productions, and delegates from abroad (the USSR, the PRC, India, and Bulgaria) accepted invitations. Such work was only possible because the MWC was able to engage large numbers of appointed activists (*idevhten songuul'tan*)—women from settlements, towns, and the countryside who devoted their time and energy in the evenings and on weekends.[26]

The celebration of the International Women's Day in 1959 showcased women's achievements and contributions to the country. Through a grandiose nationwide celebration, the MWC both revived its former branches throughout the country and proved its usefulness to the MPRP. The MWC thus obtained a new structure consisting of a chairwoman (nonsalaried) and four salaried positions: a vice president, an international relations expert, an instructor for overseeing educational and cultural events, and an editor of the women's magazine (Gerelsuren and Erdenechimeg 2014, vol. 1:19). Thus by 1960, the MWC's precarious situation was over. Financed from the state budget, it expanded its operations and gained prominence in the country until the end of socialism in 1990.[27]

The MWC gained a commanding presence in the country and mobilized women by building local branches through the grid structures of the state, by engaging local appointed activists, and by leveraging the power of the MPRP. Moreover, because the MWC influenced almost every school and organization, and cooperated with other establishments like the CMTU, and the RYL, it was able to disseminate women-promoting seeds of action throughout the country, even when the organization itself experienced stagnation and setbacks.

International and global developments further enhanced the success of the MWC and elevated its status at home. The state supported MWC's international connections in the context of the Cold War and the decolonial movement in the Third World. For instance, during the IVth Congress of Women in Mongolia in 1964, Izabella Dominguez, a secretary of the WIDF, was invited to give a speech along with other international attendees (see *The Mongolian Women* 1964, no. 3:12–15). The socialist and capitalist camps were in competition to influence the newly independent nations in Africa and Asia (see Ghodsee 2019). Women in the socialist camp were seeking allies with women in the Third World against the United States and other Western countries. Mongolia, an ally of the Soviet Union, had also contributed to this endeavor as an advocate for the benefits of the socialist system. In their presentations, the heads of the MWC consistently praised women's achievements and their equal rights and positions in society (Gerelsuren and Erdenechimeg 2014). Such advocacy was also beneficial for Mongolia, as it tacitly struggled for international recognition of its independence—that it was not a part of China and not a republic of the Soviet Union, but its protectorate. In 1965, the United Nations with cooperation from the Mongolian government, organized an international Seminar on the Participation of Women in Public Life. Delegates came from all over the world, including from Cambodia, New Zealand, and Western Samoa and observers from the Soviet Union and Great Britain. The seminar discussed legal, economic, educational, and other challenges in promoting women to leadership and strategies for improving the circumstances for women's advancement (United Nations 1966). This seminar was a crucial step for women's advancement in Mongolia, as already in 1966, the politburo had issued a decree on the promotion of women in leadership. Additional decrees followed thereafter.

During the UN Decade for Women (1975–85) the MWC gained more prestige.[28] The Mongolian government sponsored women's delegations to the UN and to other conferences by socialist organizations. The list of conferences includes the 1972 Association of Asian and African Women's Meeting, the first United Nations Conference on Women in Mexico City in 1975, the WIDF, the World Congress in Berlin 1975, the International Conference for the International Year of the Child in Moscow in 1979, the meetings of the Soviet and Mongolian women's committees, and meetings and gatherings of the leaders of the women's organizations of the socialist bloc countries (Gerelsuren and Erdenechimeg 2014, vol. 3:41–43) as well as the Afro-Asian Women's Conference in Cairo in 1961 (Prashad 2007). A representative from the MWC, Norovrentsingyn Khandbaldir, was stationed as a staff member at the WIDF and served in its Asia section.

In these international meetings the women expanded their social and leadership skills, such as networking, public speaking, advocating, and presenting professional respectable selves. Trips abroad provided opportunities to acquire cosmetics and fashionable clothes, which were scarce in Mongolia. These goods acted as status markers back home, and those who displayed them stood out from the rest of the population. Those who encountered the staff of the MWC commented on their looking like "beautiful roses" and envied their rare clothes and delicate perfume (see Gerelsuren and Erdenechimeg 2014; Batchuluun 1982). People who met the chairwoman of the MWC (1962–82), Sonomyn Udval, also noted her polished and professional appearance. Udval, according to her family members and friends, was open about her investment in cosmetics and clothes and helped others to acquire them through her travels abroad.

At the international meetings women discussed domestic and international issues pertaining to colonialism, racism, oppression, as well as resistance to war and the arms race in solidarity with their sister organizations. Together, they crafted proposals and plans for actions to garner the attention of their home governments for endorsement and for inclusion in national development. As Ghodsee (2019) argues, women's organizations in socialist and developing countries did not adhere to the Western notion of feminism. They did not believe that an independent women's movement was necessary to achieve equality of the sexes. Instead, the socialist women's organizations strived to influence the state to improve women's conditions.

The MWC leaders also understood the importance of being a part of the state in order to advance their proposals and influence the male leadership. For that, they sought status and power within the state, learned to use the rhetoric of the state, and fought for the organization's expansion and recognition. The MWC's Chairwoman Udval (1949–54 and 1962–82) was also a prolific writer and one of the most famous women in the country until the end of socialism in 1990. As well as chairing the MWC, she was a chairwoman of the Mongolian Writer's Association and a member of the national assembly, the then parliament. Udval's multiple powerful posts helped to increase the status of the MWC and expand its outreach. The MWC promoted women and made their achievements visible to the eyes of the party. For instance, during the IVth Congress of Mongolian Women in 1964, the Congress sent a letter to the Central Committee of the MPRP detailing the contributions of women in livestock herding, food production, light industries, education, and medicine. The content of the letter made it clear that the nation could not be sustained without women. From milking cows for the dairy industry—one of the key industries—to running hospitals, women were the key producers (see *The Mongolian Women* 1964, no. 3:16–17). Events like the Women's Congress, the presence of international attendees at the Congress, as well as the letter to the politburo, were some of many ways in which the MWC persuaded the MPRP of the importance of women in the country and the significance of the MWC in leading them.

In retrospect, the socialist women's positioning themselves as taking part in all aspects of national decision-making without limiting themselves to "women's issues" also explains why women candidates during democratization did not campaign under the banner of "solving women's issues." This also helps to clarify why the women voters I interviewed objected to the idea that female candidates should be proposing to attend to women's issues. "Women candidates should be attending to all national issues on par with male politicians. They should not limit themselves to solving only the so-called women's issues," argued a middle-aged woman in an impoverished rural town in Töv Province. For many women voters, the job of women candidates was to share the work of the state, not just attend to "women's issues." Such a view, indeed, had been conditioned during socialism through international connections, MWC, and, finally, through official decrees by the Central Committee of the MPRP.

Women's Well-Being and Advancing in Leadership (1960s–1990)

Due to many welfare provisions, increased rights, and promotions of women, the Mongolian state considered the country to have achieved equality of the sexes. But sometimes the legal decrees remained as abstract rhetoric (like the rest of the socialist ideology), while in practice, ordinary women's conditions remained challenging. The MWC leaders and staff were aware of this dichotomy and came up with new proposals that addressed issues specifically related to women's well-being. Although many of the hardships in women's lives were also related to the general economic situation in Soviet-dominated Mongolia, the MWC proposed mechanisms to improve ordinary women's living and working conditions, increase public recognition of women, protect maternal health, and promote women to leadership positions.

Through their appointed activists all over the country, the MWC established various clubs for local women, some voluntary, but others de facto mandatory. For instance, in the latter political clubs, women learned about decolonizing movements in Asia and Africa, racism and exploitation in the United States, and the imperial politics of other capitalist countries. There were clubs devoted to disseminating knowledge on running modern households and care, which taught women about DIY projects, child development, and nutrition. Because almost all women worked full-time jobs, many found these de facto mandatory evening clubs to be a strain on their schedules, energies, and family dynamics. But more than the content, the socializing, mobilizing, organizing events and activities, delivering speeches, advocating, teaching, inspiring younger women, and, in general, various works that are associated with leading and serving others—all helped women to develop their identities as social and political persons.

The MWC also organized women's "cultural centers" in all organizations, administrative units, industrial establishments, and collective and state farms throughout the country. They were equipped with brochures and booklets about health care, home economics, household technologies, childcare, self-care, beauty products, and nutrition. The cultural centers emphasized the idea that women were the brokers of modernity, innovation, cultured (*soyoltoi*) living, self-care, and consumption.

When the state launched a pronatal policy (1974–90), the MWC could not explicitly challenge it as that would jeopardize both the organization's position and individual members' livelihoods.[29] The MWC worked to improve women's well-being and conditions as much as they could within the state framework. After years of lobbying, it was able to get abortions legalized in 1980 for mothers with four or more children. Jigjiddorjyn Altantsetseg, who was one of the advocates, noted during our interview that the only way they had convinced the politburo to legalize abortions (in a limited way) was by demonstrating the number of women who had been injured as a result of illegal abortions. The MWC also established prenatal rooms in the countryside— places where pregnant women could spend time before checking in to the hospital once they went into labor—as many women had to travel great distances in order to reach medical services. The MWC kept watch over the adequacy of birth clinics and pediatricians and even proposed having separate pediatricians for infants. As happened in Romania and elsewhere, it also advocated for honors and monetary support for women who bore large numbers of children "for the nation" (cf. Kligman 1998; Paxson 2004; Kanaaneh 2002).

During late socialism and the period of pronatal policy, facilities for children and youth also improved. Mongolia's General Secretary (president) Yumjaagiin Tsedenbal, who ruled the country for forty-four years (1940–84), was married to a Russian woman, Anastasia Filatova. While many Mongolians clandestinely criticized Filatova's influence over her husband (and the country) and resisted her as a proxy for Soviet domination, many also acknowledged Filatova's steadfast patronage of the nation's childcare and youth education, which also contributed to the well-being and empowerment of women.

Nevertheless, aware of the lack of women leaders beyond the branches of the MWC, it was Udval, the MWC's chairwoman, who initiated a proposal for advancing women in leadership. The MWC realized that while women had been integrated into the labor force, they received few acknowledgments and awards. In contrast, heads of enterprises and local administrations, who were mostly male, presented the results of work often completed mostly by women to the MPRP and received most of the rewards. The MWC strove to find ways to reward women for their work as well.

Hence, on December 22, 1966, the Presidium of the Central Committee of the MPRP issued a Decree or *Togtool* (#338) to promote women in leadership positions in the party, state, and civic institutions. The decree states that while women represented 21.6 percent of the national assembly, they did not occupy leadership positions in institutions of the party and the state, industrial enterprises, and civic organizations. While there were enough qualified women to lead various organizations, the decree states, women had not been promoted. By the winter of 1967, following research on positions and ways of promoting women, all of the ministries (for example, Trade and Production Ministry, Culture Ministry, etc.) received an order to submit proposals with plans of action on promoting women in leadership. The attachment to this decree has detailed instructions on women's leadership placement. For instance, the first article of the attachment states that in all ministries, government agencies, and departments, either the presidents or vice presidents were to be women. Also, women should head all organizations where women constitute the majority of the staff, as well as children's educational organizations. Following this decree, the MWC identified, promoted, and lobbied for women who could assume high-ranking positions.

Conclusion: The Power of Abstract Principles

This chapter explored women as agents within the state and the strategies they used to influence larger gender politics within their limited opportunities. In the process of maintaining and expanding the MWC against the restraints and control of the male leaders of the state, women emerged as political and social subjects. I have argued that many gender-equalizing policies were instituted as part of the state's everyday practices under Mongolian socialism (1924–90), albeit with varying outcomes. These policies included admitting girls as well as boys to free and mandatory public schools, educating and socializing both sexes to the political realm, and advocating for women's participation in almost all professions at all levels. Although in practice many of the professions were gendered, and the road to leadership for women was constrained, the principles nevertheless influenced women as political subjects aspiring to a certain status and place in society. This aspiration for more education, higher status, and greater active engagement in society was propagated from "above" by the state and internalized by many women, even

though everyday life was fraught with difficulties. While considering the overall male-centered nature of gender politics in Mongolia, I emphasize that propaganda about equality in Mongolia allowed women to create spaces and to
carry out activities that transformed gender politics.

I argue that the political subjectivities of Mongolian women well into the
twenty-first century constitute a more enduring legacy of socialism as compared with economic, legal, and cultural structures and systems. Mongolia's
rapid embrace of democratic principles and shift to a market economy were
related to its wish to develop a new postsocialist identity independently from
its two neighbors, the Soviet Union and China. The notion of democratization went together with the notion of independence, both individual and
national, and this defined the policies and politics that unfolded throughout
the 1990s and for some time thereafter.

Western GOs and NGOs biased against socialism tend to operate based
on faulty assumptions regarding the socialist state as a monolithic institution
and women as having no agency under socialism. This disdain also reveals
the myopia of Western liberal feminists regarding their own ideological freedom and the effectiveness of nonstate actors and movements. The women's
organization in Mongolia had little choice but to use its power to negotiate
with the MPRP on behalf of women through the fulfillment of the tasks the
Party assigned to the women's organization and through showing solidarity and sharing unified goals with the international women's movement. The
"state policies" toward women during socialism, especially after the 1950s,
were a result of negotiations between the male apparatus and the leaders of
the women's organization, who, while fulfilling their obligations as state cadres, were also acting on behalf of the nation's women. Even with its grand
outreach, it was impossible to be inclusive of all women, as workers in the
city had needs and problems that differed from those of herder women in the
remote areas.

By attending to different issues for women, the MWC succeeded in influencing and expanding the state's expectations and interpretations about the
positions and welfare of women. That was due to the inventive ways in which
some female leaders deployed the abstract concepts of equality, modernization, and development. The dominant male group had a rather limited understanding of what women's positions ought to be. For instance, while male
leaders instigated a pronatal policy, it was the women's organization that negotiated for specialized services like prenatal rooms for pregnant women in
nomadic areas and state medals for women who had multiple children.

It is not just the direct beneficiaries of such "state policies" (select mothers
or medal-earning workers, or herders extraordinaire with thousands of heads

of livestock) who were shaped as public and social personae beyond their identities as mothers, wives, workers, and herders but also the numerous ordinary women who became the appointed activists who delivered propaganda at individual and small-group levels. Such nuances aid in understanding the state in a less deterministic, less masculine, less top-down way, and in seeing women as agents within the state. The unpacking of "state policies" reveals the construction of female subjects as public personae, which continues to influence women's political participation in the contemporary era.

Among the efforts toward advancing women, the adherence to the abstract principles of equality and its infusion into an everyday life also had a lasting effect. On a building adjacent to the Parliament in the main Sukhbaatar Square in downtown Ulaanbaatar there is an electric sign that reads *Mongol Ornoo Manduulaya!* (Glory to our Mongolian Homeland!). During state socialism's pronatalist policy period, there was another electric sign reading *Bukhniig Huuhdiin Tölöö!* (Everything for the Children!) on top of a building on a main street (Peace Avenue) of the Sukhbaatar Square. The principles associated with promoting women have, meanwhile, never been articulated quite this directly. There were no explicit messages etched on the walls near the nation's main square that announced "Women Are Equal!" or "Let's Promote Women!" Yet, having grown up in Mongolia's capital, by walking past these electric signs on a weekly if not daily basis, I also hold in my mind images of rooftop electric/neon signs promoting women, even if these may not have existed.

Why do I include feminist signs with other slogans of the state? It is possible that I saw similar messages while growing up (mostly during the UN Decade of Women), in print media, on posters, and in TV programs. I have been intrigued not only by the inaccuracy of the messages' rendition and placement, but more so by their existence in my imagination. Why would I have a feeling that such feminist signs existed or ought to have existed along with the patriotic and pronatalist signs? Theorist of images W. J. T Mitchell destabilizes the separation between physical and mental images and argues that an image is never an isolated thing, as we perceive new images in a context of other images that have impacted our minds. Mental and physical images are reciprocal and interdependent (1984, 509) and "we create much of our world out of the dialogue between verbal and pictorial representations" (531). Mitchell's theory of images helps to explain that my "wishful" imagination of a mental sign promoting women's equality is not something unfounded but a result of knowledge, and that knowledge "is better understood as a matter of social practices, disputes, and agreements, and not as the property of some particular mode of natural or unmediated representation" (520).

I contend that while not displayed via electric signs, messages that promoted women were coded in activities put together by the MWC—celebrating the best female workers throughout the nation, organizing women's meetings and conferences, celebrating International Women's Day every year, and influencing the production of feminist-themed literature, cinema, and media at large.[30] Once the state passed a general principle of sex/gender equality in the constitution of 1924, women took advantage of that opportunity to create programs that allowed them to work toward that principle.

The general principle of equality of the sexes in the constitution was abstract in several ways. It was an aspiration and a higher ideal, like much ideology during state socialism, and was somewhat detached from everyday life. Usually, the abstract principles were articulated into messages, like the two signs mentioned above. But the principle of sex/gender equality was unique. The state did not want women to be equal in all spheres (Kaplonski 2014), especially in the top leadership. However, it needed women's contributions. A direct message of equality would have challenged the male leadership, thus seriously jeopardizing the already fragile existence of the MWC. The women's organization under the MPRP (from the Women's Section to the MWC) had to operate in modest and subtle ways. Thus, the MWC (and its predecessor organizations) preferred action and implementation to propagation and announcements, not least because the nuanced work that aimed at improving women's working and living conditions was somewhat beyond the concerns of the male leadership of the party.

In being inexplicit, the principles of "equality between the sexes" were only rendered more abstract and more vague. To some extent this made it easier for the women's organization to implement its specific projects (although it also led the MPRP to claim credit for much of the outcome of the work, while the women's organization remained in the shadows). In other words, the MWC did not articulate the message in a tangible language for which someone could attack them and curb their projects. The articulation would have made the women's aspirations too explicit and vulnerable. But their actions—which were realized through the apparatuses of the state—expressed their principles in an indirect and mainly tacit way.[31]

There was a downside, however, to this low-key approach. The abstractness of the principles and the top-down implementation of the projects led most of the women (and much of the populace) who were not directly affiliated with the organization to take the projects for granted as a part of the welfare state rather than as specific efforts by women within the women's organization. Major achievements such as equal access to education, jobs, and resources, as well as paid maternity leave and childcare subsidies, became

expected and have continued to be expected even after the collapse of socialism. The work of the MWC was disseminated through established entities.
For instance, secondary schools (grades 1–10, with students ages 8–18), as well
as the League of Young Pioneers and the Revolutionary Youth League, provided opportunities for both girls and boys to develop their organizational
and leadership skills.[32] In schools and organizations there was an impetus to
allocate leadership and other positions to girls and boys on an equal basis.
For example, pioneer leaders or concert presenters often came in mixed-sex
pairs.

Several female candidates and politicians I know are former heads of their
local Revolutionary Youth Leagues, the League of Young Pioneers, and class
captains and model students.[33] It is in these early positions that they gained
organizational and leadership skills, including public speaking, persuasion,
self-presentation, networking, and mass event organizing. All of these skills
helped them pursue their later political careers. Some elements of female candidacy that Mongolians hardly question today, such as women's public presence, demonstrating confidence throughout campaigns, giving speeches on
stage, and shaking hands with voters and top leaders, are also rooted in socialism. Larger social changes during socialism—for instance, women's integration in the public sphere and official recognition of their achievements,
equal access to jobs and higher education, and women's command of a certain degree of attention and power—have become regular parts of social life
for many.

In Mongolia, the abstract principles of equality helped to generate the
rhetoric concerning the importance of women to the nation and the issuance
of decrees for the promotion of women in almost all social and professional
spheres. The rhetoric of equality created a conceptual and legal space within
which women could enter social relations that shaped them into feminist subjects of state socialism. The multiple generations of leaders of the MWC had
to advocate for maintaining the organization, convince the male-dominated
national leadership regarding the importance of women in the country, and
persuade the state concerning the need for policies for women. The political subjectivities of most Mongolian women have been the outcome of the
MWC's fight for existence against the state's constant attempt to demote and
close the organization. The women who have been a part of the MWC as its
staff and as appointed activists have become politicians specifically because
they were involved in advocacy, lobbying, crafting proposals, and persuading
the leadership.

I maintain that the formation of political subjects took place not only
through the state's structuring of time, space, and body politics (for example,

marching in a national parade) but also through exposure to the principles of equality and the inclusion of women in the public sphere, while women fought for these principles against the indifference from and oppression by the national leadership. These principles were enmeshed in state rhetoric during school meetings, articulated and discussed during parades of young pioneers, and offered when women were presented with awards at their work units and organizations' meetings and during national and women's holidays.

Female candidates during the democratic era, with their polished looks, perfected speeches, and updated power suits—the electable selves—were the epitome of the neoliberal, democratizing new Mongolia and called to mind popular Western leaders like Margaret Thatcher, Hillary Clinton, and Sarah Palin. Yet their upbringing under socialism continued to have an impact on newer generations' self-perception, self-presentation, and campaigning abilities. These women's subjectivities had been shaped as much by state socialism as by recent democratization and the accompanying new forms of global services and assistance from international organizations and NGOs. In order to understand women's experiences in democratic elections in Mongolia, I considered the impact of the implementation of women-centered policies on the subjectivities of women. Thus, the young Sosor being inspired by the revolutionary feminist leader Yanjimaa's speech to gain an education, Tsegmid's trip to Novosibirsk during World War II to deliver aid to soldiers, and the appointed activists of the regional branches of the MWC working with their neighborhood women speak to the impact of the abstract principles and the works by MWC beyond the class of privileged professionals. I have argued that the national socialist women's organization's work of promoting women through broad but indirect propaganda was, in retrospect, a form of perpetual campaigning for women's place in society, including in national leadership.

Electionization: Governing and the New Economies of Democratization

The Euphoric Country

It was May 2008, a month before the national elections, and I was returning from observing a campaign of Serjee—one of my interlocutors in the countryside (see chapter 4). A couple, whom I will call Khangai and Naraa, graciously offered me a ride back in their new all-wheel drive Toyota Land Cruiser.[1] They were political consultants, known as *piarshik* (from PR), and were working with several candidates in the area. On our way we stopped at small rural towns and service areas for meals, gas, snacks, and water. Everywhere we went, I overheard conversations about the upcoming elections and the candidates. The conversations ranged from neutral to heated, from what the candidates were wearing to the ones that were blaming and ridiculing the politicians.

After one of our roadside stops, I mentioned that I was surprised at how everyone seemed to be invested in the electoral campaigns and that the activities and conversations around us all seemed to be about elections and nothing else, even in far-flung parts of the country. Khangai replied in an emphatic fashion,

> I know. It is a complete madness, is it not? I presume in the USA or in most other places people hardly electionize (*songuuljaal*) like us. People elsewhere probably just carry on their daily lives while elections take place the way they are supposed to take place, without overwhelming every single person like here. We here electionize as a nation (*Bid end buh ulsaaraa songuuljaal*).

Khangai said the word *songuuljaal* somewhat mischievously, stretching the last set of "aa"s for emphasis, perhaps because he was pleased with his newly coined terminology. I thought that the word *songuuljaal* (electionize; or *songuuljih* in the primary verb form) quite aptly caught the current state of affairs in the country. It struck me that it was also somewhat ironic for him to say what he said because he was a political consultant himself and was contributing his share of activities to electionization. It occurred to me that perhaps he coined electionization for another reason: to describe the sprawling countrywide agencies and forces that were beyond his influence.

I adopt and adapt the word *electionization* in order to describe the all-around campaigns that have overtaken Mongolia both during the legally designated "campaign period" as well as the clandestine campaign activities during the noncampaign time throughout the four years between elections. During the campaign period of twenty-one days that precedes the voting day, the country gets saturated by images, sounds, and paraphernalia, and by candidate meetings and parades, all of which create extraordinary hype and euphoria. During the rest of the four years between the elections (outside of the twenty-one-day official campaign period), campaigning is prohibited by law and life returns to normal, albeit only on the surface. In the guise of donations, celebrations, and sponsorships of holidays, local services, and even disaster relief measures, campaigns continue in a less recognizable manner and reveal their intentions closer to the elections. Although many people figure out the intentions behind such activities well before the official election time, they do not necessarily cease taking part in them. Many of these clandestine campaign activities use the existing structures of everyday life and substitute for the services of the state and even the private sector, such as free dental clinics, free language classes, or organized scholarship competitions for international colleges. They also create additional assemblages, cultural practices, and social stratifications and subjectivities.

Far deeper than the euphoria that pervades the country during the official campaign period, electionization is an ongoing process that affects people of all walks of life, from individuals on welfare to the richest Mongolians. With the concept of *electionization*, I want to convey that elections do much more than bring new or existing elites to political power: they define postsocialist Mongolian social life itself. In this chapter I will show that electionization refers to the perpetual campaigning activities and processes that last almost the entire four years between elections and that penetrate the most intimate spheres of people's lives, forging new technologies and social networks. Electionization transforms people's perceptions and regulation of time, money, and infrastructural life, shapes subjects and subjectivities, structures agency and worldviews, and creates new classes and other social identities and forms. Electionization has become sustainable, perhaps paradoxically, because it nests inside of and on top of existing relations and state governing practices while also creating new and pragmatic outcomes not only for winners but for almost all participants in its logic. Electionization is a new kind of governing mechanism that is shaping and is indicative of a new postsocialist political formation.

Electionization has a contradictory impact on women candidates. The hype and the sheer popularity of the elections as the nation's grandest events opens the space for women candidates. Its magnitude normalizes women's participation in these races. From the outside it looks like the elections are pertinent for everyone. Looked at from the inside, however, the same grandiosity and intensity of campaigns creates obstacles for women. That is because the scale and type of campaign activities substitute for the actual governing or must resemble the work of the actual incumbents (and more) in order to garner voters' attention during the official election period. They also must continue underground campaigns during nonelection time (when overt campaigning is prohibited by law) through community and charity activities, donations, and leadership; must increase their visibility among potential voters; and they also must solidify their reputation within their parties. The incumbents have allocated funds for their districts (most likely on top of some other funds), whereas in the challengers' cases, the money comes from personal funds. As campaigns have been mostly funded by the candidates— not so much by public funding as in other countries—running for seats is somewhat like running a district with one's own resources. The system disproportionately favors incumbents and the most wealthy newcomers. Since the most profitable businesses belong mostly to male entrepreneurs who also tend to have powerful political positions and ties, most women candidates are disadvantaged financially in addition to being marginalized in male-centered politics.

This chapter illustrates the ways in which different actors—from candidates to voters to the ones who do not care—influence the perpetuity, size, and scope of mobilization of the country and the overall penetration of electoral campaigns into everyday lives. Hence, I outline the circumstances for women candidates running for elections and the expectations of the voters who want political actions and not just promises. It provides some answer to the questions of why and how it has been so challenging for women candidates to compete in elections in Mongolia. Chapter 1 showed how women's social and political presence was normalized during the second part of the twentieth century and how through the work of MWC women were conditioned as active political subjects for generations to come. This chapter presents the new circumstances during democratization and the formal and informal workings of electoral campaigns and their expansion into electionization, which has created entirely new obstacles and expectations. I hope the reader feels the scale of the electionization in order to understand the new struggles for most women candidates, which I discuss in subsequent chapters.

The institutions and activities of electoral campaigns have become the structures of the everyday while, simultaneously, the elections have infiltrated the existing institutions. I argue that in the early twenty-first century Mongolia has emerged as a new political formation that is ruled and sustained by elections and their attendant campaigns. This argument might be somewhat unexpected, as scholars of social science have been working with concepts such as neoliberalism, democracy, socialism, and so on for a long time now. In the past, political formations have emerged as a result of revolutions with a characteristic break from the past and had charismatic leaders with visions and philosophies, at the very least.

Yet emergent political formations, writes Dominic Boyer, "need not be recognizable in terms of categories drawn from the major political movements of the nineteenth and twentieth centuries (for example, anarchism, fascism, liberalism, populism, socialism). . . . [T]he quest for new forms of democracy, whether anarchic, liberal, or social, no longer seems so improbable" (2013, 284–85). Although Boyer's argument is based on his considerations of events and movements that took place in the early 2010s (the Arab Spring, the Occupy movement, neo-Bolivarianism, and others), it also applies to Mongolia. The country's postsocialist political formation is being transformed and governed by electoral practices and campaigns in an ad hoc and contingent way. As I will show here, elections have been extended far beyond their original purpose, becoming a perpetual process (beyond the official twenty-one days of campaigning allowed by law in the 2000s) and creating lasting outcomes and influences along the way. In Mongolia, the politics and, especially, the politics related to elections filter much of the economy. Through producing material items and cultural practices, and taking on economic and governing functions, elections, as events, turned into electionization as a process. Electionization is not a break with the existing political structures. It is an unexpected political formation emerging from within and an unplanned process of taking over and building upon the existing social, cultural, and economic arrangements and their accompanying subjectivities.

Electionization is a process because it is perpetuated not only by parliamentary elections. Local and presidential elections, which also take place every four years, further solidify the structures and institutions of electoral campaigns.[2] Thus, repetition and continuity constitute the basic mechanics of this emergent formation. Within the thirty years since the end of socialism in 1990, Mongolia has had twenty-four elections: nine parliamentary elections

(1990–2020), seven presidential (1993–2017), and eight local elections (1990–2020). Several districts had repeated elections due to disputes over the results. Although this book explores only the parliamentary elections, I mention the presidential and local elections here because these two additional elections with equally intense competitions, ever refining professionals and techniques and technologies, and savvier groups involved in multiple elections, also end up further priming the campaigns for parliamentary elections and vice versa. Hence, the campaigns of all three types of elections continue flamboyantly during their official campaigning period and discreetly during the nonelection period as continuous processes.

Elections are not just a loud continuous slew of events. They transform many lives in an in-depth and multifaceted way. To give a sense of the depth of electionization, let me provide an example of Khangai's and Naraa's transformation of lifestyle, income, and subjectivities. I first met Naraa and Khangai (and their three children) in 2005. With each election the family moved up the ladder in material and status terms. In 2005, they had just moved from an old one-bedroom condo in the outskirts of Ulaanbaatar to a more modern two-bedroom Soviet-era apartment near downtown. They have been advising politicians since Mongolia's democratization in 1990s, and the 2004 election was especially fruitful for them. Naraa did not drive, so she was using a taxi to get around. She no longer wanted to work as a journalist and was contemplating either running for a parliamentary seat or devoting herself full-time to writing fiction. After the presidential election in 2005 and before the parliamentary election in 2008, the family moved from their two-bedroom apartment to a posh, newly built five-bedroom condo in a gated community in the most expensive suburb of Ulaanbaatar. In addition to hiring a full-time chauffeur, they sent their teenaged daughter to a university in East Asia. Following the 2012 parliamentary election, they switched their daughter's college to one in Western Europe. When I saw them after the 2016 election, the family had bought a large piece of land near Ulaanbaatar and was building a new house. Khangai chauffeured us in his brand-new black Jeep Wrangler. "My wife's [Jeep] is white," he said. "But last year's model," he added.

Within twelve years, the family had transformed from two salaried journalists who made less than US$2,000 (in the late 1990s) a year to an upper-class family. The family changed not only economically but also in their tastes and lifestyles as well, complete with leisure travel to the most expensive destinations in the world, daily exercises and massages, and spa stays. Khangai was proud to have all the wealth and cultural distinctions to be at the top of affluent Mongolian society: a college-educated daughter living an independent leisurely life in Western Europe with her Western boyfriend, a wife who worked at her leisure, and younger children in private international schools in Ulaanbaatar.

Such a transformation might be ordinary in countries with more developed economies or even in less developed places where the roads to economic prosperity are relatively transparent and established. It also might not be a big issue in places where entrepreneurialism and the search for opportunities outside of established norms are celebrated and taken as a positive development. What makes Khangai's and Naraa's trajectory special is that they (and many other political consultants, media professionals, and research and advising groups) emerged during democratization and built their wealth almost exclusively by working in electoral campaigns. The average salary of journalists increased insignificantly since the 2000s. Most journalists in 2018 made about US$3,000–$6,000 per year while working full-time. More important, however, the opportunities that emerged with elections for certain people like Khangai have superseded many other opportunities that are expected to bring money, such as in industry and commerce. The fact that elections have become a profitable industry despite the drastic fluctuations of the economy, both when the GDP skyrocketed in 2011 and then when it came to standstill in 2015, shows that there are less visible forces involved. An election job guaranteed money when others did not. What this means for parliamentary candidates is that they must have a flow of money to sustain their campaigns and, if possible, to pay consultants like Khangai and Naraa while investing in countless other activities—a challenge for newcomers and women.

Although there is no official data on the salaries of *piarshik*s, in 2008 they made, on average, somewhere between US$10,000 and US$30,000 per campaign. (For comparison, the average yearly income for most people in Mongolia with a higher education was about US$3,000). The consultants occupied the top of the financial pyramid in the electoral economy. Other professions also emerged along with that of the *piarshik*: campaign managers, image-makers, personal assistants, media personnel, campaigners, researchers, and other personnel who did a myriad of less defined jobs related to PR, like "crawling agitation" (people who carried on casual conversations about the candidates) or checking and rechecking the voter registrations. This list only partially encompasses the multiplicity and variability of electoral gigs. Some businesses, such as gas stations, countryside hotels, and media and printing companies, which exist independently of elections, get vital profits from electoral campaigns. Elections have turned into a new economic sphere in a country that has been aching to develop its economy and infrastructure since its modern establishment as a nation back in the early twentieth century.

Short Histories of Electionization

Electionization is a compendium of local, geopolitical, and global events and processes. It is not just an outcome of adopting Western-style institutions such as democratization, free elections, and neoliberalism. Cultural practices of the recent and more distant past, multiplicity of viewpoints, revisions and refinements of election laws, discourses by NGOs, citizen groups, and political parties—all animate the ways in which electoral practices have taken hold and become embedded in the everyday life of the country.

Democratization in Mongolia in the 1990s was influenced by a shared anxiety about national independence, by conflating democracy with neoliberalism, and a belief in a transition to a system better than socialism.[3] Democratization was not only about choosing a more suitable political formation, it was also a ticket for gaining international recognition and new alliances. Such connections would, as many hoped, secure more thorough independence from China and Russia.[4] Since elections serve as hallmarks of democratization, the new democratically inclined leaders were interested in showing to the Western media the success in staging free elections. As Mongolia's declaration toward democratization in 1990 was a decolonizing move from the Soviet Union, people embraced it in earnest while knowing little about what might come next.

Neoliberalization, though, influenced democratization in a certain way. Like other postcommunist countries, Mongolia strived to meet the requirements of the Washington Consensus reforms, also known as structural adjustment policies, in order to qualify for aid and subsidies. Back in the early 1990s, the economic subsidies were critical for the survival of the nation after the Soviets declared an embargo on oil and other subsidies.[5] The opening of the country to free trade, liberalization of prices, and privatization of state assets were implemented from the top down, with little explanation, and in a corrupt and hasty manner. There was no registered resistance to this chaos and destruction as people could not foresee the massive and lingering impoverishment of entire towns and districts. First, the populace understood that it was temporary, but in some ways the "transition" almost never ended (see, for example, Buyandelger 2013; Buyandelgeriyn 2008; Pedersen 2011; Rossabi 2005). Second, in the early 1990s, the neoliberal ideology of self-sufficiency, freedom, and a right to private property resonated well with the criticisms of the culture of dependency and sluggishness, the characteristics that allegedly led to the end of socialism. The Marxist theory of capitalist exploitation, which supported socialism, was quickly forgotten. Instead, Milton Friedman's theories of free market principles became the dominating principles.[6] Third, as a part of the decolonizing efforts, Mongolia looked to countries like the United States to break from its geopolitical isolation and gain additional collaborators in the market, as with democratization. Hence Mongolia followed its expectations while overlooking the difficulties.[7]

For most of the population, especially the working class, the rapid privatization of state assets meant the ending of the nation's industries and subsequent loss of jobs and livelihoods (also see Hann 2006). As Lhamsuren Munkh-Erdene (2012) argues, as Mongolia ended its web of regulations, stability, and especially destroyed its industrial centers, it replaced its dependency on the Soviets with a dependency on Western capitalism. Both men's and women's lives underwent drastic transformation. Women's lives deteriorated more than those of men in the 1990s, since women of childbearing age were not protected from job losses in private sectors (see Robinson and Solongo 2000), the majority of the impoverished population consisted of single mothers, and women aged 35 to 55 were forced into mandatory retirement during the transition (Burn and Oyuntsetseg 2001). Fledgling capitalism with uncertainty and a new culture of risk-taking was more conducive to male entrepreneurs as compared to women, who often had caretaking obligations at home. With the shift from state production to a domestic regime, women lost the state-based support structures that used to address women's issues. In a domestic economy, the division of labor and control of the resources often tend to be more patriarchal in comparison to that of a socialist state economy, where both men and women receive paychecks. Women lost both formal and informal networks that were based on their work units. When the economy improved and became more diversified, opportunities also increased, especially during the country's boom in 2009–14, including for many women (see Empson 2020). Even though the overall standard of living improved for many, the economic boom did not change the unequal access to resources, including gendered allocation of resources.

The mass impoverishment that started in the 1990s opened spaces for political parties and candidates to offer services that were similar to those provided by the previous socialist state. They did so with the hope of building networks of supporters and receiving loyalty from the voters. Political parties also encouraged business owners to join them in exchange for political candidacy, thus building a pool of business owners to sponsor the next elections.[8] Among nomadic herders, the newly emerged politicians also engaged their existing networks of kinship, ethnicity, and locality to build new political bases (Sneath 2010; 2018, 123). Sometimes, political parties attracted residents by distributing gifts and donations and by implementing poverty alleviation programs. The recently impoverished working class had limited, if any, ways to start businesses on their own in the 1990s, because the necessary structures of banking and loans, infrastructure, and knowledge were not in place in most places and became available only slowly thereafter. Hence, subsidies, aid, party-funneled donations, and even job allocations were welcomed in most rural and semirural places.[9]

Elections from the socialist period also contributed to the prominence of elections in the democratic era. The state socialist elections served, as anthropologists argue concerning elections elsewhere, as secular political and state rituals and the venue for consolidating national symbols, structures, and narratives, as well as societal solidarity (Abélès 1988; Brink-Danan 2009; Lomnitz, Adler, and Adler 1993; McLeod 1999; Moore and Meyerhoff 1977, 14). Some older people in Mongolia reminisced about Election Day as a joyful social event to which they wore their best *deels* and suits. In the countryside, people rode their best horses and showed off their expensive handcrafted saddles and bridles. Although the ritualized festivities of socialist elections switched into a competitive frenzy during democratization, elections nevertheless were familiar events. This meant that unlike in other countries where the institution of democratic elections must promote voting rights, mount suffrage movements, and find ways to reach out to less literate voters, in Mongolia, all of these were already in place.

Mongolia's automatic voter registration, which utilized relatively comprehensive and dynamic local administrative structures from state socialism to update and check voter lists, also contributed to the voting. Every citizen aged eighteen and over (and usually registered in the State Registration of Citizens Office) would be registered automatically as a voter. I have gotten to know several district administrators who were furnishing voter lists. In the early 1990s, long before the time of digital databases, these administrators updated the lists by knocking on residents' doors and checking their registration against relevant forms of identification. These administrators were able to accomplish their tasks mainly because they were also district clerks, lived in the neighborhood, and already knew the families they were registering. By repeatedly confirming the accuracy of the registration (for the most part), these staff members brought voting closer to people's lives.[10] Hence, electionization has its roots both in local and global processes, as well as in socialist and recent democratic history. While it is an outcome of a challenging transformation to democracy and a neoliberal market economy, it is also about people's appropriation of elections into their everyday lives. All of this makes it harder for women candidates to participate, as noted earlier. The elections' impact on the subjectivities of voters takes electionization to a yet deeper level, thus bringing about the elections' function as an ad hoc governing apparatus beyond the structures of the state.

Political campaign financing is the murkiest aspect of Mongolia's parliamentary elections. International experts and many Mongolians worry that the unregulated and obscure flow of money and the corruption scandals seriously threaten the country's democracy (Burcher and Bértoa 2018).[11] The public fund-raising structure is limited, enforcement of regulations is weak and with many loopholes, and there are no mechanisms for tracing campaign transactions. Legal restrictions, such as limiting campaign duration or number of posters, that were aimed at lessening campaign spending and thus equalizing the playing field between newcomers and incumbents did not bring desirable outcomes.

For instance, in the 2008, 2012, and 2016 elections, the official campaign period was limited to the twenty-one days prior to elections, but unofficial and discreet campaigning continued throughout the four years between elections. During those four years, political parties preselected their aspirants to compete against each other for official selection later. This preselection is known as *rotatsand oroh*, which means "entering the rotation." Those *rotats* aspirants carry out precampaigning. During that time, neither the candidacy nor their prechosen constituencies in which they precampaign are guaranteed to hold up by the time of the actual elections. Thus, as aspirants precompete for slots to become the actual candidates on the ballot, precampaigns proliferate. When the time of the official campaign approaches, the structures of precampaigning are in place and ready to be elaborated upon as official campaigns. As campaigns take on lives of their own, they have complicated effects on women candidates. Especially when campaigns begin to substitute for state functions, individuals who are not already in such roles, including women, tend to fall behind. Electionization can lead to roles for women that are simultaneously empowering and precarious (see chapter 4 for an example of a woman candidate's precampaigning).

The precampaigning during nonelection time, as well as the official campaigning, create various jobs and gigs such as delivering pamphlets and making television ads. In a long process of setting up election regulation and monitoring since the 1990s, electoral campaigns have turned into businesses, colonizing the private and public life of the country and becoming the center of sociopolitical life well beyond their original purpose.[12] *Instead of the nation staging elections, elections stage, or run, the country.* Electionization is not a discrete form of governing but an ad hoc and dispersed one that is shaped and influenced by individuals who engage, resist, navigate, and make demands on the leadership. As local, global, and geopolitical forces have developed into electionziation, as I show in the subsequent sections, a variety of actors have influenced and expanded its outreach, often without intending to do so.

Candidates: More Winners Than Seats

Successful elections are those that do not lead to postelection violence, maintains anthropologist John Borneman (2011). That is achievable, he says, when the "losers" do not feel "sacrificed" but instead feel publicly acknowledged and consoled along with the celebration of the winners. The formal knowledge about elections, furnished by disciplines such as American politics and political science, Borneman (2011) argues, serves to legitimize campaigns and outcomes not just for winners but also for losers. Elections need to be well-staged and fair, and for that, new technologies, as well as the lengthy processes of registration, counting, and campaigning, also prevent losers from causing scandals and undermining the credibility of the system.

Borneman's (2011) attention to the "losers" helps us to see another perspective on the exuberance of Mongolia's electoral campaigns. Many losers in Mongolia are not "sacrificed" but share a form of winning in their own niche of electoral practices. Given the precampaigning that often lasts almost all four years after the official election period of twenty-one days, the winning in a niche way is still a gamble. Private sponsorships and funneling one's resources into campaigns leads to financial losses and distress among those who lose the race.

However, many (but not all) candidates are neither so idealistic or ignorant as to assume they will win, although that is the goal of most. Elections in Mongolia are no longer self-contained formal events focused only on the outcome for voters. Rather, elections present opportunities and outcomes that are relevant to various candidates whether they are incumbents or new to the arena. I am not arguing that there are no losers or that everyone who competes for seats benefits. But the difference between losers and winners is not black and white. The "winners" are not just those who win seats. Many candidates who did not win seats gain in various ways and degrees along the way. For example, an aspirant might construct a new building in his district. Then he would tell voters that if they elect him, the building will be turned into a community hospital, in which case, the district will benefit. But if they do not elect him, then the building may end up being a shop, which will benefit the owner. The candidate does not fully lose, even if he or she fails to win a seat; he or she has attracted customers through the platform of elections. In this fashion, many Mongolians have appropriated elections, and especially campaigns, as opportunities beyond voting or competition, thus expanding the meaning of elections.

In other cases, the candidates running for office are not in the race to win to begin with, but participate instead to distract the attention of the electorate, to shield certain other candidates from attacks, or to split the vote for a potential winner. Such candidates lose in the sense that they do not win any seats. Yet, such candidacies are often paid by the opponent of the main competitor and these could be called "winning" races because their function was simply that—to distract or split votes. Moreover, a candidate running for a seat might give the impression of personal autonomy and control over his or her performance during the official campaign period. There are certainly candidates who fit this description. But for the most part, a candidate from a major political party is just the face of a larger team. Much gets done by the hierarchical structure and centralized orchestration. Candidates' districts and their compatibility, in-party competitions, and connections, as well as the candidates' cultural and financial aspects are often taken into an account and preorganized and negotiated by various influential people. Therefore, losing or winning is not always a big surprise for a candidate. For instance, Oyungerel, a politician, told me that women with strong opinions get exiled to "incompatible" far away rural districts, so their losing is almost inevitable.

Even some of the candidates who are expected to win seats but then do not still might gain other benefits, such as name recognition to be "banked" for the next election, higher posts in state or private institutions, knowledge of the craft of campaigning, or enhanced personal networks. The nonwinners gain certain credit and placeholders for the future, such as the probability of getting an equivalent of an appointed position. The alternative is simply nothing.

Indeed, an SMS message received on the cell phone of one of the winners—shared with me during my fieldwork—shows that an election is not just a competition for seats but potentially a scramble for all kinds of state power and resources. This was a message from one candidate, a former incumbent, who lost the 2012 election to another who had newly won a seat (they were not competitors in the same district but were in the same political party). "Is there any way to give me one of the ministries? I prefer X or Y," wrote the losing candidate to the winner. "If someone else has taken up those ministries, then, can you please create additional ministries, like either A, or B, or C, and give one of them to me or, better, a combination of B and C? What other ministries and state agencies are still awaiting their heads?" The winning candidate read the message aloud to me, complaining that now everyone wanted something from her. Although the message-sending candidate did not win a seat or a ministerial position, his business career flourished within influential international and national circles. Although it could be argued that such opportunities would have come without his political visibility, it certainly did not hurt, especially since advanced age can go against one's advancement.

These Mongolian examples illustrate how participants create side opportunities and make elections relevant to individuals beyond the main political purpose of choosing leaders. Hence, while I agree with Borneman (2011) that elections proliferate because of improvements, or alleged improvements, in managing the losers, especially with technology and knowledge, I also argue that elections have been popular because their benefits *sometimes* go beyond the winners of seats. It is possible that there is essentially nothing for a candidate besides the allure for a gain. He or she may never become a seat winner, or a niche winner, or simply obtain a buildup for their next steps. Still, running for a seat as a form of gambling is also a choice and one which exacerbates the phenomenon of electionization. I will further explore the candidates' experiences in a section on power-holders toward the end of this chapter.

Voters: Expect Actions, Not Promises

Electionization would not be possible without voter participation. The rate of voting in Mongolia is one of the highest in the world. Even with the turnout declining since the 2000s, on average, it has been around 70 percent.[13] Such a participation rate is surprising given the populace's disillusionment with political leadership, corruption scandals, and allegations of electoral fraud. Instead of being indifferent, much of the populace remains engaged.[14] The state's violent suppression of the organized protest in the aftermath of the 2008 election did not stop Mongolians from demonstrating on the streets and continuing their political engagements through the use of social media.

Why do people vote despite their disillusionment with the elected leadership and integrity of the electoral mechanism? Anthropologist Mukulika Banerjee (2014) is also intrigued by the high voter turnout rate in India despite the populace's dissatisfaction with political leadership. Banerjee (2011, 81) explains that Indian voters are active because they are also aware of the positive aspects of elections, such as elections being entry points for new political players. But more than that, elections have gained a sacred place in public life in India (Banerjee 2007). India's Election Day is an extraordinary event that "creates time out of time, a carnival space, where the everyday reality of inequality and injustice is suspended, and popular sovereignty asserted for a

FIGURE 2.1. Voters waiting for a candidate to start the voter outreach meeting. Ulaanbaatar, 2008. Photo by Nerguigiin Baasanhuu.

day," thus creating superstructure that matches the abstract moral standards that are not always followed during regular times (Banerjee 2014, 3). Scholars such as Scott Simon (2010) and Michelle Obeid (2011) also argue that elections help marginal and ethnic communities engage in dialogues with the state and potentially create transformation. All these views are relevant for Mongolia as well. With electoral campaigns reaching out to almost every corner and connecting with individuals in order to attract them for voting purposes, much of the rural population no longer feels as left out of modernization as before (fig. 2.1). The "election period" that is filled with campaigns sometimes even creates a Durkheimian-style collective effervescence (1995, 212–17).

In addition to the affective forces that animate the voters and propel them to cast their votes, campaigns bring both symbolic and pragmatic opportunities in the forms of gifts, donations, and political actions. The phenomenon, whether it is called "vote buying," or "corruption," or "patronage," has many components and visions. For instance, the voices of prodemocracy groups and individuals who critique these actions often replicate, although not always, Western institutions such as the Asia Foundation and associate gifting and donations with corruption and the erosion of democracy (see, for instance, examples of that type of criticism and disdain by Ledeneva 2006;

Tuya 2012). Scholars have noted a complexity of the so-called corruption and how certain actions can be filed as corruption even though they might be related to inadequate legal and political circumstances. For instance, the allegations of corruption in the 2004 election in Mongolia, during which each political party revealed the inadequacy of rules, designs, and the previously existing structures, had put to question various tactics that were labeled as corruption (Bayantur 2008; Tuya 2005). Sometimes, even seemingly respectable, and thus unquestioned, practices, like maintaining heritage, is a form of corruption, although labeled differently (Herzfeld 2015). Patronage in higher political circles is different from gifting to voters during campaigns, although some extensions from the former might continue to ordinary voters. The relationships among the former are about loyalty and tight reciprocity. When it comes to voters, the connections are larger, looser, and with less notable direct obligations. Corruption cases related to electoral financing are also an issue of a different category.

This section considers gifts (*garin beleg*) such as food items, clocks, calendars, mugs, books, camping gears, and other items that get distributed in abundance during electoral campaigns. It is understandable why many Mongolians criticize gifts and donations and refer to it as "vote buying," even though there is little evidence that people sell their votes and remain loyal to whoever distributes gifts. It also suggests a certain degree of social and temporal boundary-making by more educated groups. They adhere to the rules and laws of democratic institutions and see the gifting as a form of feudalistic and, therefore, outdated and shameful actions, all of which is juxtaposed to their own identities as modern and progressive. These more educated groups see the voters' acceptance of gifts as weakness and as betrayal of their fellow citizens' efforts to ensure electoral fairness. As Michael Herzfeld (2018: 54–55) explains, in the cases of Greece and Italy, the disagreements as to which acts constitute corruption emerge due to a differential uses of temporality. For some who value older forms of loyalty to patrons, the illegality of patronage does not exist or is at least harmless. It tends to dissipate against the doctrine of original sin. But others "adhere to legalistic understandings of virtue . . . and wish to scale all moral and legal judgement up to the state's domain of competence" (2018, 54–55). The younger Mongolians are engaged in keeping up with the current temporality, which, in their view, is also about legality, national pride in the context of international stage, and insuring a competent society.

A good example of the young people's efforts to stop campaign gifting is a 2019 exhibition of political gifts that was organized by the Center for Social and Political Education and by students at the Political Science Department at the National University of Mongolia (Namuun 2019). The in-person and photo exhibit featured a collection of bowls, clocks, calendars, coffee mugs, and food items. The comments under the articles express abhorrence toward voters who "sell votes" and some wonder why people sell their votes for such negligible items. The exhibition curators mainly blame the candidates for [attempts at] "vote-buying," and their blame carries less of an assumption that voters sell their votes for trivial items such as clocks and mugs. But they attempt to stop the process altogether lest it become a normalized vehicle for more serious deeds.

Some people, including politicians, Western observers, tourists, and NGO members comment that a distribution of resources through "gifting" may not be bad if that is the most efficient channel given the absence of other ways. In response, many Mongolians, however, including the people who receive the gifts and donations with enthusiasm, are critical of such channels and prefer more official and transparent structures of services outside the electoral sphere. As Marissa Smith (2018) states, "feeding" in the context of political campaigns, is not seen as a necessary act of political power. The public perceive of politicians as amoral overall, and symbolically file them into a different category, such as national or moral outsiders, like the reincarnations of the Chinese (Abrahms-Kavunenko 2018, 35) or carriers of bad karma (138).

In other words, there is a desire, especially among younger generations, to prevent elections from becoming a vehicle for (or a substitute for) some other institutions and services. This desire recognizes the structural imbalance, the system's inadequacy, and the unequal access. In places with a more traditional patronage system, such as India (Piliavsky 2014), Kazakhstan (Werner 2002), and Kyrgyzstan (Ismailbekova 2017), patronage is a mechanism of social protection. In a similar way, although relatively new in Mongolia, the gifting and patronage have become a form of safety net against uncertainty despite their own unevenness. While the inadequacy of the state services (especially the shrinking of the welfare state due to neoliberalism) is a form of structural violence on a geopolitical scale, their substitutions through elections are not laudable either. The gifting is not sufficient to replace livelihoods and the patron-client relationships among voters only masks this larger structural violence while also further perpetuating the inequality and, in some cases, the violence to local and parochial spaces. In other words, while the proliferation of gifting is understandable, it is also not a system to rely on especially as a part of a livelihood.

Gifting is also about social integration and not just about material resources. Lars Højer (2019) argues that integration is based on reciprocity, and a refusal to reciprocate leads to animosity and exclusion. Hence, participating in receiving a gift is not just participating in an economic transaction with the campaign but also about being integrated socially, which is necessary for survival in Mongolia, especially when exclusion leads to further social and economic impoverishment (Buyandelger 2018). In the electoral context, however, integration takes a form of assemblages (*süljee*) that is expected to support the candidate but also generate demands and expectations. Hence, gifting creates a space for open-ended expectations based on the network integration. What emerges as a side effect of campaigning, then—in addition to politicians attracting voters—is a multitude of interdependent and shifting hierarchical networks of politicians, local power-holders, and voters. Many voters are actively engaged in these connections, partly to deal with the neoliberal unpredictability and to create additional social landscapes. Voters, then, have steered the campaigns into a social, political, and economic practice beyond the original purpose of electing an official.

Gifting, however, does serve a particular electoral purpose. As Lauren Bonilla and Tuya Shagdar (2018) argue, electoral gifting is a mechanism through which the locals evaluate the candidates' moral and professional standing, whereas the candidates demonstrate their capabilities and access to wealth as a glimpse into the future. Such a practice of gifting, although termed "vote buying" by the more educated middle class and, in general, widely criticized, is not just a cultural obligation to reciprocate. Bonilla and Shagdar (2018) argue rightly that the classic Western theory of the gift that emphasizes the obligation to reciprocate is based on the premise that voters have an independent individual judgment that can be kept uninfluenced. Their insight is telling, given the fact that campaigns are active and plentiful, and the electorate is exposed to all kinds of influences, from ideological to pragmatic and from promises to tangibles. In Mongolia, where individuals are largely a part of the whole, an individual's choice is often already half someone else's. Even though some campaigns strive to create a sense of obligation to return, voters develop their own impressions based on a variety of factors.

Campaign gifting is related to the dynamics of the larger governance structure that has become symbiotic with electoral campaigning. Elizabeth Fox (2017) argues that Mongolian elections have inverted the logic of the vote-return exchange. In most democracies, candidates are elected based on their promises, which they strive to fulfill after they have been elected to office. By contrast, Fox argues, in Mongolia, the voters evaluate the candidates through gifts or political actions before the election. More, since most people are aware that politics requires knowledge of the rules and competition requires attracting voters, they evaluate the candidates not only on their honesty but also on their ability to work within the system and on the attributes that are necessary to compete in the system.

Hence, gifts and patronage may not be desirable for many, and they are against the fundamentals of the Western democratization; yet they persist and thrive despite criticisms and efforts to curb them via official and unofficial channels. This paradox is beyond pragmatism and cynicism. This type of paradox, as Michael Herzfeld (2015, 531) argues, is one of the most fundamental practices of being a part of a nation-state. "Nation states achieve their best chances of survival when their functionaries connive at practices that violate the official ideology and morality of the state itself—the principle that [he has] called 'cultural intimacy'" (Herzfeld 2005). Mongolians participate in democratic elections through activities that are nondemocratic by Western standards. By doing so, they engage in cultural intimacy—an allegiance to the group, small and large. This allows people to be democratic as well as belong to their locality, kinship, and all things societal without becoming a Western-style society of "autonomous" individuals governed mostly by the rule of law.

Moreover, empirically, there is a difference between gifting and vote buying. Anastasia Piliavsky (2014) makes it very clear by delineating gifting as a deliberately visible public activity that is done with great pride and fanfare, whereas vote buying is done at night, secretly, and not through gifts but cash. Sneath (2006) argues that gift-giving in Mongolia is an enaction of social roles and marks the relationships of obligation and duties. Bonilla and Shagdar (2018) argue that gifts carry the identities of the giver (for example, noodles or calendars) to show not only the success of the businesses or activities but also the time (namely, at the end of a harsh winter). In addition, gifting, unlike a television ad or a media pamphlet that is distributed by tossing such into front yards or near the *gers* (felt tent) of the constituents, often requires face-to-face presence. Giving gifts, especially in public, such as during campaigns, is a gesture of acknowledgment of the receiver's presence.

When overt campaigning ends prior to Election Day, electoral campaigns slowly reemerge in the quiet spaces of everyday life after the dust of the elections settles down. While the hype of overt campaigning certainly magnetizes voters, the activities that take place in quiet mundane life are just as important. Because electoral campaigns appear at and sponsor community events, like New Year parties for children and Lunar New Year parties for the elderly, offer free language lessons, distribute aid packages, and even take credit for securing public funding for facilities such as a local swimming pool, they are a part of everyday life. By participating in the campaign of gifts and political actions, the voters contribute to turning elections into electionization.

This situation further strengthens the power of the wealthy and especially that of incumbents while marginalizing new political candidates, including women, most of whom have fewer resources than male candidates. Nevertheless, some people depend on elections for important things in life like getting free dental care offered by a campaign or securing a tuition payment from a new candidate.

New Electoral Economies: Giggers and Election Experts

Economic activities that develop as part of campaigns also help illuminate why and how elections persist despite the populace's disenchantment and cynicism toward political leadership and the loss of the integrity of electoral mechanisms more broadly. This section shows that elections impact people's economic lives from different strata, create new socioeconomic layers, consolidate existing ones, and create new professions and relations, as well as hopes and resistances. Tangible outcomes aside, the versatility and scale of the creation of hopes and dreams, from the national to an individual level, is a crucial aspect of electionization. I move from the elections generating affluent groups to how they impact the have-nots. The economic differences I describe below might sound familiar or even expected for most of the world, but they are relatively recent in Mongolia and should not be taken for granted. Elections turn into electionization as they become an integrating force while also being a tool for social stratification and an exclusionary mechanism for guarding the power of the ruling groups.

Some of the campaign gigs, especially those that fall between consultants and street agitators, are reminiscent of jobs in a neoliberal gig economy, where individuals need to piece together different activities to make a living. For instance, my main informant Radnaagiin Burmaa's local political party campaign office hired an announcer for her group's voter outreach meeting. She was eloquent and used laudatory poetic language to excite the voter crowd. After a few sessions, however, she disappeared. We learned afterward that a different campaign had hired her. Another skilled student was working for Burmaa's campaign as an organizer and campaigner. He then found another candidate to work for and started juggling the two opportunities. The myriad of posters, flags, LCD screens, campaign offices, leaflets, brochures, and TV ads that dominated the daytime provide extra work for the underemployed and for established businesses to strengthen their finances.

In addition to gigs, elections officially employ a steady number of full-time staff. The GEC staff numbered 20,174 in 2008, 15,549 in 2012, and more than 20,000 in 2016.[15] In addition, there are people who work for political parties and individual candidates' campaigns, ranging from accountants to drivers. Consider that three different sets of entities—the GEC, political parties, and candidates—all employ their own staff, managers, advocates, and service personnel. Moreover, parties and candidates consistently employ media, research, and propaganda workers, and draw on extra labor for fund-raising and voter outreach efforts. It is important to consider the scope of employment opportunities, from part-time to full-time, against the bleak picture of employment among the impoverished low-wage earning population, which mostly come from the generation of workers who had been laid off during neoliberalization given structural changes in the economy. Such a scope of employment—gigs and full-time—of workers is a real financial strain on newcomers and women candidates. The most loyal people are those who already work for the candidates on a regular basis either for their businesses or NGOs as it is in their direct interest to keep the candidates successful. This means that the candidates who already have larger everyday bases (namely, businesses, NGOs, and social media followers) also have bigger electoral campaigns. For that reason, sometimes, candidates establish NGOs or businesses (especially media or polling related) in order to aid their candidacy.

Although patronage in higher political circles prevents authoritarianism given that it creates strong *fraktz* (factions) (see Radchenko and Jargalsaikhan 2017, 1035), it is not the same across different circles and different places. Unlike India or upper-level circles in Latin America, in Mongolia, patronage is not a stable institution with a reliable structure and established past. Overall, patronage, if it takes place, can be oppressive with respect to ordinary people, especially in small settlements and towns, where people's political affiliations are public. With each election and shift of political power from one party to another, many opportunities and especially jobs, even the most ordinary ones, migrate from the members and followers of the losing party to those of the winning party. Since, for some people, their jobs and other resources are linked to the power of their "patron" (that is, an elected parliamentarian), there is a tendency for some people to become ardent political advocates for their candidates. At the same time, however, as the candidates' or parties' victory is not guaranteed, voters strive to benefit from the campaigns as much as they can. This dependence, for better or worse, fuels electionization and empowers political parties that have come to act as job-allocators—reminiscent of the former party-state.

The populace, however, has appropriated elections in order to navigate such political and neoliberal instabilities, especially, the four-year-long *tsiikl* (cycles) of hiring and firing at jobs by the winning party. For instance, in order to deal with unemployment due to the opposition party being in leadership,

FIGURE 2.2. Campaign Workers in 2008, Ulaanbaatar. Photo by the author.

some families join both of the two major parties (for example, the husband joining the DP and the wife the MPP) instead of both staying loyal to one party. That way, when the winning party refuses employment, aid, and subsidies to the supporters of its opponent, the family would not be stranded without a living for the next four years. It is by fusing together political power and allocation of resources and opportunities that political parties find a niche to influence and subsume large portions of the population into their support base. Hence, neoliberal politics were crucial in influencing the citizens' dependencies on political parties, whereas the latter began gaining much power and influence especially through elections. More than political events, elections have become influential forces in many people's everyday lives.

Working for a campaign in various capacities has become an expected gig. A large contingent of campaign workers, especially for the candidates' individual campaigns, are college students who are not only attracted to making money but also to the socializing, promises for job opportunities, and general excitement. The nonstudent low-income or impoverished residents, mostly on the outskirts of Ulaanbaatar, however, were more dependent on campaign gigs and other less visible and unguaranteed opportunities for improving their livelihoods (fig. 2.2). Research has shown that in the United States, the new shared economy, or gig economy, benefits mostly the middle class with means and skills far more so than the people on the lower rungs of the socioeconomic ladder (Heller 2017). The unpredictability and shifting opportunities, and the temporal nature of the gigs during elections, do not replace traditional jobs for extended periods of time for people who need them the most. "The proliferation of the temporary is . . . a fundamental feature of a new kind of capitalism" argue Rebecca Empson and Lauren Bonilla (2019). In that line, the prevalence of gigs in elections makes them stand in for nonexistent private businesses and add to existing ones, albeit temporarily. Regardless, electoral campaigns have gained a vivid place in capitalism—as capitalist undertakings—even if they do not substitute for some of capitalism's roles. Hence, the gigs and gifts are entrenched in electoral campaigns as a part of the everyday, which contributes to the transformation of elections from political events to structuring forces—electionization.

The meager salaries of campaign workers in poor residential areas do not preclude the workers from walking all day along the dusty streets of the outskirts of the city under a merciless sun, carrying stacks of print magazines and leaflets, being ridiculed by skeptical residents, and sometimes even being attacked by suburban watchdogs. Political parties tend to be keen on working closely with the resident campaign workers, as they often can provide important informal knowledge about the local electorate and in some cases even impact their neighbors' voting choices. Hence, often both the candidates and the campaign workers can be on the lookout for opportunities to be useful to the other party, although nothing is predictable or guaranteed. For the campaign workers, their formal low-paid gigs can be doorways for potential opportunities. Some opportunities may not even lie with elections but come up later from having made a closer connection with the local district head and other people in power. Thus, working for a candidate's campaign by distributing pamphlets for a meager salary is a kind of a placeholder—a way to occupy a space for potential opportunities. Hence, campaign workers can be thoroughly invested in their posts; getting into fistfights in the middle of the street and electoral office workers "sharpening their tongues" and pulling up their sleeves if wrestling becomes necessary. Individuals and groups become so invested (after months or sometimes years of being involved in preparations) that the election becomes a self-constitutive, self-generating event.

In addition to distant hopes, electoral campaigns provide immediate rewards and returns. By working for a campaign, these residents get closer to the candidates' political actions that substitute for governing services and the welfare state. Because the campaigns sometimes do tangible and direct governing, the electorate has come to use the campaigns to seize these benefits even if they are minuscule, such as salaries as well as banquets and lunches.[16] For instance, at the end of the official campaign period in 2008, the

FIGURE 2.3. The reception under chandeliers for the DP members and supporters in 2008. Photo by the author.

DP organized a dinner reception for all its campaign workers. Since I was shadowing a DP candidate, Burmaa, I joined the reception with her campaign staff. As soon as we entered the restaurant—one of the biggest and most elegant reception halls in the country, we lost sight of each other. Crowds of people were in an uproar, shoving and shouting. I could smell roast meats and sausages, hear the clanking of cans, but all I could see were empty reception tables covered with sparkling white high-end linens. I saw no food, and no one was eating or drinking. Once I caught a glimpse of a waiter bringing in a tray of what looked like cans of soda. People around me shoved even faster and for a moment I lost sight of the waiter. The next moment I saw that his tray was empty. I scrambled through the crowd and found Burmaa and the rest of her staff near a stage and near larger-than-life portraits of DP leaders. I got on the stage for a minute and saw a giant crowd under crystal chandeliers shoving and grabbing for sausages in various parts of the reception hall before the party leaders drew their attention from a podium at which point the crowd broke into loud cheers (fig. 2.3). I did not see where the food went or how much of it there was. The next morning, campaign staff said they saw people at the reception stashing sausages and other foods, along with canned sodas, in their purses, bags, and even hats to take home. I also heard that the chairman of the DP was also shocked at the famished and desperate state of the people.

Whether related to distribution of resources or teaching free language classes, these clandestine campaigns create spaces, networks, opportunities, and sometimes even pressures and necessities to vote. It is the everyday infusion of campaigns that transforms elections into electionization.

The Ones Who Do Not Care: Subjectivities and "Social Songs"

Sociologist Chua Beng Huat, explaining the persistence of elections, writes that

> Across Asia an election is a cultural "event," distinct but nonetheless in continuing with the flow of everyday life of the local population. . . . If a candidate is to appeal to the electorate for votes, his/her campaign activities must draw on elements of the "popular" culture, the cultural practices of the masses, in order to draw emotional and rational resonances from the electorate. (2007, xii)

Chua Beng Huat's note contributes an additional, more cultural explanation as to why elections persist. Elections do not just draw on culture. They *transform* that culture, and through it, the subjectivities of the people. Electoral campaigns in Mongolia have pioneered and influenced many popular fashions, such as the genre of the "social song," which came to my attention on another drive with Khangai and Naraa to another electoral constituency.

We were driving in a remote and barely populated part of the country. The trucks and cars we passed had campaign advertisements on them. The billboards still stood along the road. At one point, Khangai, who was driving, turned on the radio. We heard a song by Javkhlan, a singer who became quickly known for spreading the genre known as the "social song" (*niitiin duu*), which can be categorized as soft pop with traditional Mongolian tunes. "Javkhlan is working [singing] for the campaigns nonstop these days," Khangai announced and immediately turned off the radio, as if he already knew that his passengers were more interested in talking with each other than listening to songs. Even in the remote countryside in the middle of nowhere, we could not escape electionization. Social songs, I knew, had been popular in the 1960s and 1970s and now seemed to be becoming so again. They started as *zohiolyn duu* (authored songs) but their popularity resembled either folk or pop songs; hence, they also became known as *niitiin duu* (social songs). Even though the term *authored songs* is technically more correct than *social songs*, the meaning of the latter better suits the phenomenon.

The social song grabbed my attention in a more substantive way when one day in the spring of 2008 my twenty-one-year-old cousin told me that she had become a big fan of social songs. I was a bit surprised. My hip cousin and "social songs" were incompatible, at least from my point of view. I associated social songs with slightly older people, people at least in their thirties. That was partly because social songs created a vibe of calmness, stillness, a sense of tradition; sometimes the singers even wore traditional garb. The rhythm and flow of the songs, slow and mellow, dictated certain bodily conduct as well— gentle smiles, seriousness, smooth gestures, and dignified looks. The songs were also about moral correctness, love for one's homeland and parents, and the beauty of the surroundings. But what I knew about my cousin was the opposite of those songs: rebellious, edgy, and hip, she was into Korean pop, disco and dance clubs, Madonna, and Jennifer Lopez. That spring she asked me to bring her a new J. Lo perfume from the United States, and the year before that, the latest edition of Nike sneakers. Social songs were emotional and deep, and people sang them while sitting together at tables over meals and after a few rounds of drinks. But if my jean-clad cousin (who had refused to wear a knee-length skirt to go to a ballet performance because such skirts were "for grannies") was into the dignified "social songs," that meant the campaigns were effectively impacting people's subjectivities.

The extent to which these songs influenced electoral choice is less important. There are plenty of people in Mongolia who do not vote and consider elections an unnecessary institution. Some of them are financially independent because they have families living abroad who supply them with cash.[17] Others are disenchanted, yearn to migrate, and thus they imagine their future somewhere else. But even those people cannot fully escape the campaigns and their impact even if that impact is not political. My cousin was amused by the stories about the campaigns but was not interested as much in who might win. For her, the valuable aspects of campaigns were hanging out (and singing) with her friends at the outdoor concerts that were part of the campaigns. Yet these concerts were having an impact on the subjectivities of young people.

The social song was in demand all over the country in the 2000s. No anniversary, graduation party, or organization picnic went without people, young and old, learning and singing songs of that genre. Because of this popularity, a parliamentary candidate, allegedly, sponsored the singer Javkhlan's concert for US$100,000—an astonishing amount by most standards—in order to receive instant recognition among the electorate in his constituency. Since 2000, election law has prohibited entertainment as a part of political campaigns. But the campaigns found ways around the law: instead of a candidate sponsoring a concert during his/her campaign event, the concert was arranged as a gift from a supporter of that candidate to other supporters (*demjigchees demchigchided*). The performers also found ways to give gifts of songs to the supporters. By 2008 and especially by the 2012 election, prohibitions against mixing campaigning and entertainment were enforced by civic groups that emerged as "election watchers," but some candidates and supporters still found ways around those prohibitions.

Remarkably, Javkhlan ran for a seat in the 2016 election and became an MP, demonstrating Chua Beng Huat's (2007) insight that elections are cultural events that must appeal to people both emotionally and rationally. Javkhlan's campaign was unique in its entertaining as well as ideological scope. Dressed in Mongolian traditional garb that included handmade boots and a simple herder's hat (which are also the clothes he wears when he sings his social songs), with longish flowing hair, Javkhlan walked his camel caravan, complete with carts with wooden wheels, along the roads of his prospective constituency.

Although there were plenty of critics who saw Javkhlan's deeds as a call to reject modernization and return to a primitive past, it was a welcome spectacle for many others. Javkhlan's performance of a traditional lifestyle spoke deeply to many Mongolians' nationalist sentiment to respect traditional heritage, which was further fueled by resistance to foreign mining activities. Resource nationalism—a claim to assert control over resources on the nation's territory—that stemmed from an anxiety about losing the national subsoil resources to foreigners and a fear of assimilation had contributed to the already strong nationalist sentiment during economic downfall after 2013. Thus, this example shows that not only do elections impact the subjectivities of the voters, but also potential candidates as well.

Javkhlan's success in staging a unique campaign, which was both nationalistic and masculine, can be hypothetically contrasted to the campaigns of most women candidates who tend to be seen as modern and somewhat Westernized (baruunjisan). Chapters 5 and 6 discuss how women candidates' identities tend to be contested by the voters. For the women themselves, the choice of self-presentation is always a gamble. Women candidates can be perceived as too feminine or not feminine enough, too old or too young, or too aggressive or too timid. The social song and Jalvkhlan's ascent to Parliament reveal an interconnected influence of elections and cultural practices on a variety of subjectivities, including how very particular aspects of gender play a crucial role in electoral choice-making. Such preferences, as discussed in chapter 3, also illustrate how at the moment of social stress and uncertainty, there is a tendency for gender essentialization.

Power-Holders and Campaign Promises

What follows illustrates the ways in which the power-holders (incumbents and influential challengers) utilized elections as a stage to transform the sentiment of the nation during election of 2008. Electoral campaigns became stages from which the ruling group placated the resisting citizens into accepting mining (primarily gold but also coal and other minerals) as a narrative of the future. This act of using elections as a platform for changing a collective sentiment on a national scale (and not just as a road to political power) is a powerful indicator of elections' structuring force.

Mongolia's excitement about mining started in the 1990s, peaked in the early 2000s, and then began transforming into a complex set of reactions combining criticism, resistance to foreign capital, environmental protection movements, and anxiety about the competency of the government to manage the national wealth.

This section explicates how mining and elections have become mutually constitutive entities that generated both economic activities as well as dreams and frustrations that have defined the lives of Mongolians since the early 2000s. In 2008, the two main political parties, the DP and the MPRP, made campaign promises to distribute *anticipated mining revenue*—the unconditional cash—to the citizens (figs. 2.4 and 2.5). The MPRP promised to grant each Mongolian the "Motherland Gift" (*eh ornii hishig*) of a million and a half *tugrik* (about US$1,270) and the DP promised a "Treasure Share" (*erdeniin huv'*) of one million tugrik (about US$847).[18] The campaign promise was fulfilled: the MPRP, which promised more money, won the election. This was one of the most striking examples of electoral campaigns making promises that resembled the characteristics of the welfare state. But this resemblance was not just a goal to get elected to power. As I learned later on, it was also a way to convince the populace to move forward with the mining agreements.

From the perspective of an anthropologist studying parliamentary elections, the politicians offered cash promises mainly to present themselves as respectable leaders and to attract votes. It was a crucial time to be in political leadership and to continue to benefit from their leverage on all things related to mining. Mining and politics were already interconnected. For instance, 90 percent of one of the biggest coal transporting companies in Mongolia, Tavan Tolgoi Trans, is controlled by D. Bat-Erdene, a member of Parliament representing the DP (Naughton and Ullman 2008). Although unevenly, many politicians have direct connections with mining enterprises either through licensing or production if not through ownerships of various parts of mining or related enterprises. I also heard from many people that money from mining constituted a large share of campaign sponsorship. Since much of campaign financing remains discreet, it is impossible to provide concrete examples to back up this speculation. As elsewhere, mining in Mongolia is a controversial and a complex endeavor that goes hand-in-hand with the ongoing remaking

FIGURE 2.4. Front and back of the MPRP's campaign promise flier of the "Motherland Gift." It was distributed to voters as a part of their campaign materials.

of the country's legal, political, and economic infrastructures, especially in response to the populace's reaction to foreign enterprises and the national leadership's oversight. Overall, I was certain that political parties used mining both as resource and as a magnetizing promise of a bright future in a modernist way in order to aid their electoral success. Mining enabled elections.

"It is the other way around," my colleague, social geographer Lauren Bonilla, said to my surprise. Since 2002, she has been studying the social and environmental implications of mining in Mongolia. In her extensive study, Bonilla (2017) suggests that the mining industry and the government (including the candidates who were expected to join or remain in leadership) used elections as a platform to regenerate the waning hope for a better future that was associated with mining in the 1990s and early 2000s. In other words, electoral campaigns were used as a platform to regain the populace's trust in the national leadership's ability to carry out proper management. This search for consent was necessary because, starting in the mid-2000s, there has been a nationwide reaction against mining, a critique of foreign investment-friendly minerals law, and a debate over the mechanisms of the agreement in regard to Mongolians' share of the mining revenue (Bonilla 2017, 155–56). In order to continue the groundwork and eventually launch the extractions in the largest mining deposits, various agreements have waited to be signed by the Mongolian government and foreign companies.

However, the populace's reactions and citizen resistance suspended the signing of those agreements as they required a revision of the law. The politicians were now working with a new awareness about "a new national consciousness about the cultural and economic value of subsoil resources" (Bonilla 2017, 155). One of the main reasons for the increase of citizens' awareness was the deeds of Ivanhoe Mines president Robert Friedland who, upon discovering the Oyu Tolgoi deposits, began promoting mining to Mongolians and helped ignite dreams about the country becoming the next Saudi Arabia.

FIGURE 2.5. DP's campaign promise flier "Treasure Share." It was distributed to voters as a part of their campaign materials.

However, his work of conjuring investors by advertising Mongolia abroad was denigrating and exploitative, and it disconcerted Mongolians. Robert Friedland (2005) made exaggerated claims that Mongolia was a treasure chest, with attractive taxes, no local resistance or NGOs, and little concern over environmental degradation. Although protests against mining and foreign investment soared and the state made changes to better control licensing, capture windfalls and rents, and to regulate foreign companies, the state nevertheless remained committed to having foreign-invested mining in a neoliberal setting (Bonilla 2017; Hatcher 2014). The state went as far in its support of mining as to charge the heads of the resistance movement who protested amending the law that protects water and forest resources with terrorism (Bum-Ochir 2019).

Simultaneously, as Bonilla (2017, 157) states, the state also had to appease the populace and "assuage their anxieties about becoming emptied of resources by foreigners." Bonilla's arguments about the politics of mining in the 2000s help explain not only the intensity of the electoral campaigns but the content of the candidates' presentations at the voter outreach meetings. Different candidates had appropriated the cash handouts as the ticket to the future and presented different versions of the scheme.

The cash distribution was framed by the idea of human development as a necessary condition for the development of the nation. Hence the Human Development Fund was established by the government. Also, for liberal and neoliberal advisers who had historically been hostile to the state and who had propagated free market ideas, the distribution of money to citizens was seen as a way to prevent the concentration of wealth in the state or in other entities. It was understood as a democratization of spending and an equalization of revenues.

There was, however, even more nuance behind this promise of cash distribution. Cash campaign promises were also directly related to the US government's neoliberal policies. Even before mining revenues became the subject of campaign promises, the Mongolian government in 2007 was negotiating a $284.9 million US foreign aid program called the "Millennium Challenge Compact" (MCC). The MCC was designed to reduce global poverty through economic growth (MCC 2008). In order to receive these funds, Mongolia needed to demonstrate its commitment to three criteria: good governance, economic freedom, and investment in citizens. Along with the MCC, Mongolia was also going to implement the UN's Millennium Development Goal (MDG). After signing an agreement with the Millennium Challenge Compact at the beginning of 2008, the government declared that one of its main commitments was to distribute parts of the mining revenues accumulated in the Human Development Fund as Motherland Gifts. Right after that, government representatives went to Alaska to explore the logistics behind the Alaska Permanent Fund's redistribution of hydrocarbon revenues directly to Alaskan citizens in the form of annual payments by check. In other words, the cash campaign cash promises were a part of a larger context of socialist, liberal, and neoliberal policy schemes and coordinating values (some historically conditioned, others recently implemented). From the point of view of the study of elections, the campaign cash promises were also tools to maintain power, pacify citizens, and exclude political opponents and newcomers. The cash promises were the Mongolian version of, to borrow Amel Ahmed's (2013) term, an "exclusionary guard," which refers to the tools of the ruling elite to secure their power by dominating various aspects of elections. In this case, elections were the power-holders' stages on which to sway public perceptions on issues like mining and the country's future.[19]

There was, however, no cash available for distribution. "The election promises were not based on an exact calculation of mineral revenues accumulating in the state treasury from existing mining projects. Rather, generalized expectations of future mineral wealth animated them" (Bonilla 2017, 320). Both the state-controlled mines (namely, Tavan Tolgoi) and foreign-investment mines (namely, Oyu Tolgoi)—two of the most potentially profitable mining enterprises—were only in the development and construction stages and not yet in production. To finance the Human Development Fund, the government negotiated a long-awaited mining agreement with Ivanhoe Mines in 2009. The agreement included a US$250 million payment to the government of Mongolia, ostensibly drawn from future mining royalties, specifically intended to fund the 1–1.5 million tugriks of cash transfer promises made during the 2008 election. Even though the government called the US$250 million a tax prepayment, the monies were actually a loan to be repaid to Ivanhoe Mines/Rio Tinto between 2014 and 2016, with interest exceeding US$24 million (Kohn and Humber 2013).

The money from the Ivanhoe Mines was not enough to distribute the promised cash to all of Mongolia's 2.7 million citizens. People received smaller installments and were kept waiting for more. Meanwhile, major mining projects were postponed. To continue to finance the Human Development Fund, in 2011 the state-owned coal mining company signed an agreement with Chalco, a Chinese aluminum company. Chalco agreed to pay the Mongolian mining company US$250 million upfront in exchange for four million tons of coal from the Tavan Tolgoi deposit (Kohn 2013). The agreement was extremely opaque. Chalco assumed the money they were lending was going to finance the construction and development of the Mongolian state-owned company. The government extracted US$200 million for the Human Development Fund.

Both Ivanhoe Mines and the Erdenes Tavan Tolgoi Company had to halt construction and lay off workers, thus creating a massive disruption to the Mongolian economy. The coal companies trimmed and delayed salaries and had little money to invest in environmental programs and community relations projects. Unable to operate, they also fell deeply into debt. There was a third source of money to finance the Human Development Fund for cash distribution: the older, established state copper mining corporation Erdenet, which had been built in collaboration with the Soviets and which had been almost the sole revenue builder for the nation since the second part of the twentieth century. The Ministry of Finance demanded US$28 million in dividend payments and more in royalties from Erdenet. This put the corporation in a financially vulnerable position. Both Erdenet and the coal mining company Erdenes Tavan Tolgoi were implicated in international scandals regarding avoiding their payments, resulting in negative media attention, which in turn impacted Mongolia's reputation among international investors, bank lenders, and donors (Choi 2010; Kohn 2013).

The campaign promise and cash distribution devastated the country's economy. People received some money (less than the promised amount), but in the next few years, the country ended up paying off the massive debt, losing many international investors, and losing any hope for improving its collapsing economy in the foreseeable future. Instead of the nation running elections, it is fair to say this was a case where the elections ran the country (this time close to bankruptcy).

Conclusion: Governing the Political Time

I have described electionization here—electoral campaigns taking over social processes and private lives, influencing subjectivities, and directing economies and livelihoods. From extravagant campaigns on the streets to a cultural force that transforms subjectivities, electionization manifests in a myriad of ways. I highlighted the experiences of major groups: voters, candidates, professionals, workers, and people who end up being influenced culturally if not politically.

We can see the manifestations of this force in campaigns decreasing the urban-rural divide into continuous political time, songs that transform subjectivities, tastes that create class, gig and gift economies that integrate, as well as through economic devastation that had developed from an election promise of cash allocation from mining revenues to the entire populace. What we learn from all these electoral campaigns is that in order to participate in this electionization, a candidate must already govern the constituency and do the job of legislatures before they become members of Parliament (if they become such at all). The extravagant campaigns with unlimited expenditures might look like the hallmarks of democracy and a sign of an open and free competition. However, due to the privatization of campaigns, and a murky financing structure, most women candidates and most newcomers to politics fall short in participating in campaigns. In exploring why elections remain prominent and why electoral campaigns take over the people's sociopolitical lives, I engaged with various scholars, whose work illuminated nuances and provided abstract theorizations of the problem. Their studies are helpful conceptual tools for analyzing the Mongolian situation.

In a context of neoliberalization of the economy, Mongolians have appropriated democratic elections as a platform for generating resources and conducting useful transactions. Hence, elections with their multitude of venues for opportunities, and clusters for various productions, tend to have more winners than the seats. While a legislative seat is the main goal of the candidates, the tiered and expansive electoral process affords room for many other smaller winnings. One of the important aspects of electionization is the tacit role of the previous state socialist structures and practices in mobilizing, registering, and tracking voters (or people in general). Therefore, the high voter turnout, which is the main premise of democratic elections, happens to be accomplished partly due to the legacies of the totalitarian structures.

So the answer to the question of why elections are such extravagant events and why people vote rests not so much in appeasing the losers, as Borneman (2011) argues, but by making elections into a widespread land of opportunities, promises, and hopes on various scales. In addition to being festive events, elections also have turned into everyday structures in order to ride on the existing structures of time, sociality, and infrastructures. By revealing the history of democratization and simultaneous neoliberal reforms, I showed the development of competitive elections against the drawback of postsocialism "shock therapy" for the impoverished working class and the appropriation of elections by candidates and voters. The more flamboyant the overt campaigns are and the longer the discreet ones, the more difficult it gets for women candidates to participate, even if they have a great deal of creativity and prowess. Overall, elections as time-regulated events have turned into perpetual structuring forces, thus making it challenging for women candidates to participate in the competition.

Finally, electionization as a sociopolitical formation-in-the-making has created an additional homogeneous political time for the nation. Many rural and suburban groups often feel outdated and left out of modernization, development, and integration (Plueckhahn 2020; Smith 2020). These groups feel that they occupy a different time, historical and developmental. This time is necessarily hierarchical with Ulaanbaatar, the capital, being closest to global modernity, and then different parts of the country occupying different times.

In addition, similar to many so-called preindustrial societies, different groups in Mongolia carry out their lifestyle activities based on distinct times that are beyond the clock, such as seasonal, weather-based, and livestock tending. These times are conceptually similar and not hierarchical. For instance, the weather change dictates travel planning and duration of nomadic herding communities everywhere in Mongolia. But the shared concepts do not yield homogenous time in practice, as the weather in different parts of the country is uneven. Hence, herders in southern provinces might move to their winter pastures later than those in the northern provinces. Depending on a location, the types of livestock prevalent in the area, and the kinds of dairy products that the people make, the times for mobility and daily and seasonal activities are heterogeneous.

The political time of electionization, however, brings the country into a synchronic mode like other social and political events that take place regularly, such as the start of the new school year on September 1 and the associated nationwide supply shopping period two weeks before. This homogenous political time adds to this existing multiplicity of times among various groups in Mongolia. Election campaigns—posters, media, the candidates' meetings with voters, the voters' discussions about the candidates—gather the entire country into a single, synchronous political moment, one that obliterates the time lag that usually characterizes flows of information from center to periphery, from city to country. The usually delayed access to information and goods on the periphery has long been a source of regional anxiety, one that perpetuates a sense of marginalization. In such a context, a relatively simultaneous, although temporary, access to information, resources, and even meetings with candidates during campaign season lessens the sense for many people in remote areas of being left behind. The Civic Will Party's political message was to bring that good time of equality and prosperity to everyone, as they expressed it on the poster of a candidate by the name of Chimediin Bazar (fig. 2.6).

During the nonelectoral period, time feels more linear, similar to what Carol Greenhouse has glossed as "Marxian time as history" (1996, 2). Yet, even when campaigns are absent or quiet, the infrastructures that were built for them during the election period—the rich media ecology, the social assemblages and networks, and political party local branches—still remind voters

FIGURE 2.6. A message at the top of a campaign poster of a Civic Will Party: *We Bring the Good Times That Prioritize Our People*. 2008, Ulaanbaatar. Photo by the author.

of the next elections. Most important, the political time is an affective force on people's subjectivities—people structure their lives around anticipation of elections. That is because of the near seismic shifts that occur in people's lives every four years of the *tsiikl* (cycle), when political parties sometimes switch in leadership and when most of the state jobs and regulations migrate to the members of the winning party.

During election campaigns, on the other hand, experiences of time in Mongolia come closer to a Durkheimian sense of time as a collective representation of social experiences, characterized by social rhythms or cyclicality that produce an aura of social cohesion without consensus, marked by "collective effervescence" (Durkheim 1995, 212–17). To a limited extent, campaigns in Mongolia are a form of collective representation that brings the experiences of diverse groups, actors, and regions into a single temporal frame. This Durkheimian notion of social time as a collective representation that brings into relief the linear time of the neoliberal, postsocialist condition is an important characteristic of electionization. For it is within this time that people—and, significantly, the women candidates at the heart of this book—experience the meanings and outcomes of elections.

This political time has been generated through the ways in which electoral campaigns and voting link "concrete individuals to the social whole, giving . . . societies a means of reproducing themselves" (Greenhouse 1996, 3). The most basic aspect is the connection between candidates and potential voters that emerges as the beginning of additional social relations, economic production, mobility, and discussion. The posters and broadcast media seem to edit candidates' ethnic, class, and regional identities (Smith 2020), promoting instead a homogenous and upper-class Mongolian identity. As in state or official performances, most candidates and advocates speak the official national dialect, the Khalkha, and the male and female candidates wore business suits while campaigners were clad in T-shirts, thus adding to the homogeneity and formality of the electoral performances. Only the voters themselves represented diversity through their variety of clothing, dialects, accessories, and other possessions.

Electionization has also been evident from "seasonal" semirevolutionary activities in public up until the postelection riots and violence in 2008. (With the government suppression of riots in 2008, such gatherings ceased. Then, with the advent of social media, such gatherings moved online). Throughout the 1990s and 2000s, each spring, following the celebration of the Lunar New Year, political life awakened after a cold winter in the nation's capital. Known as *khavrin sindrom*, or "spring syndrome," new political parties, social movements, and individuals launched demonstrations and protests in the city's main public squares, calling the public to criticize and resist the current political leadership.[20] This yearly "syndrome" was somewhat reminiscent of the early days of the democratic movement and the subsequent revolution in the spring of 1990, which also included these elements. During electoral contests, political symbols reproduced the excitement of the revolutionary past, memories of which were recalled through quasi-annual spring events and prepared people for the upcoming elections, thus maintaining the political atmosphere among the populace outside of official politics. Such political events were usually well covered in the media, especially in the news, thus enhancing a sense of national belonging and unity among newswatchers, evoking memories of past mass gatherings, and creating a sense of "eternal revolution."[21]

SurFaces: Campaigns and the Interdependence of Gender and Politics

The (In)Substance of an Epoch

Images of women are equally common in the state propaganda produced during socialism and in the advertising of the market economy in the age of capitalism. Both systems developed their own image regimes—the predilection for certain styles and points and the exclusion of others. The socialist state depicted women as revolutionaries, workers, and mothers (fig. 3.1), as a part of the state's regime of governing the identities and roles of its citizens. Carnal or material desires were absent from such depictions. Contemporary advertising of the market economy, by contrast, identifies women with goods and tends to frame women as objects of desire in order to promote consumption. After almost a century-long struggle for equality, we continue to be surrounded by images of women that are misleading in the way Virginia Woolf (2019 [1929]) noted when she contrasted glorified images of women with their difficult positions in real life. Both the state and advertisers have used images of women to forward their respective goals with insufficient attention to women in actual life.

In contrast to their ubiquity in socialist propaganda and consumer advertising, images of women are scarce in today's campaign posters, an absence mirroring women's scarcity in politics. In May 2008, I shared an SUV with a small group of campaign workers traveling to one of the rural provinces where I conducted my research. We passed row after row of male candidates' portrait posters perched on the buildings in the town center as well as plastered on shop fronts, market entrances, and the walls of apartment buildings. Then, as we arrived at the intercity highway, we saw countless billboards with photographs of well-groomed, dark-suited male politicians, temporarily replacing the usual advertisements for carbonated beverages, cosmetics, and luxury cars. I did not see a single poster of one of my interlocutors, the female

FIGURE 3.1. A socialist mural on an apartment building in Ulaanbaatar, 1993. Photo courtesy of Christopher Kaplonski.

candidate who was competing in that constituency. Despite her efforts to promote her candidacy, her posters were absent in her district and on the roads that led to it. Women had better chances of being elected in urban areas—or so it was assumed. But then they might face proportionately stronger male competitors, higher campaign costs, and less room for posters. Popular urban districts with more powerful candidates came with more crowded campaign surfaces.

It is no coincidence that electoral campaigns fight for surfaces in order to reach voters. The German social philosopher Siegfried Kracauer, who witnessed the transformation of mass culture and its explosive representations in the pre–World War II Weimar Republic, notes that surfaces express a society's most substantive state of being. In his seminal work *The Mass Ornament* (1995), he states:

> The position that an epoch occupies in the historical process can be determined more strikingly from an analysis of its inconspicuous surface-level expressions than from that epoch's judgment about itself. Since these judgments are expressions of the tendencies of a particular era, they do not offer conclusive testimony about its overall constitution. The surface-level expressions, however, by virtue of their unconscious nature, provide unmediated access to the fundamental substance of the state of things. Conversely, knowledge of this state of things depends on the interpretation of these surface-level expressions. The fundamental substance of an epoch and its unheeled impulses illuminate each other reciprocally. (1995, 75)

I take Kracauer's insight as a license to dwell on the surfaces of the electoral campaigns, their materiality and sensorium. Even though his suggestion is based on a study of one instance of *mass ornament* during the Weimar Republic— the ambivalent irreality constructed by the synchronized movements in tiller girls' performances—his call to attend to surfaces applies equally to postsocialist Mongolia. Kracauer argues that the mass ornament is an end in itself. It is a kaleidoscopic pattern made by choreographing the movements of people's bodies and it has no substance beyond itself. I argue that campaign media, and street posters in particular, although having little motive beyond attracting voters' attention, still foster a particular understanding of gender that is influenced by the politics of the moment. In other words, even though the posters were meant to have a finite purpose, they expose much more than they had intended.

In this chapter I illustrate how posters reveal the ways politics and gender are mutually constitutive. I do so by exploring the meanings and stories behind the ubiquity of the form and the banality of the content of campaign posters. Posters need to be understood as being only one type of item in the larger ecology of media campaigns. Thus, I start this chapter by inviting the reader to walk with me through the streets of Ulaanbaatar. My goal is to have the reader feel the sensorial saturation and surreality of the posters within the context of other media forms during the electoral campaign of 2008 and with references to the election of 2012 and 2016.[1] I ask why poster images are so prominent in Mongolian (and many other) elections. How did certain electoral designs and circumstances influence the 2008 election's posters (and other media)? What can we discern from the form and content of these posters about women's participation in politics and the connection between the representation of gender and its lived practice? How do campaign posters reveal and even shape gender as a representation that is also temporal and intersected with class?

My search for answers to these questions inspired me to probe how free elections, which are democracy's most valuable practice, also happen to be an outlet for anxieties surrounding gender inequality. Taking off from the insights by Joan Scott (2018) and Claude Lefort (1988), I uncover the ways in which new and existing understandings of gender are being tweaked and reaffirmed. In doing so, I argue that the campaign posters demonstrate electionization as a sociopolitical formation that builds mostly on existing content and values that are coupled with the newly available automated mechanical reproduction of images. I show that the posters tend to seek safe, familiar, and risk-free content, but they strive to make up for their banality through the magnitude of their reproduction. The safe content conveys paranoia in the political arena, whereas the ubiquity displays frenzy. Thus, seemingly benign images reveal electionization's affective and structuring forces. Campaign posters contain invisible contestations by political parties and individual candidates. Many tend to be ambivalent about the appropriate gender norms to inscribe on their posters and their actions are also influenced by the economics and pragmatics of technological reproduction. Through ethnographic analysis of the events that unfolded behind select images, I show the coconstruction of politics and gender, and how the media representation reveals and conceals the in-person gendering of campaigns.

The Surreal Ecology of Campaign Media

Posters of male candidates made their way to the most remote places. Halfway through our ten-hour journey from the country to the city of Ulaanbaatar, we stopped for a meal at a roadside restaurant in the middle of nowhere. A giant portrait of a candidate covered the restaurant's entire front. While we ate our *tsuivan* (steamed noodle dish), beef noodle soup, and *huushuur* (fried meat pockets), we watched campaign advertisements on a wall-mounted flat-screen television. The restaurant was empty, but at the same time, we were surrounded by walls covered with additional portraits of candidates. For a split second I could not help but feel watched by the candidates even though the pictures were just that, pictures. When we left the restaurant, I noticed that the lone felt tent (*ger*) next to the restaurant—probably the home of the restaurant's owner or manager—also displayed candidates' posters, all male. In the campaign consultants' SUV, we talked about the electoral campaigns and listened to popular songs used by various campaigns. Visually and soni-cally, we were immersed in electoral campaigns in the vast emptiness of the Mongolian steppes.

We arrived in Ulaanbaatar after midnight and found its streets populated with posters but otherwise empty. I stood in front of the Wrestling Palace—a round building that was covered in posters hanging down like curtains from its roof—and I was overcome by another bout of eerie feeling as these giant post-ers were gently swinging in the breeze as if they were about to take off on their own. I looked at other streets. The city electorate was known to be friendlier to female candidates than the electorate in the countryside, and one could find portraits of women candidates among those of the men. Campaign materials were everywhere. Entering the elevator of my apartment building, I faced a wall covered in campaign posters. In my apartment, piles of materials from the twenty-two candidates competing in my district sat on the dining table and in boxes underneath: magazines, brochures, calendars, business cards, newspa-pers, fliers, and postcards. Campaign materials have been diverse and some creative: toys, table-top games, food items, wall clocks, coffee mugs, and candi-date names on toilet paper. Here, however, I concentrate on campaign posters.

The next morning, I walked the streets. Within the two weeks since my departure, they had turned into a theater stage for campaigning. The three- to five-story buildings from the mid-twentieth century that faced the main streets of the city had been turned into displays for posters of individual can-didates and political parties. The tops of the buildings, their walls, and their doors were covered with portrait posters. New billboards were erected on lampposts and building tops. Most vertical spaces except for windows were taken and thus one of the consulting companies, MAXIMA Consulting LLC, had created freestanding posters as shown in figure 3.2. Even when the elec-tion law of 2016 and 2020 prohibited billboard posters and posters on build-ings and on walls, leaving only designated areas along sidewalks on certain streets, human posters (*hun plakat*)—humans carrying posters—and poster stands filled the horizontal spaces as well (fig. 3.3).

FIGURE 3.2. Budeegiin Mönktuya's poster stands arranged by MAXIMA Consulting, 2008. Photo by Nerguigiin Baasanhuu.

FIGURE 3.3. Poster stands instead of billboards placed high upon lampposts in Ulaanbaatar, 2020. Photo courtesy of Yadamsurengiin Khishigsuren.

Campaigns use every possible media and technological strategy to attract voters. Many media outlets originated coterminously with elections, and more than 74 percent of media outlets have a political affiliation (Gruska, Dreyer, and Renzenbrink 2016). For instance, the country expanded from one television station (Mongol Televiz), which broadcasted on one channel in the late 1980s, to 131 channels, without including local stations, by 2020. Like television, Mongolia's media ecology has been diversified and has expanded into every possible domain. The campaigns utilize techniques that include voter outreach meetings announced via loudspeaker; campaign offices in *gers* are scattered in courtyards of apartment buildings; LCD screen-mounted trucks; passenger LCD screens in taxis; cell phone communications; radios and boom boxes; and gifts and promotional items, such as wall calendars and coffee mugs. They also rely on television and radio programs, newspapers, magazines, postcards, and social media, including Facebook and Twitter (these became especially important around the time of the 2016 election).

I sensed that the visual takeover extended to the sonic realm when I walked past a convenience store that blasted out prerecorded campaign advertisements. Loudspeakers in different parts of the city announced the voter outreach meetings of candidates and encouraged potential voters to attend the meeting. Candidates' speeches at one of the meetings in the city center echoed through the streets as they spoke on the microphones. The evenings were especially spectacular with free open-air concerts in the city's large public squares.

That day I was heading from downtown Ulaanbaatar to Bayangol district, which is a western wing of the city. I combined my errands with observations of the campaign posters of these two districts. As I entered a taxi I had flagged down on the street, I saw a small individual digital screen that was placed on the back of a passenger seat to play campaign advertisements. This was the first time I had witnessed such an individualized high-tech campaign targeting practice in Mongolia. I asked the driver about the "small TV" for the passengers, and he mentioned that it was new and all taxis now had one installed. For a few moments, I was glued to the personalized screen blasting at my face rerunning a candidate's campaign. As I lifted my eyes from the screen to the street through the taxi window, I saw vans and cars that were fully covered in life-size stickers with candidates' images, bearing the words "We trust . . . ," "We support . . . ," "Let's vote for. . . ." Finally, giant LCD screens mounted on the backs of trucks airing campaign media signaled the speedy techno-modernization of Mongolian media (fig. 3.4).

Mobile and dispersed campaigns gave the impression that campaigns were amorphous entities filling any available free space. While that was true,

FIGURE 3.4. "A mobile campaign center" featuring an LCD screen in Ulaanbaatar, 2008. Photo by the author.

many campaigns also had firm headquarters locations and were housed in brick-and-mortar buildings and in *gers*. Officially, campaigns were composed of multiple interrelated tiers and an accompanying bureaucratic infrastructure. First, the official election administration by the General Election Commission (GEC) consisted of three tiers: the district/constituency (*düürgiin khoroo*), the district (*toirgiin khoroo*), and the subdistrict (*hesgiin khoroo*). These administrative units also organized the polling stations, furnished voter registration lists, and carried out much of the advocacy work. Second, there was a centralized political party campaign that was usually housed at a party headquarters and overseen by the party head. The political party campaign was independent from the administration of the GEC. However, it worked closely with all GEC tiers, especially with the constituency-level (*toirgiin khoroo*) campaign. Third, there were the candidates' personal campaign organizations, almost entirely self-financed. Candidates often had to donate money to their parties to sponsor campaign activities.

Mongolians use a Russian word, *shtab*—a command center—for a campaign office. Many affluent candidates had multiple *shtabs*. I mention them because they are sites for posters and much more. They are spaces for dynamic campaigning through media, meetings, discussions, food and tea, and entertainment. The campaign *shtabs* took various forms. Some were housed in apartments and in *gers* (fig. 3.5) built in front of the apartment complexes.

Once, within one block I counted up to seven different campaign *shtabs* of different candidates: two on the first floors of apartment buildings, three as specially built *gers* in the courtyard of those apartment buildings, and two more inside small family shops that were right next to those buildings.

Conversely, I counted numerous campaign *shtabs* of one group from the MPRP, which ran in a centrally located constituency of Bayangol district. The group consisted of four members. First, I saw their *shtab* inside my friend's apartment complex, then near a shopping center, then in a building of the district's MPRP office, and then inside a high school. It appeared that many of the constituency's twenty-eight subdistricts (*heseg*) had a *shtab* for this par-ticular group. In addition to these group *shtabs*, each of the four candidates also had their own *shtabs* throughout the constituency area. A notable one was that of a former education minister, a woman candidate, whose *shtab* was housed, appropriately, adjacent to a bookstore. In addition to their *shtabs* (as a group and as individuals), where they erected their posters, flags, and cam-paign messages, they also placed their posters on the constituency's major roads, streets, sidewalks, businesses, and service centers.

Indeed, in the beginning, I had not realized how ubiquitous that group's campaign posters were until I started encountering them everywhere, to the

FIGURE 3.5. A campaign *shtab* in a courtyard of an apartment complex, 2008. Photo by the author.

FIGURE 3.6. Candidate posters on Peace Avenue (main thoroughfare), Ulaanbaatar, 2012. Photo by the author. The 2012 election also had ubiquitous posters as had been true for the 2008 election.

point of wondering if I had gotten lost in that part of the city and mistakenly returned to the same place I had started out from. I kept seeing the same poster of four candidates almost everywhere I went. Because of the concentration of service centers and businesses in that constituency area, it just happened that many of the errands I did that day were within its perimeter. Several times I paused to look back and forth at various landmarks to make sure I was in the right place. The MPRP group of four candidates I just described was a part of Bayangol district's candidate pool of thirty-one people. The remaining twenty-seven candidates, both independents and from different parties, also had their own group and individual *shtabs* as well as visual and sonic media, voter outreach meetings in various public locations, mobile campaigns on trucks and in vans, and campaign advocates carrying flags, wearing uniforms, and distributing media. A sense of getting lost due to the redundancy of the posters of the same candidates was the third and truly surreal experience of all three similar feelings within the past twenty-four hours. I felt haunted by the same images appearing in front of me over and over, trapping me in a labyrinth. It was the excess of these posters, about which I elaborate more carefully in the following section, that was one of the most surreal aspects of the experience.

Moving on, in addition to posters covering every inch of vertical space (in 2008 and 2012) (fig. 3.6), the city was festooned with flags of the competing political parties. A profusion of flags, although not of that scale, was a well-known practice from socialism. In an article entitled "Gloomy Thoughts on Festivities," journalist Tserendorjiin Dashdondov (2003) criticized the excessive production and swift liquidation of national flags. It was a misuse of the state's already constrained funds, he wrote. For every holiday, the State Factory of Beautification and Ornamentation (*Goyol Chimegleiin Üildver*), which was located next to the government building, manufactured flags anew only for them to be erected for three days and then destroyed. In democratic times, different political parties produce their flags in various venues at home and abroad. In addition to the flags erected on the streets, balconies, and trucks, large crowds of campaign workers carried flags around the city.

The media onslaught signaled that electoral campaigns had resurfaced more overtly after proceeding for the greater part of the four years between parliamentary elections in a clandestine manner, disguised as local community events or a free course on a foreign language. Now voters were realizing (or had their guesses and rumors confirmed) that the sponsors of their language classes and holiday events were also their constituencies' electoral candidates. The surface went deep. This section introduces the larger campaign media ecology and describes the ubiquity of the campaigns specifically by emphasizing the onslaught of posters. I have described three instances of eeriness. The first was during a meal in an empty restaurant surrounded by moving and still images of the candidates. The second surreal moment was on arriving in the city at night in empty darkness save for giant posters swinging in the breeze. And the third was getting lost in Bayangol district, where it felt like the posters were haunting the place. These feelings are subjective and I relay them to the reader to convey their ubiquity, intrusiveness, and their surreal excess.

The Magnitude: Why So Many?

The explosion of campaign posters is just one example of the larger media ecology that has come to dominate the life of the country. From the point of view of democracy-promoting institutions, the multiplicity of portrait posters was a hallmark of free democratic elections. With inflated prices during campaigns, the posters were also a manifestation of the economic boom that the country was experiencing from mining licenses, anticipation of future revenue, and foreign investment. Although posters—portrait posters in particular—have served as the hallmark of electoral campaigns since democratization in Mongolia, the 2008 election relied on posters in a particularly intense way. Important changes in the 2008 electoral legal system stimulated

the explosion of campaign media in general. The number of electoral constituencies was almost three times greater in previous elections: there were
seventy-six in 2004 but only twenty-six in 2008. The constituencies, which
almost tripled in size in 2008, also changed from single-member to multiple-
member districts. The official campaign period was shortened in 2008 to only
three weeks, although the exact length had varied in the past. Hence, the candidates tried to make up for the shortened time and the enlarged voter base
by using as much media and technology as possible.[2] The 2008 legal changes
certainly had a strong impact on the number of posters. However, these legal
changes were not the sole cause of the primacy of posters, which had been the
key medium during other elections.

The frenzy of posters and the proliferation of campaign media at large
substantiates what French philosopher Claude Lefort (1988) calls "democracy
empty locus of power." Unlike in European monarchies, where the space for
the sovereign power is always determined and occupied by physical bodies,
in democracies, with a representative system of government (a parliament),
"the locus of power becomes an empty place. . . . It is such that no individual
and no group can be consubstantial with it—and it cannot be represented"
(Lefort 1988, 17). This emptiness is unavoidable, asserts Lefort (1988), because
the elected representatives do not embody the community.

Lefort (1988) argues that totalitarianism tries to eliminate the space between the people and power and merge the two. While this argument might
be based on earlier aspirations of the revolutionary ideology of communism,
totalitarianism in real life was very different. Alexei Yurchak (2015) and Mayfair Yang (2018) show that Lenin's and Mao's corpses, in the Soviet Union
and in China, respectively, have been treated like those of sacred emperors.
Lenin's corpse, especially, was an object of continuous scientific renewal; 77 percent of his original body has been replaced with other matter and the Lenin
Mausoleum has a laboratory solely dedicated to the biotechnology of maintaining Lenin's body (Yurchak 2015).[3] In Mongolia, the bodies of revolutionaries Damdinii Sukhbaatar and Marshal Choibalsan were kept in a mausoleum
and revered even without sophisticated embalming techniques (Delaplache
2010). In addition, Mongolians' notion of the state (tör) as an abstract and
divine entity remained intact during the socialist state. The state as a transcendent and external entity was and remains separate from the state as a set
of institutions. In other words, totalitarianism did not eliminate the space between the people and the sovereign ruler.

With democratization, the space between people and power lessened,
particularly through free elections, but the sense of emptiness in the "locus of
power" in Mongolia increased. Mongolians' focus on Chinggis Khan as a part

of nationalism and a popular discourse about a need for a powerful leader (*hüchtei udirdagch*) suggests the anxiety about a lack of a tangible ruler.[4] The bodies of the former rulers were taken out of the mausoleum and buried (Delaplache 2010), which had physically emptied the symbolic site of power. And the new, uncertain democratic leadership had led to disappointments and worries about the nation. The frequency and multiplicity of elections (parliamentary, presidential, and local), each every four years, further exacerbates the sense of emptiness at the seat of power in both abstract (the transcendent) and often actual rulers. In democracy, the stable figure (or face) of a sovereign ruler is replaced by "a set of disembodied abstractions: state, nation, citizen, representative, individual" (Scott 2018, 9).

From a sociocultural perspective, therefore, the portrait posters strive to fill the empty space for a body of a ruler. There is a connection between Lefort's (1988) idea that the place of power in democracy is empty and uncertain and the explosion of posters as a metaphorical attempt to fill that void. Posters try to avoid uncertainties through certain techniques. For instance, photographic styles invoke former authoritarian rulers, and "enframements" (that is, positionings, placements, etc.) (Spyer and Steedly 2013) that mark, announce, and put a face to power. I argue that the goal of each poster is *enfacement*; it seeks to fill the void by covering the public space and, by extension, viewers' minds with a face. In elections, faces are tools, although for women, especially, the presentation of bodies is also important.

Posters seize attention by intruding into public spaces and making them into political spaces. Although the candidates also saturated television, internet, and print media, viewers could switch channels or websites and they could dispose of campaign magazines and brochures. Posters in the streets take up visual space. At least in Mongolia in 2008, viewers had few opportunities to take posters down, although occasional vandalism was tolerated. Even then, attempts to disfigure a poster can help it reach more viewers and extend the life of the image. Posters "fight" for attention through a crude replication. For the most part, posters remained statements rather than becoming "image-events," which are "discursive and affective engagements across a diverse public" (Strassler 2020, 9–10).[5]

Enfacement: Dull Images and Risk Takers

In 2008, 2012, and 2016 election posters, male candidates were presented in passport-style photos and sported sleek, side-parted short haircuts, collared light-colored shirts, and dark suits.[6] These choices were purposefully safe in order to conceal any hint of personality that could be ridiculed or critiqued.

They emulate authority and status. A political consultant from Russia who worked in numerous countries in addition to Mongolia told me there are strict rules for political posters: they must be sharp, minimalistic, and invulnerable to interpretations or misreading: "No distractions, sentiments, or embellishments." To use the words of sociologist Maurizio Lazzarato, the posters must produce "invariance" and "univocality," unlike artistic images, which strive for "multireferentiality" and "polyvocality" (2014, 72). The posters fit with how Ernst van Alphen (2013) described the transformation of images in our surroundings since 1990: "An explosion of images and implosion of meaning." The posters were there, to borrow W. J. T. Mitchell's words, to occupy a space and demand a *presence* before making any specific political demands (2012, 10).

Monotonous electoral posters are not unique to Mongolia. Even though laughter and the carnivalesque (Klumbyte 2014) and the acts of blurring a distinction between parody and sincerity (Boyer 2013) are some of the ways in which people engage with politics, scholars note an increase in "the performative reproduction of the precise forms of authoritative discourse" at work in other parts of the world (Boyer and Yurchak 2010, 182). Dominic Boyer and Alexei Yurchak (2010) have observed that political discourses in the late socialist Soviet Union in the 1970s and 1980s and in the late liberal United States in the 2000s exhibit a common tendency toward self-referentiality, repetitiveness, predictability, and an overcrafting of the dominant style of representation. As Yurchak (2007) explains, such uniformity stems from the 1950s, when authoritative texts in the Soviet Union adhered to the objective laws of language and conveyed only a literal meaning independent from context; language was, according to the state, impermeable to subjective interpretation. Visual styles also became normalized and subsumed in a system of "hegemony of representation" (Yurchak 2007). In the 1980s, such representational forms (even with sarcasm and mockery), exploded in volume. Boyer (2013) has also observed that in the United States and elsewhere, political discourse has become more formal and more homogeneous. At the same time, corporations have monopolized the media infrastructure, all of which has led to the proliferation of specific representational forms and an oversimplification of content.

The posters' homogeneity in Mongolia, partially, is related to the parliamentary candidates' liminality. Aware of the power of their superiors, most candidates, including women, chose the style of those who had been elected previously. But voters' potential criticisms were the most paralyzing and prevented experimentation and individuality in posters. Candidates were careful to avoid appearances that might lead voters to question their appropriateness as MPs. Many posters were produced by the political parties' centralized management, which relied on a limited number of production studios, and that contributed to the posters' similarities. Furthermore, as noted above, the 2008 election had multiple-member districts, which means that instead of one candidate from each political party competing in each constituency, multiple candidates from the same party competed against one another in addition to competing against the opposition party for the same seat. During that election, the political parties emphasized "group performance," which further encouraged members of the same groups to craft posters with coordinating images.

The political parties used authoritative and standard images to convey nostalgia for the socialist era's unity and stability. In a similar way, political engagements in postsocialist Eastern Europe (Gal and Kligman 2000; Creed 2011; Burawoy and Verdery 1999) often take the "form of socialist practices of iconography" (Greenberg 2006, 197), which emphasizes the unity of the people, such as representations of the young pioneers (2006, 194). In Serbia, such socialist forms of iconography "formulate new sites of political belonging that avoided interest-based politics and fragmentation endemic to liberal democratic modes of governance" (Greenberg 2006, 182). Similar to the Serbians, some Mongolians associate democratic practices with political instability, a fragmented nation, and incompetent leaders. Hence, the uniform portraits were meant to evoke a sense of stability, predictability, order, and—most important—the powerful political leadership of the socialist era. The portraits could tap into that nostalgia even if few voters had any desire to return to socialism.

Consider a poster at the MPRP's city headquarters. It consists of portraits of twenty MPRP candidates, with the party chairman's portrait in the middle of the row. The message underneath the banner reads: "Let's support Bayar and his entire squad." Older Mongolians who came of age during socialism will connect the phrase to a popular children's novel, *Timur and His Squad* (1940), by Soviet author and World War II hero Arkady Gaidar. The story is about young people engaging in civic service and taking care of their community during the war. Much of the post–World War II generation in Mongolia knows of Timur and his friends as moral exemplars. On the poster, the word "entire," added in front of "squad," puts additional emphasis on unity. The MPRP flaunted "unity" as its political identity against the DP, which was associated with the democratization that brought fragmentation and chaos.

The location and timing of the posters was even more important than their content and revealed the candidates' economic and political might. Patricia Spyer and Mary Steedly (2013, 19) use the notion of "enframement" to explain various techniques of positioning, accessorizing, and improving an image and ways of connecting it to its surroundings so that its intended viewership will appreciate it properly. In the context of elections, the billboards are the main forms of enframement for the posters and keys to the viewers. The billboard positioning accomplishes as much as the content and quality of the images. The billboards on main streets, which not only attract crowds but also come with audiences who actively view and discuss the billboard images among their own circles, are rented months ahead of campaign times at rates several times higher than normal.

Hence billboards, regardless of content, convey distinct political messages. The best placed billboards often sport the most powerful candidates. Since most candidates do not learn about their candidacy and district assignments until a couple of months before the elections, only leaders with leverage over district assignments can plan where they will locate their advertising. In 2008 and 2012, billboards ran out fast and many candidates had to install new billboards and scaffoldings for their posters, thus creating new visual surfaces. These campaigns were dexterous, but they were spending money to acquire these new surfaces and losing valuable poster time in comparison to the candidates who had reserved their billboards ahead of the campaign rush. The older billboards became key signifiers of power. They also tended to endow candidates with the status of a "microcelebrity" (Marwick 2015), solidifying their preexisting power.

Individual posters are "enclaved" images that should dominate the viewer's memory and exclude competing images (Spyer and Steedly 2013, 21). The overcrowded collection of posters, however, did not produce a clear memory of any particular candidate that the campaigns hoped for. Instead, the posters' intrusive placements, omnipresent sizes, monotonous content, and repetitions resulted in sensory overload. Many people told me that they were "fed up with campaigns," "felt nauseated," "felt fatigued and wanted to move to the middle of nowhere." Ironically, instead of "hailing" the voter-subjects, in some cases posters repelled viewers.

Female candidates who managed to erect their posters and *enframe* them for the public's view formed a select minority. With stylistic uniformity and standardization, they mostly wore power suits, accessorized by scarves and subtle jewelry. The women on these posters tended to be incumbents or former parliamentarians or else they occupied high-profile positions in political parties or were influential in business. Similar to their male counterparts, they strived for safe and properly political images that were invariant and not open to interpretation (for example, fig. 3.7).

FIGURE 3.7. Mönkhtuya's 2008 campaign posters, as arranged by MAXIMA Consulting LLC. Photo by the author.

In comparison, the women candidates who were mostly new to politics, independent, marginal, and not wealthy, struggled to break into the campaigns (for example, Jurmediin Zanaa, discussed in chapter 5). If they managed to place their posters, these posters were not uniform, minimalistic, or univocal, like "proper" political posters. Instead, these new candidates chose images that showed variety and individual preferences. They were marginal, but they were also risk-takers.

Radnaagiin Burmaa, a first-time candidate from the DP in 2008, had her picture taken against a background of flowering white Monos or Bird Cherry (*Prunus Padus*). Burmaa offered a perspective outside of the mainstream and did not adhere to the posters' need for clean, sharp, and nondistracting images. Instead she concentrated on the purity, honesty, and freshness associated with the color white. The bird cherry bushes flowered for only a few days in early summer, and Burmaa waited for the right day when the flowers were at their peak. To my mind, it added to her style and the distinctiveness of her poster, although one consultant (who worked for a different candidate) remarked to me that Burmaa's poster was not "properly political" because it had flowers and was "too soft."

Another female candidate in 2008, Gantömöryn Uyanga from the Civic Movement Party, selected a photograph of herself in a pensive mood. She was immediately criticized. "A weird picture," someone said. "Why is she so lost in her thoughts (*bodlogshrood l*)?" The portrait attracted attention, not always sympathetic, partly because her poster diverged from the neutral and plain pattern espoused by the political consultants and instead stirred disquiet in the viewers (fig. 3.8). The most unusual poster came from the Civil Movement Party in the 2012 election campaign. It featured a map of Mongolia with the party's

FIGURE 3.8. Gantömöryn Uyanga, from the Civil Movement Party, 2008. Photo by the author.

FIGURE 3.9. Election poster for the Civic Movement Party, 2012. Photo by the author.

thirty-eight candidates populating it. Strikingly, thirty-six of thirty-eight candidates were women. The poster was unique and did not fit with the expectations of a professional political consultant, which was exactly the point (fig. 3.9).

If the uniform content of the portrait posters reminded voters of bygone state socialism in the context of a competitive election, posters were part of a dynamic exchange. The campaigns constantly reproduced, renewed, and (re)placed their clients' images in dialectical relation to those of their opponents. On the one hand, the magnitude and the uniformity of these posters were pragmatic outcomes of the competition, a response to electoral design with larger constituencies, and situated within a particular historical epoch. On the other hand, these posters revealed the unconscious substance of the state of things, to use Kracauer's (1995) term. They communicated the politicians' paranoia of going forward and taking risks and, simultaneously, a search for safety in the familiar. This speaks to electionization as a formation that is constantly spinning in politics.

Deep Surfaces

Historian Joan Scott (2018) takes off from Lefort's (1988) notion of democracy's empty locus of power and argues that as democracy creates anxiety about the instability of power, it tends to encourage the naturalization of the sexes as a form of certainty against uncertainty in democratic leadership. She argues that politics downplays the concept of gender while choosing to capitalize on the notion of sex. And the "naturalized belief in the . . . differences of sexes provides legitimation for the organization of other social and political inequalities; in turn the legitimation invoked by politics, establishes the immutability of biology" (Scott 2018, 8). "It is precisely at moments of great political instability that invocations of gender . . . appeal to deep psychic investments," says Scott (2018, 10). She writes that the biological differences between the sexes "as a ground for politics is one of the legacies of modernity" and tends to exclude women from the political arena while legitimating masculinity as the embodiment of power (10). As Scott puts it:

> It is not that gender and politics as established entities come into contact and so influence each other. Rather, it's that the instability of each looks into the other for certainty: political systems invoke what is deemed the immutability of gender to legitimize asymmetries of power; those political invocations then "fix" differences of sex, in that way denying the indeterminacy that troubles both sex and politics. (2019, 25)

Scott's argument resonates with the electoral campaign politics in Mongolia, especially in regard to what makes an electable woman candidate. While I agree with Scott that, in theory, the political power aims to solidify gender norms into predictability for further legitimacy, I found that in real life, this process can also create a more dynamic transformation in gender. This relates to the indeterminacy of gender norms to begin with, especially at the time when gender in Mongolian society was transforming rapidly from a more fixed and top-down regime to a more pluralistic and market-oriented one. Moreover, the women candidates were actively seeking certain forms of femininity while rejecting others, thus perpetuating the transformation in gender. In the following, I illustrate, ethnographically, how campaign images reveal the interdependence of gender and politics and how women candidates strive to gain confidence by adopting certain qualities or attributes that are either already associated with being a proper man or a proper woman or that get gendered in the process. I show that transformation of gender does not always lead to its naturalization per Scott's (2019) argument. On the contrary, women candidates' embodiments of cultural traits, particularly education and skills, keep them in the sphere of culture, although with little guarantee of seats in the Parliament. Although highly valued, culture, which is acquired and human-made, remains secondary to "nature" due to nature's association with powers that are beyond human activities.

FIGURE 3.10. "Let's Elect the Democracy Trio" poster, 2008. Photo by the author.

Campaign images communicate emerging understandings of gender and women's impact on politics. They show that elections are highly gendered processes—specifically, one can see how gender is being utilized, transformed, and presented by electoral campaigns. Women tend to be framed not so much vis-à-vis men, but often as assets, subsidiaries, or as enhancers in a battle for seats among male candidates. In response to this, many Mongolian female candidates choose carefully how they are being represented. The repertoire for creating official feminine looks in political posters remains narrow and women work around the familiar authoritative representations by bringing subtlety to their looks. Posters tend to hide that struggle, but the stories behind the pictures reveal a dynamic negotiation of gender and politics.

In 2008, a poster from the DP, "Let's Elect the Democracy Trio," featured Burmaa and two cocandidates: Elbegdorj (chairman of the DP) and Bayarsaikhan (a businessman and newcomer to politics) (fig. 3.10). The poster was an assemblage of three passport-style photos against a white background. Each candidate wore a navy suit. Since the suit colors blended into each other, one did not immediately notice that Burmaa was placed behind the other two (male) candidates. "It is a strange picture," my discerning research assistant Baasanhuu wrote in her research diary on first seeing the poster when it was placed on the street. "The two men are squeezing Burmaa from each side."

FIGURE 3.11. The MPRP poster featuring "the gentlemen" who let the lady be in front. 2008. Note that there are no names written under the candidates. The two male candidates are well-recognized politicians in Mongolia, whereas the woman, a medical doctor, is newer to politics. Photo by the author.

Later, I looked closely at the picture and saw that the two male candidates' shoulders were placed over Burmaa's shoulders.

When I saw Burmaa in person, she exclaimed: "The two men of our parties pushed back the only woman cocandidate [in the group]!" "I told [the cocandidates] to look at the poster from the MPRP and learn how to be real gentlemen!" Burmaa said, referring to a poster where a female candidate was standing in front of two male cocandidates (fig. 3.11): "They know how to treat their women properly, I told them."[7]

Burmaa was also upset because in the picture she appeared a darker shade than her actual skin tone. In contrast, the pictures of the male candidates were of a slightly lighter shade. "How could you do that?" Burmaa noted to Elbegdorj during a meeting. "You [fellows] made me look pitch dark while making yourselves look lighter!" she protested. (Later on, the poster was replaced with ones that had somewhat better photos, although still accentuating the male candidates.) Most Mongolians favor lighter skin tones over darker ones, especially when judging a woman's attractiveness. The physical attractiveness through the skin tone was also interwoven with a host of values associated with modernity and class that in turn conveyed the background in education and professional status. As in most of East and North-East Asia, in Mongolia, darker skin is often associated with lower social status, rural life, and little education. For Burmaa, the poster felt like an attack on her candidacy, as she was foregrounding her qualities as a leader and an educated professional. Many people, including Burmaa, found the association between skin tone and other characteristics outdated and discriminatory. Yet, at the same time, Burmaa and other politicians were aware that much of the populace would automatically associate a lighter complexion with urban professionals. A darker skin tone required the viewer to make an extra cognitive step to make that connection. The candidates agreed that campaigns were not the place to fix voters' prejudices.

In a few days, the trio had another photo session, during which Elbegdorj tried to correct the previous mistakes: positioning and skin tone. The skin tone was easy to get right. In the subsequent posters, Burmaa appeared with her light complexion. But the positioning continued to be an issue. The problem was Burmaa's height. "It is impossible to have Burmaa in front," Elbegdorj said to me. "She towers like a camel!" Elbegdorj was just about an inch shorter than Burmaa and Bayarsaikhan was perhaps a fraction of an inch shorter, if at all. However, they strived to create a poster that fit the gender stereotype of men being taller than women, even though all of Mongolia knew of Elbegdorj's smaller stature (which did not prevent him from becoming one of the most popular politicians). Together with the photographer, they choreographed a photo session. The trio would walk together at an angle that would downplay Burmaa's height and make the men appear taller. They spent a frustrating evening walking back and forth in front of the photographer. Yet, the photos from that session did not appear on a poster.

Instead, two additional posters were made. One was another assemblage in which Elbegdorj appeared the tallest, Bayarsaikhan slightly shorter in the middle, and Burmaa the shortest. The heights conspicuously reversed reality, and the poster did not hide that it was a montage. Unlike in the first poster, Burmaa was placed up front and with a more realistic complexion. In the second poster, the trio was photographed while appearing to have a conversation against the background of the city's *ger* district. The picture took advantage of the natural environment. The men stepped up on the rocks for a slight elevation, which instantly solved the height issue. The picture showed the candidates only from the waist up, so you could not see their feet on the rocks (figs. 3.12 and 3.13). The poster reaffirmed and reified the stereotypes of gender that were based on biological attributes: men's tallness and women's light complexion. Socioculturally, the respectability of gender was also at play: the men let the woman be in front of them. The candidates' negotiation of the attributes of gender on these posters affirms Joan Scott's insight that gender and politics are unstable entities that look to each other for self-affirmation and

FIGURES 3.12 AND 3.13. Newer versions of "Let's Elect the Democracy Trio," 2008. Photos by the author.

naturalization of sexes. Yet, Burmaa's professional background as a leader in civil society and her reputation had complicated the situation.

If Burmaa's height was such a threat to Elbegdorj's performance of masculinity, why did he, the DP chairman, choose her as a cocandidate? He could have chosen from a multitude of candidates—including smaller-statured women—whose presence could have enhanced his masculinity in a more natural way. But Elbegdorj chose to run the election with Burmaa. Burmaa's credentials, as I discuss in the next section, were more valuable to Elbegdorj than one might have predicted.

The Honest Gender

Campaign posters included not just a pictorial image but also texts, such as candidates' names, a slogan, and the name of a political party. "Let's Elect the Democracy Trio" appeared above the portraits of Burmaa and her cocandidates on the poster she abhorred, which showed her skin tone as darkened. The candidates' full names were listed at the bottom of the poster. The poster also included three adjectives meant to describe the group: Honest, Civic, Dynamic (*Shudarga, Irgenleg, Erch Huchtei*). The choice of these three adjectives merits scrutiny. The first two words, *honest* and *civic*, resonate with how Burmaa's party leadership used some of her credentials in the campaign.

When the DP chairman, Elbegdorj, came to one of the voter outreach meetings and introduced the other two cocandidates, he noted Burmaa's intelligence and honesty and her service to civil society. The third word, *dynamic*,
relates to the chairman's assessment of Bayarsaikhan at that same meeting.
Elbegdorj accentuated Bayarsaikhan's youthful energy as a man in his thirties
and described that energy as an important asset for the country.

   There are stories behind those words. Burmaa was known as a person of
high integrity, especially in urban educated circles. Her reputation for honesty had three primary components: her long history of work in civil and
social organizations, her recent political career, and her gender. Her reputation had been enhanced by her legal fights against Parliament Speaker Tsen-
diin Nyamdorj, who edited several laws, including the election law in 2007,
in a manner that was deemed unconstitutional. After repeated accusations
by Burmaa and her colleagues, Nyamdorj was found guilty and was ousted
(Undarya 2009). The media followed the process closely, thus accentuating
Burmaa's reputation as an unwavering opponent of dishonesty.

   The second component of Burmaa's reputation for honesty came in part
from her status as a newcomer to politics. Compared to many long-term politicians who eventually lost credibility through association with one scandal
or another, Burmaa's overall reputation was untainted. She was unrelated
to any disreputable politicians or corruption cases, and because she owned

no businesses, she had no conflicts of interest. Burmaa's competitors could gather no fodder to launch a "black" PR campaign against her. Such "cleanliness" was rare.

The final component of her reputation for honesty involved her gender identity. A popular (but contested) rhetoric that women politicians are less corrupt than their male counterparts further accentuated Burmaa's characteristic as an "honest" candidate. In the 1990s and 2000s, the campaign to promote women in politics drew on this stereotype of women in their attempt to pass the 30 percent quota for women among candidates running in parliamentary elections and to prepare the passing of the Law on Promotion of Gender Equality. Overall, in the context of politics, women as a group were termed as *shudarga* (honest).

So, all these factors considered, Burmaa could not be "cleaner" as a potential politician. In contrast, Burmaa's two male cocandidates, Elbegdorj and Bayarsaikhan, were getting hammered by "black PR." During his candidacy in the 2008 election, Elbegdorj was accused of corruption, lying, and making unfilled promises (Bodoo 2008; Erdene 2008; Süren 2008; Tsogtgerel 2008). The *Century News* (one of Mongolia's periodicals), meanwhile, published an editorial about Bayarsaikhan entitled, "The Ecologist Bayarsaikhan Is Caught" (Bat 2008). The editorial disclosed that Bayarsaikhan's doctorate degree on ecological sciences was a fraud and that he had betrayed his former party, Citizen's Will, by joining the DP. While it is impossible to prove that the "halo effect" of Burmaa's integrity was sufficient to increase Elbegdorj's votes, it was certainly important that at least one of the cocandidates did not exacerbate the media's attack on him. Burmaa's reputation helped her gain a candidacy in the elections regardless of the result. Burmaa's political cleanliness and a reputation for being an honest person, as I detail in the following section, was crucial for the DP as well as for its chairman in participating in the election.

The Civic Defense

On the "Democracy Trio" poster, the second word—*Irgenleg*, civic—pointed to another set of Burmaa's assets. Considered as one of the founders of a civil society following democratization in the 1990s, Burmaa commanded outright respect in civil society. She earned the nickname "*Irgenii Burmaa*" (Civic Burmaa) because she established civil society groups and NGOs promoting women in politics. Because she established a center for voter education, one of her friends urged her to run in the 2008 election as "Voters' Burmaa."

In anticipation of the 2008 election, civil society groups had been mobilizing against corruption. The Civic Coalition (*Iregnii Evsel*), a group that emerged from civil society, was competing for seats in the election.[8] The Civic Coalition's campaign argued for the eradication of the two larger parties, the DP and MPRP, as they had been accused of corruption. This means that some of Burmaa's acquaintances were now against her political party. Uyanga—a member of the Civic Coalition, a female journalist, and now an electoral candidate—was especially inclined to speak out against Elbegdorj, the chairman of the DP.

According to the rumors that circulated in political circles, there were some who claimed that Elbegdorj chose Burmaa as his cocandidate in order to "shield" himself from attacks by civil society, especially those involving accusations of corruption. I was skeptical that such "shielding" was possible, especially regarding an issue as heated as corruption. However, an impromptu event supported this view, when Burmaa indeed shielded not only Elbegdorj but also the DP.

On the afternoon of June 19, 2008, Burmaa was invited to participate in a debate show on "Corruption" at the Mongolian National Broadcasting station. The show would broadcast live at 9:00 p.m. that day. All eleven political parties competing in the election were invited. Initially, Elbegdorj (as chairman of the DP) was slotted to participate, but he withdrew at the last minute.

The opportunity was a double-edged sword for Burmaa. The screen time, usually reserved for higher-profile politicians, was rare and valuable, especially since it was being offered free of charge. But participating in a debate on corruption could also hurt Burmaa's candidacy. The DP and its leadership were being accused of corruption, and Burmaa was being thrown into the front line of defense. "The small [political] parties will attack us, the big parties," said Burmaa. Uyanga, from the Civic Coalition, was also participating in the show. While it was unlikely that Uyanga could surpass Elbegdorj in votes, many people speculated that she was there to split the vote and to weaken his chances of winning. For that, she would use this opportunity to confront him. But what would happen if Burmaa went to the interview instead of Elbegdorj? "Uyanga cannot attack me [no association with corruption], but if she attacks the chairman [Elbegdorj], then an outright defense would not be possible," Burmaa said.

After much hesitation, Burmaa decided to go. Anticipating a heated debate, she gathered the booklets on the DP's financial disclosures and electoral spending, just in case they proved useful. She was one of the first to arrive at the broadcasting studio—a large well-lit circular room—and took the center seat (fig. 3.14). As other participants arrived, they greeted each other. Some could not hide their respect for Burmaa and some even appeared intimidated by her. Others expressed amazement. "What a clever move for the DP to send

FIGURE 3.14. A debate on corruption. National Broadcasting Station, June 19, 2008. Burmaa is in a white jacket at the center-left. Uyanga is at the same desk. Photo by the author.

Sister Burmaa!" they said, half-joking (meaning that they were aware that Burmaa was sent to defend the DP). When Uyanga entered the room, her eyes widened for a quick moment, then she came up to Burmaa, respectfully extending a handshake: "Hello, Sister Burmaa! Oh, *of course* the DP sent *you*! [*Medeej Ardchilsan Nam taniig l yavuulani sh dee!*]" she exclaimed with a gentle smile but without hiding her disappointment.

As Burmaa anticipated, the two main parties were the targets. The first question: How will your political party fight corruption? Each participant could address the question in two minutes. Burmaa was one of the first to answer. She argued that the law on corruption was incomplete and that it needed an amendment that addressed a conflict of interest. The next three participants argued against her idea of amending the law by saying that additional laws were of no use because law is too abstract, and people do not abide by the law. Instead of another law, they suggested implementing mechanisms to encourage people to obey the law, such as increased salaries for civil servants (who are the most corrupt, as the participant argued) or creating citizen watch groups within the government.

Uyanga, as anticipated, directly condemned the two main parties, the DP and the MPRP. "The two big parties are incapable of fighting corruption. We have no other way to eradicate corruption but to remove the two parties from the leadership, and bring citizen monitoring into the government leadership," she argued. As an example of corruption, she mentioned how one of the main parties' chairman had made a mutually beneficial arrangement with a younger businessman to run for this election. (This could be seen as a direct allusion to the DP's chairman.) The second question followed: What innovative changes do you suggest in implementing the law against corruption? Uyanga responded by continuing to criticize the two major parties. "The anticorruption law is being implemented among midlevel positions. Instead, it should scrutinize the large 'sharks,' like the political party leaders, and high-level state officials," she noted.

Despite the expectations of Burmaa's staff, the debate did not turn into a volley of accusations. Except for Uyanga, almost no one directly attacked the DP. Burmaa let the program participants debate the causes of corruption (that is, the low wages of civil servants) and possible remedies (increasing civil servants' salaries, changing attitudes, stepping up citizens' vigilance). When a show host posed a simple question—Does your party have a genuine desire to fight corruption?—a representative from one of the smaller parties accused the DP of corruption. In response, Burmaa lifted up a couple of brochures from the last two years that she had brought with her, titled "The DP's Financial Statements." "We must begin with financial disclosures. All political parties were asked to submit their financial statements to the monitoring office. Where are yours? [I] do not remember your party submitting anything. These are the statements from our party." Seeing these publications, other participants sank in their seats. Burmaa did not offer any explicit defense of her party. However, she rescued the party by bringing up the work that she did to fight corruption, and the monitoring work that the Voter Education Center conducted on the DP's financing. It was Burmaa's representation of the DP, her appearance in person *biyeree* (in her body) to substitute for the chairman of the DP, that mattered most. Her presence alone prevented the representatives of other parties from further attacking the DP and its chairman on the National Broadcasting Station. Gender and politics influenced each other: the DP was saved and the honesty and civic-ness of the female candidate was proven, at least within the DP, and reconfirmed to the public.

Expanding the Surface

Although I spotted the "Let's Elect the Democracy Trio" poster here and there, I could not find Burmaa's individual poster on the main street in Ulaanbaatar. Of the three DP candidates, Bayarsaikhan had the largest number of posters.

His passport-style portraits were all identical, varying only in size and placement. Some were placed high on a pole, others on newly made billboards
right on a grassy, tree-filled roadside berm. The billboards, about the height
of an average person, had been placed about twenty yards from each other
and were visible to both pedestrians and drivers. I counted about fifty billboards with Bayarsaikhan's portrait in the space of two city blocks. If you
looked at them from one end of the street, they made a perfect row. If you
were coming down the street, you would encounter one every few yards. This
redundancy gave Bayarsaikhan's billboards the most advantageous placement, creating a miniature world of their own. Unlike the posters hung from
tall buildings, their tight spacing excluded all competitors, so that no other
candidate's media could share the space with them. Posters featuring Bayarsaikhan's portrait also appeared on building walls and streetlight poles; the
repetitive concentration of his posters was one of the densest. Campaign advertisements greatly outnumbered commercial ones. Repetition was one of
the techniques campaigns used in the hope of maximizing visibility.

When I entered Burmaa's office, I saw a gathering of her campaign staff
at a small round table discussing what appeared to be an upsetting issue. A
friend of Burmaa's from high school who had been volunteering for the past
few days had discovered a big pile of Burmaa's posters (letter size) for distribution thrown in a trash pile the night before. These were posters of Burmaa
on her own without the two other candidates. The friend rescued the un-
soiled copies and brought them to the office. Insulted and worried, Burmaa's
friend wanted to understand why anyone would throw the posters away. She
explained that she saw it as a moral attack on Burmaa as a person and not
simply an effort to damage her candidacy. Everyone was concerned, but Burmaa gently steered the conversation toward the many other tasks that needed
to be done in her campaign.

One of the most urgent tasks was to produce additional posters. Almost
everyone in Burmaa's *shtab* was worried about the scarcity of her posters
compared to those of the other candidates competing in the Chingeltei district. One large poster featured Burmaa against a background of a flowing
Mongolian flag. Stylistically, this poster was similar to the other candidates'
posters—the univocal portrait posters covering the city. The second poster
was Burmaa in front of the flowering bird cherry bush. Burmaa also decided
that a third poster should reflect her commitment to voters, as demonstrated
by her initiating and directing the Voter Education Center (NGO). Her campaign motto was "Voters Preside over Governing" (*Songogch Ta Töriin Ezen*).
She chose a photo from one of her voter outreach meetings. She appeared
fully surrounded by local voters, children, and campaign workers holding

FIGURE 3.15. Campaign workers in uniforms, 2008. Photo by the author.

her portraits, flags, and posters. The image made a dramatic contrast with her rivals' campaign posters, which featured the candidate alone.

In the next few days, the number of posters on the streets continued to grow, as more candidates tried to secure some space among the campaign of images. Various candidates began creating campaign surfaces by having people wear campaign paraphernalia with the portraits of the candidates. The campaigns engaged their staff, volunteers, or paid individuals to wear T-shirts with the portraits of their candidates, turning humans into posters at the height of the competition. These human-posters delivered flags, marched in public rallies and parades, attended gatherings and speeches, and distributed print media. The campaign began valuing people more as mobile images than as individuals. The blue T-shirts and caps of the DP campaigners and the red uniforms of the MPRP dominated street scenes. Interlacing the blue and red were the colors of individual campaigners: I spotted large groups of young people wearing uniform purple, orange, green, and gold T-shirts with matching caps, some with portraits and others with names of individual candidates printed on their paraphernalia (fig. 3.15).

Burmaa's campaign staff feared her campaign was too modest, her posters still too few, and tried to convince her to commission a large campaign sign. At first, Burmaa refused because there were so many logistical questions, including where it would be possible to install a poster of approximately 10 ×

FIGURE 3.16. Burmaa's largest poster, 2008. Photo by the author.

7 yards (the size of a three-story building). Then she happened to talk to one of her old friends about the idea. He owned a small construction company, and had a ten-story building under construction in Chingeltei district, where Burmaa was campaigning. He offered her the use of most of its wall space for her poster. Making a poster the size of a three-story building in one piece was technically not feasible, but the poster-making company printed the poster out in pieces, transported them, and glued them together at the site. I was standing with Burmaa next to the building when we realized that without a metal frame to hold the poster, it would soon be soaring in the wind. Burmaa had no money left to pay for metal scaffolding and framing. The poster

survived without a frame for longer than we expected, although one of its corners constantly flapped in the breeze (fig. 3.16).

Conclusion: Triangulation of Images

Although campaigns have relied on print and other media since the inception of democratic competitive elections, in the 2008 Mongolian elections candidates' images gained more significance than ever. Given the enlarged constituencies that year, candidates were no longer able to carry out enough face-to-face meetings with voters. They turned to media as a substitute and relied heavily on their images' mimetic effects. They began relying more on images to connect with viewers than on their ability to provide charismatic performances in person. The restrictions on the number of pages produced by a campaign and the fear of the populace's criticisms, among other concerns, led to the reproduction of "safe" images that were mostly reminiscent of the established mundane portraits of former socialist leaders.[9]

Through a mechanical repetition, most images strived to attain what Michael Warner (1992) calls publicness or metapopularity—when popularity reaches a point where the attributes of the individual are no longer crucial. The fact of popularity, or the popularity of one's popularity, as it were, gives the image an extra value beyond the qualities of the image itself. The viewer alone does not decide the significance of the candidate (Warner 1992). The viewer is no longer alone with the image: a triangulation occurs between the image, the viewer, and the viewer's sense of what others feel and perceive. This triangulation of image, viewer, and context produces the sensorial saturation and shared hype and concern that characterize electionization. Kajri Jain's (2007, 298) assertion that "mass cultural image[s] serve as mediums of contagion, like air, water, and bodily fluids," helps us to perceive the power of images for the public, especially the imagined public that is a part of Warner's triangulation of image, viewer, and the context. Hence, images are a part of the surface of electionization.

By 2008, the nation had shifted from a mostly meeting-based electoral process to an image-dependent one. With the expansion of constituencies, the crucial democratic elements of the campaigns—the dialogues during the voter outreach meetings—were now no longer the primary tools for candidates, although they remained the preferred part of the campaign for voters. To some extent, voter outreach meetings continue to exist as a possibility for a reciprocal relationship between voters and candidates. But a reliance on images greatly diminishes the role of what could be regarded as a form of rational-critical discourse in which candidates are forced to hear voters' complaints, criticisms, and requests. Instead, the campaign of images is a form of domination that prevents the transformation of both parties (candidate and voter) through communication. In a campaign of images, voters are treated, at best, like viewers and consumers and, at worst, like "dystopic or dysfunctional others of particular modernities" who are expected "to submit to [the images'] dictate" (Jain 2007, 298). Voters are treated as having little or no influence on candidates. Yet, candidates are worried about the populace's disparaging criticisms, even if they appear impermeable. Most candidates tend to concern themselves with the publicness of their images, which strengthens their confidence in their candidacy but not always the confidence of voters in them. Previously, small-scale voter outreach meetings in local cultural centers or schools generated an intimate but also more realistic sense of the ways in which candidates were perceived by voters. In contrast, large-scale, lavishly staged, and preorchestrated meetings with thousands of voters in concert halls gave the candidates a feeling of euphoria, self-adulation, overconfidence, and even a false sense of victory. There was a disconnect between voters and candidates in those large-scale meetings, as they rarely featured dialogues with or spontaneous comments from townspeople. The fact that the candidate on the stage during those mega-meetings needed to be projected on a large screen shows that the image (even in real time) was a necessary object. Consistent with the campaign of images, such large-scale meetings were one-directional: they expected voters to listen, admire, uptake, and be molded—not so much the other way around.

The campaign of images made legible a peculiar but not unexpected political transformation. Because the campaign of images required massive investments, and because electoral campaigns were largely privately financed, the campaigns gained a double role as unofficial "exclusionary safeguards" (Ahmed 2013) intended by the ones in power to keep challengers out of Parliament. In the United States and many other places, campaigns are financed through fund-raising—a practice that hardly exists in Mongolia, or does so only covertly. It is also not surprising that in the United States, with its longer history of capitalism, political candidates would be expected to finance their own campaigns. The situation is different in Mongolia, where individuals or organizations in control of large sums of money have emerged relatively recently, since the end of socialism. Most newcomers have no access to the structures of popularity that are free for incumbents, who enjoy the advantages of routine media presence, exposure during public events, and access to public funds for infrastructure and services that some incumbents present to their constituents as the result of their special efforts. In such an unequal competition, only the most well-positioned and wealthy newcomers are able to compete with existing incumbents. Given the gender disparity in wealth, female candidates are in a doubly disadvantageous situation, competing against money and against male-dominated politics. The 2008 election raised the bar for campaign expenditures partly due to the expansion of the districts, which required more resources for reaching voters compared to previous elections when the constituencies were smaller.[10] This also allowed images to take precedence over the quality of the candidates. The connection between media, power, and elections became even tighter. The elections became less democratic and the formation of a ruling elite took place in conjunction with the campaign of images.

The rare images of women on political posters are outside of the media regime and differ from typical images of women on TV and in ads, magazines, and other media, many of which emphasize physical attractiveness, wealth, and commodity consumption, all in line with market capitalism and new forms of conspicuous consumption. Political posters are out of sync with this kind of gendered regime of images. As the political regime has changed from a socialist totalitarian one to a market in the past thirty years, the regime of images also has transformed, and most profoundly for women. As there were almost no women political leaders during state socialism, they were also absent from the political posters of the national leadership (all the central committee members were men). Ordinary and sometimes celebrated women appeared in posters geared toward the populace as moral models. Women in those posters, along with men, were often examples of inspiring workers and selfless mothers.

Hence, the images of women candidates on political posters during democratization are unique and at the same time incongruous with the existing regime of power and the regime of images. Their existence is notable but puzzling for the larger public. Instead of career women, the current regime of images disproportionately favors the young and attractive: fashion models, beauty queens, and trophy wives. These are the images that dominate public spaces, entertaining and enticing. It is against such a regime of images that women candidates strive to gain a presence in politics. As Joan Scott (2018) argues, democracy's empty locus of power exacerbates the anxiety about the country's rulership. This leads society to revert to the safer and naturalized notions of masculinity versus femininity, thus privileging sex over gender. What my ethnography has shown in this regard is something rather surprising. While the images of men tend to stick to more biological markers of strength and thus appear neutral in cultural terms, women's images are often adorned with cultural attributes that take attention away from their biological characteristics. Hence, "honesty," although a genderless attribute, became associated with women during elections in 2008 and 2012. It is difficult to gauge the extent to which this attribute enhanced women candidates' electability. Yet it must have been helpful, as in the following elections, some of the prominent male politicians have adopted "honesty" as their attribute in order to override their tainted reputation in the past.

Backstage:
Inside (Pre)-Campaigning Strategies

A New Candidate: Beyond Gender

The absence of Serjee's campaign posters in her constituency—a rural town I call Bumbat—was especially glaring given the ubiquity of posters and the extravagant onset of the official campaigns.[1] Absences are revealing, and this one was particularly intriguing. I kept asking myself as I entered Bumbat toward the end of my daylong journey: "Did Serjee fight for poster space? What went on in the background of the campaign that she could not have a single poster on the street?" Together with Serjee's consultant (and his family), we drove from Ulaanbaatar to Bumbat to spend a few weeks with Serjee as she campaigned for the first time.

Upon our arrival, we checked into the town's main hotel. After a long night of discussion about Serjee's opponents in the consultant's one-bedroom suite, the next morning Serjee met us in her own suite. It comprised a large living room for meetings, a bedroom, and a spare room for her assistants. In front of a large mirror, Serjee was finishing off her makeup from a tray that was almost as big as the top of the hotel's writing desk. The consultant complimented Serjee on her outfit, an ensemble that consisted of an A-line dress and a matching coat.

We arrived early for Serjee's first meeting, which was with the local women's group.

"Oh, my dear women!" Serjee exclaimed, rather dramatically, as she entered a large room where a dozen women—including the leaders of her political party's local branch of the women's group—also had arrived early in order to prepare for the meeting. "Let's make a circle with all the chairs," she said energetically and confidently, and started to rearrange the furniture. Serjee's "my dear women" (*mini hüühnüüd ee*) sounded warm but firm. It felt too personal for someone who was just getting to know these women. Yet, she ignored the women's surprised expressions and continued to haul the furniture and instruct them at the same time. Serjee's style of connecting with people was somewhat outside of the expected norms. Usually, candidates act courteously and formally, and they hardly ever try to be one of the locals. Serjee was quick to enter their circle.

Serjee's candidacy presentation to a group of more than fifty women comprised her plans to create more jobs in the constituency, to take care of the poor and vulnerable, and to fight corruption at the national level. After she finished, her consultant stood up and gave a short speech advocating that the women should vote for "this new candidate," who was standing for election for the first time. He emphasized that "this slim and petite woman has great potential in politics." And he added: "Give her a chance and see what she will achieve and bring to you all, as all the other candidates are your familiar middle-aged male candidates and you already know what to expect from them." He told the gathered women that their choices were crucial. "That is because an aggregate Mongolian voter," he said, "is a *woman* in her late twenties and early thirties. And," he concluded, "it is hard to believe that *you* women do not support your own kind."

In retrospect, the consultant's gendering comments were particularly revealing, as Serjee's preparation for her campaigning was based on mobilizing her political party's women's groups as her base. That is why she also felt immediately frank and at ease in managing the local women from the moment she stepped into the meeting room. Yet her campaign in Bumbat was a mystery. Why was she holding an introductory meeting with the local women this late—right before the elections? Why were there no posters and other visible campaign materials in the town center? And why was she living in a hotel suite during her campaign as opposed to renting a more long-term residency? All of this led me to unravel the complex activities that take place during the four years that precede the campaigns—the precampaigning period—and which influence the official campaigning. Indeed, the visual and auditory takeover that saturates the electoral landscape, which I discussed in chapter 3, does not immediately reveal the work of precampaigning that must take place before and beyond the legally designated twenty-one-day campaign period.

Thus, in this chapter, I examine Serjee's precampaign and campaign experience in running for seats and its influence on individual subjectivities, group identities, and the politicization of everyday life. It is an example of how a single person's efforts to become a parliamentary candidate are entangled with and influence wider sentiments, social dynamics, and subjectivities: that is, they can *electionize* the people and places surrounding that candidate. Serjee's story—her campaign activities, her choice of supporters and the ultimate outcome of her campaign—is particularly revealing of the ways in which electionization is a gendered and a gendering process: it builds and expands on social and political institutions, it mobilizes groups, and it recreates certain forms of femininity and feminism. Serjee aspired to be independent from the economic patronage of her male colleagues, unlike some other women candidates, as she put it to me. The fact that she sponsored her own campaign and insisted on demonstrating, whenever possible, that she was an autonomous subject helps to emphasize that women's lives are not entirely constituted or influenced by men, even in the male-dominated elite politics.

Serjee's campaign also illustrates a more common aspect of the female candidate's situation: the struggle to compensate for less than sufficient funds through clever strategizing and networking activities. Serjee's precampaigning and campaigning demonstrate that the activities of female candidates are indeed associated with leadership, power, persuasion, and independence albeit often different from those of male politicians. Their activities also do not correspond to media representations of women in politics in Mongolia as loquacious and weak. The qualities interpreted as positive in men, such as persuasiveness and persistence, are turned into negative qualities in women, such as pushiness and aggression (see Togtohbayar 2008).

By examining Serjee's experiences, I argue that the very practice and process of campaigning, which encompasses building fame, authority, and support, has become a socially legible and broadly influential "technology of gender," to borrow Teresa de Lauretis's (1987) formulation. Electionization in Mongolia creates the conditions by which gender is constructed through representational and self-representational strategies alike. Serjee incorporated what could be called technologies of power politics (that is, mobilization, persuasion, and directorship) into the technology of gender: she mobilized women and built a hierarchical system of support, which she used in turn to gain more access to power, and maintained her existing power through exchange and negotiation (until an opponent took over her constituency).

Serjee's case is particularly illuminating as it reveals some of the multiplicity of the technology of gender. Her strategies were geared toward acquiring power in order to move beyond the existing gender system. In the existing politics, for the most part, women's attributes tend to be developed and inscribed in relation to men, especially powerful ones. Even though Serjee could not fully escape this realm of gender and power that is based on male dominance over women, she built much of her relations by connecting with other women in a hierarchical manner and by simultaneously defining her autonomy in relation to her male leaders and colleagues. Serjee strived to manage her surroundings in politics in a way that would minimize her dependency on her male colleagues as much as possible. To do so, Serjee built her dominant support through hierarchical connections with women both up and down the power ladder and by gaining a formal leadership position with her party's women's organization. By commanding other women—through formal structures—she stood on a par with her male colleagues and restricted their patronage and domination.

This case shows that technologies of power, as a part of the technologies of gender, are not limited to a conventional domestic realm or even to a more nebulous woman-identified notion of "community" (see Bowie 2008; Wolf 1960). Serjee and other female candidates operate in spaces of formal politics that have been associated with male power, like women in the London Stock Exchange (McDowell 1997) or on Wall Street (Fisher 2012). However, unlike the strategies that Linda McDowell and Melissa S. Fisher describe for such women—which are considered quintessentially feminine, like being risk-averse and applying long-term planning rather than focusing on short-term gains—Serjee's strategies are not necessarily based on such female stereotypes.

Instead, she tried to create resources for exchange within her party and ascend through the ladder of an institutional hierarchy. Some of her strategies are reminiscent of the socialist era's mobilizations and management of the masses: forms of ideological enticement that encourage solidarity and collectivity through symbols and inspirational language. Other strategies, such as taking the initiative in changing the structures of institutions, confronting leaders, and bartering her services with senior colleagues, are new, entrepreneurial, and speak to a competitive market economy. Serjee's overt unapologetic demands and confrontations with her male colleagues and women superiors are a new set of dispositions that are neither traditionally Mongolian nor reminiscent of the socialist period. She refused to entertain gentle requests, use apologetic language, mold herself to the situation or mood, or find the right tunes for anyone (*aya oloh*) to get things done. By eschewing these expected feminine performances, Serjee was leaving the attributes of gender aside while trying to build new ones. Serjee's refusal to tame her outspokenness, candidness, and openness—with her male and female leadership and women followers and staff members—is new and almost "foreign" to some people who are used to more reserved and restrained ways. "Who slams the door of the [boss's] office?!" Serjee asked me rhetorically. "That is unheard of and people scold me and call me names for doing that. And yet I was right and after a long while the [boss] acknowledged that!" she told me. What follows is an account of Serjee's precampaigning and campaigning strategies, tactics, and activities, which reaffirm that technologies of gender are not separable from technologies of power.

Made with Politics

Listening to Serjee's interview narratives, in which she outlined her path as a politician as well as her tactics and strategies in running for Parliament, I have come to understand that she saw her candidacy as an integral outcome of her life trajectory and the expectations that already surrounded her. Serjee had spent her adult life, for the most part, among people who were either in politics, entering politics, or expected to enter politics at some point. Like many women candidates I met, Serjee was confident, eloquent, and, in general, fluent in being public. Despite being one of the younger candidates, she was very comfortable in an executive position: she delegated various tasks to others, congregated people around herself, and devised plans and solved problems in meetings in front of her superiors, staff, supporters, critics, and unacquainted audience as well.

Many personal and social factors influenced Serjee's decision to go into politics. One major aspect of her interest in politics was related to the recent socialist and postsocialist events and their outcomes: state socialism routinized political participation as a part of everyday life and normalized women's presence in politics (see chapter 1), and the democratic movement of the 1990s attracted individuals who had been less visible and less powerful under socialism. Serjee falls into the category of a newer generation of politicians who have been affected and pulled into politics by the democratic revolution of the 1990s. Western feminism's emphasis on self-actualization, empowerment of women, and independence helped her to realize her own potential as a leader. She had also repurposed some aspects of socialist feminism, especially mobilization of women. In other words, being a politician for Serjee is based on a conglomeration of social, feminist, historical, and theoretical understandings of her position in Mongolian society. She has come to live *through* politics.

Serjee found both instant gratification and social-emotional satisfaction in electoral politics. In the aftermath of competing in the election, she made clear what the most rewarding aspect of the experience was: "Being nominated as a candidate." It was the sense of recognition, belonging, and achievement that was the most memorable and valuable to her. Her step-by-step tactics and strategies indicate that she defined herself through action and getting results. Her identity as a politician and the surroundings that shaped and were shaped by her reveal the extent to which elections have affected Mongolian subjectivities. Some candidates, including Serjee, articulated their reasons and their paths to candidacy as both expected and desirable, which speaks to electionization as a structuring force and not a time-bound event.

I observed Serjee during some difficult moments, and I was struck by how easily she managed the challenges she faced. A mutual friend, who introduced us, marveled at her persistence:

> I do not know how she meets all the demands that her party puts on her. The party requested a large sum of money as a "donation" for granting her permission to run as a candidate, and she got that money. When the party ordered, "Organize this and that event," she organized them. Then the party said, "If you want to remain in the candidate pool, send fifteen women abroad for a leadership training course." Serjee arranged the trip for fifteen party women to the United States, all at her own expense. If I were told to do these things, I would have a nervous breakdown, or just quit the candidacy altogether. Serjee came from a rather poor background and her first job was as an assistant in the service industry, where she had to do grueling and dirty work. Maybe because she had such a hard life in the past, she puts up with all these hurdles.

The scope of Serjee's expenses, at least to the extent that she revealed them to me, would be considered modest compared to those of other, richer and more powerful politicians. Her campaign spent money on television and radio ads, posters and campaigners, and gifts and infrastructural contributions to her target constituency, including playgrounds and bridges.[2] The extensive activities that Serjee organized were targeted to specific groups and exemplify one representative strand of the country's electionization. In the election of 2008, about 340 candidates competed for seats. But before these individuals received their party mandates and permission to embark on the official twenty-one-day campaign, about three times as many *gorilogch* (aspirants or precandidates) spent as long as two full years competing for the mandate. Inside the major political parties, this unofficial and usually clandestine precampaigning is known as *entering the rotation* (*rotatzand oroh*). Here rotation is basically meant to express being on the way to actual candidacy. One of the two major parties, for instance, operates with an initial pool of over two hundred aspirants—almost three times the number of parliamentary seats, which is seventy-six. In other words, by the time the campaign begins, hundreds of people around the country, in various political parties and local groups, as well as independents, have already been hustling and competing to secure nominations but with no guarantee. As Serjee was especially diligent in her preparations, her example helps us imagine what it is like when multiple politicians conduct similar outreach activities in one constituency.

Strategies and Tactics

Serjee may in some respects be a representative case, but she is also singular in other ways. Unlike any other female candidate I observed, she directed her activities toward women and women's organizations as ways to build support and consolidate votes. Serjee was a feminist in the sense that she believed in the mutual support of women, counted on the power of female solidarity more so than on the patronage of powerful men. Thus, Serjee's attention to women both as a resource for her political career and as beneficiaries of her political and economic support distinguished her from other candidates. Serjee empowered herself by mobilizing other women in a hierarchical way and that also expanded the role of women specifically within the rigid formal structures of male-dominated political party.

Serjee's preparation for campaigning combined features of creative agency that Michel de Certeau describes as *tactics* and *strategies*, the one often enabling the other in a dialectical fashion. De Certeau calls a strategy "the calculation (or manipulation) of power in a relationship that becomes possible as soon as a subject with will and power (a business, an army, a city, and scientific institution) can be isolated" (1984, 36). In other words, formulating a strategy presupposes the possession of power comparable to that of one's competitors. Strategy "seeks first of all to distinguish its 'own' place, that is, the place of its own power and will, from an 'environment'" (1984, 36). A place of one's own is important in order to "capitalize acquired advantages, to prepare future expansions, and thus to give oneself a certain independence with respect to the variability of circumstances" (1984, 36). The implementation of successful strategies affords a mastery of both time and place—what de Certeau calls a *panoptic practice*—which enables further mastery of time through the reading of space. The reading of space further enables one to manipulate time. The mastery of time and space generates and legitimates the knowledge that further sustains itself (1984, 36).

By contrast, a tactic is a "calculated action determined by the absence of a proper locus" (de Certeau 1984); it is organized within the grid set out by dominant power. The tactician has little chance to maneuver in and out of this territory, and thus is unable to plan and implement a general strategy. A tactic has no way to "stockpile its winnings," but uses opportunities, takes advantage of "cracks" in the dominant system, and is an art of the weak (1984,

37). Obviously, in an election context, political parties and legal codes pre-determine much of the candidates' strategies. However, individual actions diverge depending on their identities, resources, and power.

In the case of Mongolian women's electoral participation—and in Mongolian electionization more broadly—it is crucial to observe the difference between strategies and tactics. Through strategic practice, female candidates aspire not just to win elections but also to fundamentally reshape a male-dominated political arena and, in the process, redefine female political sub-jectivity. Yet because they are entering electoral politics with a dominated (if not subaltern) status, they must also work to secure tactical advantages, ac-cepting the conditions of an androcentric political culture and their received subject positions within it while still maneuvering to eke out political gains. In this sense, the dialectical relationship between paradigm-shifting strate-gies and structurally determined but nevertheless agentive tactics indexes the complex reality that female candidates must navigate and constitutes a lo-cus of resourceful decision-making in its own right. From a methodological standpoint, attending closely to the way this dynamic unfolds in the life of a focal individual offers rich insights into the circumstances in which other candidates, male or female, inevitably find themselves—and, indeed, this is an approach taken by other feminist ethnographies of women's agency (see, for example, Ginsburg 1989; Ahearn 2001; Mahmood 2004).

While de Certeau's (1984) notion of strategies versus tactics is useful in thinking through the activities of female candidates, each aspect needs fur-ther elaboration in the context of electoral campaigning. That is because campaigning involves influencing the perceptions, thoughts, and subject-positioning of others primarily through face-to-face interaction and through working in spaces that do not always have delineation between one's own or that of the opponent. Oftentimes, the main battles are about transform-ing the subjective stances and positioning of others. Hence, I would like to break down de Certeau's notion of strategies into what I call *affective* and *architectural*. Throughout her experience as an aspirant and as a candidate, Serjee employed a suite of *affective strategies* that were meant to transform the perceptions of people in necessary ways, especially in acknowledging Serjee as a politician, a candidate, and a capable individual. Sometimes these were self-defenses against oppression and unfairness and consisted of a variety of speaking engagements, such as reprimanding her competitors during meet-ings for defamation, refusing to be roped into paying for her corunner's cam-paign services, and defending her time slot on the stage from other candi-date's encroachments. Sometimes, these affective strategies were to promote herself, such as negotiating with her superiors and convincing her staff members. At other times, affective strategies were about managing her own feelings and emotions, such as persevering through a drinking party that was necessary for her networking or not feeling resentful about letting a senior colleague take a position she was striving for.

Along with the affective strategies throughout her experience, she also employed what I call *architectural* strategies. These architectural strategies overlap closely with de Certeau's notion of *strategies* and included the following: self-preparation to become an electable candidate; clearing the legal and structural obstacles to her candidacy (in particular, helping to legislate the 30 percent candidate quota); securing her space (that is, finding and fighting for a constituency); consolidating her organizational power in the party and in her voter base through the party's women's organization; and eliminating or minimizing her foes. All these strategies are large-scale ones and involved creative management of space, time, human capital, and influence, as well as an accumulation of knowledge that Serjee would use during the official campaign period. These larger *architectural strategies* were permeated with *affective strategies* on a daily basis.

As the reader will learn, in her precampaigning journey, Serjee had to give up her achievements and move into something new altogether. This change was beyond her control. She then had to switch from adopting strategies that allowed her a panoptic gaze over her own territory (à la de Certeau 1984) to mostly *tactics*, which are limited to reactionary efforts in someone else's territory without being able to command the space and see her opponents. Here I am interested not in assessing the success or quality of the outcome of certain strategies or tactics but rather in demonstrating how women's tactics and strategies in male-dominated spaces shape their senses of themselves as agents, their subjectivities, and do so within the space-time of electionization.

Affective Strategies: Knowledge Work, Night Work, Drink Work

Affective strategies are not temporal and permeate throughout Serjee's campaigning. Thus, with almost each step Serjee employs some form of affective strategy in order to move forward her campaigning. However, I devote this section to some of the most distinct examples of affective strategies that stem from incongruity between being a woman and expectations in working in male-dominated politics. Serjee envisioned her preparations for candidacy in several areas: knowledge, family support, and building networks, among many others I discuss in subsequent sections. In order to gain knowledge—the first precursor for candidacy—Serjee attended the national workshops and international seminars that were designed by several international foundations, including the UNDP, to prepare female political candidates. There she learned about democratization, candidacy, and the place of women in politics. Then she started working for them by delivering capacity-building workshops to women in different political parties. Through such teaching she also gained public speaking and presentation skills. Through her workshops she met women from different political parties and learned about their situation with their respective parties and about the parties' internal politics.

After careful consideration, she joined a political party she believed suited her values and disposition. Once a member, Serjee began her electoral experience by working for other members' campaigns and started learning campaigning skills, such as communication techniques, use of media for self-promotion, and advocacy. In doing so, she encountered the importance of several concepts and practices that she used in her speeches and incorporated as her political and personal orientation as a candidate and as a person. These included the following:

negotiation—*zövshiltslöl*
problem-solving—*asuudal shiideh*
gender equality—*genderin tegsh erh*
vulnerable groups—*emzeg bülgiihen*
poverty reduction—*yaduurliig buuruulah*
political empowerment of women—*emegteichudiig uls tord chadvarjuulah*
quota—*kvot*
voter registration list—*songongchdiin neriin jagsaalt*
receptions—*hüleen avalt*
event—*arag hemjee*
team work/performance—*bagyn toglolt*
forum—*forum/hural*

These terms suggest the rapid socioeconomic transformations that enveloped Serjee and potentially developed her as a politician. They are indicative of the period of the late 1990s and early 2000s, during which the presence of international organizations in the country increased, as did the language of human rights, women's issues, and women's rights. Because of the impoverishment of women and their social stratification due to the transformation in employment and family structures, there has been much discussion about the development of policies for women, strategies for poverty reduction, and plans to empower women in the political arena. It was the time that preceded the establishment of the 30 percent women candidate quota. For women like Serjee, the 2000s (before the election of 2008) were an exciting period filled with dreams about further democratization and the possibility for women's greater impact on politics and policy-making.

Unlike some women candidates, Serjee had a husband who was enthusiastic about her ambitions, which was conducive to her competing for a seat:

> My husband is my *red fan* (*ulaan fen*)! He encouraged me to pursue my ambitions and he also told me that I should really think hard about running for Parliament. "It is a big commitment and responsibility," he said to me. "Will you be able to spend long stretches of time not seeing our baby?" My child was only an infant back then. He also said: "You will have to give up your day job for a while and be content with a reduced income." And one day he asked me: "If I get sick and my heart stops, and you are on a campaign trail, what will you do?" I said to him: "I will come to you, of course!" He said: "Then, you are not a politician! You are supposed to think about the people and the country, not about your personal life!"

While, unlike many women, Serjee had a supportive home life and had considerable freedom to pursue her political career and networks, she encountered serious problems at work. The first difficulty was working with men in her party, especially at the leadership level, which entailed joining them at regular nightly gatherings after work for drinking and discussing politics.

> During almost all meetings, our [party district] boss would open a bottle of vodka and share it with the visitors and staff. He was very popular and drew a big following. The [district party] center was always partying. "That is the only way to get the work done," he told me. I disagreed with him for the entire time. When I worked closely with the upper administration, I had to sit with men at the meetings and participate in drinking. This was a problem for me because I do not drink vodka, only beer and wine. In addition, we would celebrate every holiday, event, and anniversary with receptions and outings. I was against that kind of expenditure. I told our boss that I want to do training sessions and workshops and teach people skills and deliver knowledge instead of spending the resources on galas and receptions. He said that I had no idea how politics worked. When I moved up in the political hierarchy, my boss instructed me to take the women for a weekend outing to a mountain resort. But I just rolled my eyes at him and other women who were also talking about that.

Despite disagreements over work style, Serjee's boss was interested in supporting her career in politics. Serjee demonstrated her exceptional ability to mobilize women in the party and prepare a workforce that would be deployed at the most critical moments during electoral campaigns and especially during disputes over voter registration lists. Plus, with the 30 percent women candidate quota under discussion (before 2007), the party bosses were interested in the most electable women, lest they lost those seats to their opponents. Hence, Serjee's boss was supportive of her. But his support came with an expectation to lead a particular work style and lifestyle that was not only incompatible with but almost detrimental to her as a woman, mother, and wife:

> Initially I sat at the meetings and did not drink. Then I quickly realized that when there was a sober person present, the men felt under surveillance and got paranoid. They stopped talking freely and openly and did not share all the nuances that I needed in order to participate in politics! So, I taught myself how to drink hard liquor without passing out! Otherwise, they dropped me from their circle and I was constantly left out without any updates. There was no way I could be in politics without the information from the tight circles. But the funny part was that they talk about the most important things at around 2 a.m.! These men live their lives as if they have no families of their own!

As a mother of a young child, Serjee was trying to be home by 7:00 p.m., but most days she managed to get home only by 10:00 p.m. She worked at her day job, then spent late afternoons and evenings in the district party office, before rushing home. But she was getting left out of important actions and decisions when she did not join the night meetings. Serjee would often get phone calls demanding her presence, but sometimes she could not determine if she was really needed. Sometimes, during these casual night meetings over vodka, things remained ambiguous until a decision was reached at the last moment. Since meetings often ended inconclusively, she started skipping them. As a woman, Serjee also felt awkward at meetings attended almost exclusively by men. Most were married but some were separated. "It was not a good situation at all, and I did not feel right," she told me.

Once she did not join the night meetings for over a week. Back then, she was the head of the women's organization of her district's party branch. She was busy during the day organizing—and self-financing—different events but was going home at nights. Then, one day, she heard that the district party was going to replace her as its head. She had neglected to update her bosses about her work, and this shocking development was the result of the waves of rumors that followed.

Another time, Serjee was absent from the night meetings for a week as she was helping to organize a large forum in a resort outside of Ulaanbaatar. It was a lobby for the 30 percent women candidate quota legislature that would help women to gain a better foothold in politics. She was still nursing and thus traveled with her baby. After the forum, which was a great success, she returned home at midnight. At 2:00 a.m., her boss called and told her to come to the office. "We need your voice immediately," he said. "We are changing the composition of the headquarters and you need to come and vote." Serjee resumed attending the night meetings and started coming home at 4:00 or 5:00 a.m. "My husband then told me that he trusted me and that he was not worried about me coming home that late. But he said that he could not accept me drinking alcohol with my colleagues." Serjee tried to explain how drinking was a part of the job if she wanted to be a successful candidate, but her husband remained unhappy about that.

Although working with men on a regular basis was necessary and Serjee continued the meetings, she preferred the visible, structured, and official work of leading the women's group of her party. Leading a women's group—however aggravating, resource-draining, and labor-intensive it had been—was the work she felt fitted best and thus there was less affective work of being a misfit and a need to constantly internalize the discomfort, embarrassment, and logistical difficulties that had no other outlet than herself. The issue with working with a small circle of male politicians in an obscure time and space was that it was based on a gender-based incongruity, which was beyond her skills, knowledge, and efforts. The affective work of being a misfit was much harder than the physical and emotional exhaustion from working in other visible and legitimate spaces of building up the women's groups. There, Serjee employed her skills, knowledge, and genuineness without reservation and awkwardness.

Architectural Strategies: The Fight to Get a Constituency

In addition to affective strategies, which became the most notable for establishing her presence in her party's leadership circles, Serjee employed what I called architectural strategies. These were large-scale steps she needed to take in order to become nominated as a candidate. They include paving a legal road to the candidacy, such as a 30 percent female candidate quota, and claiming a constituency within her party, which required that Serjee occupy a high position within her party's leadership scheme.

Serjee was a keen participant in the 2005 effort to pass the 30 percent female candidate quota. After the enactment of the quota, she began working as a lobbyist for changes in the election law in order to make conditions more favorable for women's full participation as candidates. Yet, as I mentioned in the Introduction, Parliament repealed the quota at the end of 2007. Official and collective strategies for increasing the representation of women at the legislative level had failed. Now women aspiring to be candidates were mostly on their own and entering a realm of tactical rather than strategic action. Nevertheless, despite the repeal of the quota in 2007, Serjee continued her planning for the 2008 election.

While contributing to the work of legislating the candidate quota, Serjee was also working toward becoming nominated as a candidate in her party. (The work with the leadership circles in her party, mentioned in the previous section, was also a part of networking toward that goal.) Because it is the political parties that nominate the candidates to the General Election Commission (GEC), competitions for candidacies within the political parties are constant and ongoing, known as *rotatsand oroh* or entering a rotation. Candidates for parliamentary elections begin competing well before the official campaign period (about two years on average), indicating that electionization has an enduring effect long after (and before) official campaigns. The aspirants are expected to make donations to their party and maintain a high profile among voters in their probable, although not guaranteed, constituency for precampaigning. Importantly, in order to ensure an actual nomination for a candidacy before the elections, aspirants are also expected to have an administrative post or membership in their party's National Committee, its leadership body. In addition, women also seek leadership positions within the women's organization (Union of Women) of their respective political parties.

In order to be nominated as a candidate, Serjee needed to find a constituency. To do so, however, she needed to be in leadership posts in her party's National Committee and Union of Women. It was a chicken-and-egg problem. The constituency and leadership posts were "tied" together, but there was no prescribed sequence as to which was supposed to come first. In order to get leadership posts in her party, she needed a constituency—and vice versa. Thus, she had to start from nothing by taking advantage of opportunities as they emerged along the way. While candidates do not always reside in or come from their constituencies, it is common to campaign in one's parents' constituency.[3] Serjee needed to start her (informal) precampaigning and garner enough support to be able to demonstrate to her party that she could be a viable candidate.

Serjee's first attempt to find a constituency was in Selenge province. As she was about to leave to start her campaigning there, however, Saraa, president of a well-known women's NGO, dissuaded her from going. The NGO was highly regarded and well known for promoting women's rights and supporting the involvement of women in development and politics. Saraa told Serjee that she herself had been on the party's National Committee for many years and was planning to run for a seat in Selenge in the 2008 election. Saraa told Serjee that because Serjee was still very young, she had time to find another constituency. But Saraa herself was more senior. Out of respect for this senior member of her party who was also a well-regarded NGO leader, Serjee decided to look for another constituency.

For her second attempt to find a constituency, Serjee consulted the chairman of her political party, who suggested Sukhbaatar district in the city of Ulaanbaatar. Sukhbaatar was a constituency of the "big boys": its representatives had gone on to become prime ministers, party chairmen, and mayors. Serjee decided that even if she were to lose, it would still be an honorable candidacy. In order to be nominated in Sukhbaatar, she needed to be elected as the district representative to her party's National Committee.

In preparation for the National Committee election, Serjee organized and sponsored numerous activities, parties, workshops, and lectures for party members of the Sukhbaatar district. She told me about her first attempt to be elected:

> Two additional women were competing for that position. I was surprised that they were doing nothing to promote themselves: no meetings, no activities, no contribution to the local branch of the office. I guessed that they had their membership fees paid by male party members, as many women tend to do. I was independent and did not lean on men for help. So I was hoping to win.
>
> When the election was held at the National Committee meeting, we introduced ourselves. Then during the Q and A, one woman got up and started attacking me: "Serjee," she said, "do you not have a constituency? Are you not a Selenge person? Why are you here? And what is your address? What is your phone number?" So I got irritated and said, "I am not answering these personal questions. If you need this information, then I can provide it to you personally, not during the National Committee meeting. I think our party should eliminate such requests." When I said that, she began aggravating the situation by saying: "Hey look everybody, she has not answered my questions. Who does she think she is?" She created a negative atmosphere. So when the time came to vote, I started receiving SMS messages that said: "It is clear that you will lose." "Withdraw your name." "Withdraw your name before it is too late." I did not withdraw my name because I wanted to see my score. Of ninety votes I won forty, and that was a very high score for me.

Serjee lost the first round. However, a few months later, two new positions opened on the National Committee, one in Sukhbaatar (where she lost for the first time) and another in Selenge (where she had previously declined to compete). In Selenge, Serjee had no competitors, but in Sukhbaatar she still had to compete. She had been warned: if she lost in Sukhbaatar district for a second time, she would probably not have a third chance. Serjee chose Sukhbaatar, mainly because it was a concentrated urban district and she thought it might be easier to bring it under her influence.

This time, in order to compete for membership in the National Committee from Sukhbaatar, Serjee decided she needed to win over Sukhbaatar district's branch of the party's Union of Women. To do so, she volunteered to organize the Union of Women's national convention. Two hundred women arrived from ten different provinces and elected leaders for the regional branches. Serjee became the head of Sukhbaatar district's branch, as she had hoped. As soon as she was in control of the district branch—"the existence of which was rather ambiguous," as she put it—she began to revive it and made it into a center of activities and events.

However, all Serjee's competitors turned against her. It was impossible, she recalled, to organize any activities or to complete any projects because some of her former competitors occupied executive positions under her. The administrative structure of the Sukhbaatar branch was hierarchical: Serjee was the head, and then came the vice president, then the executive committee, the executive officer, and other officials. Serjee realized that as head she was communicating only with the vice president, who exercised the most influence—the de facto power—over the rest of the organization. The head was cut off from the rest of the organization by the vice president. While for many politicians the "symbolic" (*belegdlin*) role of district branch head was enough, Serjee needed direct influence over the members of the district, and she needed to oversee the executive committee and the officers.

In order to exercise power over the entire branch, Serjee petitioned the city office of the party's Union of Women (which oversaw the city's nine district branches) to transform the administrative structure of the organization, at least in her own district. She explained that as head, she wanted to have more direct involvement with the committee and executive officers. She flattened the vertical hierarchical structure into a horizontal one by putting the executive committee, the vice president, and the executive officer under her headship. This connected her to all three bodies directly. With the new structure, Serjee was able to further her priorities in collaboration with the executive committee and the officers, even if the vice president did not support her.

After transforming the structure of the organization, Serjee began a series of activities. During the national Mother and Child celebration on June 1, 2006, her chapter of the party's Union of Women distributed gifts to two hundred poor families, organized a public children's concert in front of the main cinema, and distributed one thousand free ice creams to the audience. Then, together with the Lady Center (an image-making and lifestyle center consisting of a PR service, health club, dance studio, modeling agency, and consultancy services), Serjee organized training for her party's female members in image-making, self-development, and self-care. She made sure to choose a luxurious venue with upscale meal and coffee services for her workshops and gatherings so as to impress the attendees. As she said: "If I organized *nice* things with two meals and coffee breaks with pastries, then people were extremely happy to attend. Most have not seen such luxurious training and lecture sessions." Serjee paid for all these activities out of her personal funds. Within a few months, she had consolidated her image in the district and her institutional power within the party and within the women's organization.

Thus, when the next election for the party's National Committee came up, Serjee won a position without a major competitor from Sukhbaatar district. At this point, she was the head of Sukhbaatar district's Union of Women for her party as well as a member of her party's National Committee. Her process of consolidating power within the regional framework of a political party by mobilizing female social networks (despite competition from other women) and feminine imagery illustrates the complex interplay between structure and agency at work in female candidates' preelection maneuvering. In some sense, her tactics within female-oriented political arenas constituted a long-term strategy for establishing a power base that would eventually allow her to exert influence decisively in male-dominated electoral politics. In the following section, I will show that the process through which Serjee consolidated her own position of power also established her female supporters—and, by extension, women in general—as prominent actors in electoral politics. In so doing, I will demonstrate the extent of a single new electoral precandidate's influence on creating a political public, shaping subjectivities, and activating political life as a part of the electionization process.

A Panoptic Practice: Building the Base and Capital

After obtaining the two positions that were necessary to support her candidacy (the head of her district's Union of Women, and member of her party's National Committee), Serjee became the vice president of her party's branch in Sukhbaatar district. All the other district vice presidents in the party were men. Serjee was the first woman to contend for that position and win. If the other two positions made her candidacy possible at all, this third one was meant to establish her as a leading contender for a parliamentary seat.

Due to Serjee's constant activities, Sukhbaatar district had become the informal center of her party's Union of Women in Ulaanbaatar. Serjee became famous throughout the city's other eight branches. When the time came to elect the next president of the Ulaanbaatar branches (comprising all nine districts), the other district heads suggested her for the position. Serjee hesitated. It was necessary to remain influential in Sukhbaatar district because she was planning on running for a seat in the 2008 election from that constituency. In the end, she decided that it was also her duty to take over the presidency of her party's Union of Women in Ulaanbaatar. To do so, she had to resign from Sukhbaatar district's headship post. She continued her activities on a much larger scale and brought together the women of the nine districts under her direct influence. In addition to the activities she organized, Serjee was proud to see the members of the party's Union of Women come together as a single political community under her leadership.

Serjee was gaining recognition in her party at large. As the president of the party's Union of Women, she often attended large-scale party events accompanied by numerous women dressed in the same uniform and carrying flags or balloons. In this way, Serjee demonstrated to her party that she had power and capital to exchange or share. Specifically, she had established a mass of followers to work on electoral campaigns as advocates, administrators, and as a backstage staff to organize events.

Serjee had consolidated resources that were needed by others as well. Party members began asking her for favors that involved the services of members of the Union of Women. For instance, during a parliamentary reelection campaign for one of the city constituencies in the mid-2000s, her party's candidate asked for her help. "They would ask me," she said, "Serjee, give me fifteen women to work on my propaganda. Or something like, please send us some of your women to organize this or that event." Serjee knew that one area of weakness for her party was the voter registration list. This was because all neighborhood-level administration was in the hands of the opposing party. Serjee's party thus had no direct access to the civic registration lists and needed to be especially vigilant in checking voter registration lists against actual voters. When Serjee was asked for help, she sent several hundred women to comb through the records. The women found that the existing voter registration lists included both deceased and absent voters as well as multiple registrations for people with two or three residencies—all creating potential fraudulent voters. The women were able to eliminate such inaccuracies, which contributed to the victory of Serjee's party's candidate in that election. Serjee was pleased that she had trained the women to be useful campaign workers and that she was an asset to the party. "I finally had the male leaders ask me for favors. I finally was in possession of valuable things that they needed. It was good to be asked."

Most important, as Serjee originally intended, she had consolidated a base for her campaigning. "I was planning to get at least a hundred women from each of the nine districts, nine hundred women in total. I planned on dressing them in the same uniform and staging a quiet women-supporting parade in Sukhbaatar district." Those women would distribute literature promoting Serjee's candidacy and her message that the country needed a clean government. The women would ask members of the public if they agreed with the idea of a clean government, and if so, then they would ask them to wear a particular scarf as a sign of support for that message and for Serjee herself. "The goal was to create the sensation that the district of Sukhbaatar was supporting my candidacy in its entirety," Serjee said. This was one way she envisioned her official campaign right before the election. In other words, Serjee's preparation was to become an integral part of the local environment by getting out on the street and contributing to the visual landscape, the general soundscape, and public sentiment. Her effort to mobilize and expand women's groups brought women into the electoral process as active participants beyond voting.

So far, based on de Certeau's (1984) delineation of tactics versus strategies, many of Serjee's actions can be seen as strategies. For de Certeau, strategy is derived from the actor's mastery of her "own" territory, as well as an ability to calculate, plan, and foresee. Having one's own territory also means having a place in which to accumulate one's own achievements. Serjee's step-by-step takeover of her party's Union of Women for Sukhbaatar district and the accompanying increase of support for her were accomplished through textbook-style strategies (in de Certeau's sense). (It should be noted that her participation in establishing an official path for women candidates through the 30 percent candidate quota—though later revoked by Parliament—and her help in passing a law to encourage women's participation in elections were also forms of "strategy.") Getting a place of one's own (that is, a constituency) where one can securely invest energy, time, and resources in preparation for official campaigning was the supreme goal for everyone planning on running for election, regardless of gender. That included incumbents and challengers. While de Certeau's distinction between strategies and tactics can be too prescriptive, it nevertheless helps one to think about the positions of female candidates and their agencies as fluid, dynamic, and creative. In addition, as de Certeau noted, a space of one's own helps one to plan and predict future steps by exercising a panoptic vision. It also helps one to accumulate achievements and resources. In Serjee's case, once she gained a constituency, she also was able to consolidate her voter base and expand the number of women under her leadership as the head of her party's Union of Women. All of these were architectural strategies that were also enmeshed with affective ones. Yet, things were about to change dramatically and not for the good for Serjee.

Resorting to Tactics: Internal Competition and Debasing

Constituency placements are not guaranteed until the last moment due to intraparty competition. Thus, regardless of how hard a person precampaigns, there is always a danger that someone with more influence in the party and more resources to impress the party leadership as well as the voters can take over one's constituency. In that case, all the money, effort, and time one has spent can dissipate into thin air.

In the summer of 2007, a new female member was elevated to the party's National Committee. Serjee tried to find out if she would be competing in the election, even going so far as to directly question the party chairman. Everyone, including the woman herself, claimed she was not going to compete. Serjee supported her in the party until she learned that the newcomer was, in fact, going to compete in the election—and in Serjee's own constituency, Sukhbaatar. The woman owned a business and was one of only a few women in politics who could rival businessmen in terms of resources. As Serjee told me, she could not match this newcomer's financial resources:

> When I learned that she was contending for my constituency, I stopped supporting her. When I, as the president, stopped talking to her during meetings and gatherings, the women [from the Union of Women] openly ignored her. It was awkward, but she was also tough and persevered! With the help of her money, she was able to persuade all the male leaders to her side. The party leaders saw, however, that when it came to voting for candidates during the party board meeting, she would lose and I would win. Thus, the party leaders, especially Sukhbaatar branch's leader, told me that I ought to find another constituency and let go of Sukhbaatar. I resisted. I said that this was unfair. But then I realized that even if I won at the board meeting, the party leaders were not going to support my candidacy in Sukhbaatar. I had to find another constituency three months before the election!

Meanwhile, tragic and unexpected events in Serjee's personal life coincided with her troubles in the political sphere. In January 2007, she arranged a trip to the United States where she accompanied fifteen women of her party in attending a leadership workshop. On the fifth day of the workshop, Serjee received word from Mongolia of her husband's sudden death. She quit the workshop and traveled back home. By February, overtaken by grief, she was unable to attend to her campaign or other duties. Since the party's nominations for constituencies took place in March, Serjee lost the most valuable time for consolidating her candidacy within the party. She also regretted leaving the headship of Sukhbaatar district's women's organization to become the city president. In retrospect, she speculated that had she remained in Sukhbaatar, the newcomer might not have dared to contend for that constituency. As it was, though, during that time the new contender became more influential within the party leadership. "It was ugly," said Serjee. "After I lost my husband, the party leadership began doubting me as a political candidate. They suddenly began comparing me [unfavorably] with the other contender, who had more money than I did." Moreover, the leadership decided that it was a bad idea for two women from the same party to compete for the same constituency. Serjee was asked repeatedly to go to another constituency. After much heated discussion, she picked Khentii province.[4]

In Someone's Territory: Watching Campaigning as Governing

Having lost the constituency where she had worked for over a year and where she had consolidated her campaign base, administrative apparatus, and voter base, Serjee ended up in someone else's territory. In Khentii, she had to resort to *tactics* while giving up her planned *strategies* because she had to operate in someone else's space and follow the rules of others.

She was unacquainted with the members of the Khentii branch of her party and unfamiliar with the local branch of the Union of Women. The party branch organized the *shtab* (command center) for the campaign in its own way, but Serjee had a different plan, one that they did not support to the extent that she needed in order to promote herself. "Since I did not know the people in the branch," she said, "whenever I tried to communicate with them about my plans, they pushed me away."

The constituency had three seats, for which Serjee's party was floating two candidates: Serjee, the challenger, and a male incumbent named Samdan. In addition to their personal funds, most incumbents can earmark public funds specifically for campaigning or use the public funds during their campaigning. While it is impossible to trace the sources of MP Samdan's campaign money, his voter outreach meetings were geared toward solving individual constituents' social and economic problems. The local branch of the party's campaign *shtab* organized voter outreach meetings for both Serjee and Samdan. If Serjee imagined that her meetings would be about explaining her vision and plans as a future member of Parliament, Samdan had an entirely different approach.

When we arrived to the voter outreach meetings in the mornings, Samdan performed the work of resolving individual problems (*asuudliig shiidej ögöh*) like a welfare agency. In morning meetings with voters (from 8:00 to 11:00 a.m.), he set up an outdoor office with a table and a chair to sit with several assistants working next to him. When the constituents came to talk to him about their problems, he mostly delegated one of his assistants to help that person to put in written requests or petitions (*örgödöl*). Oftentimes the constituents already had a written petition with them. Sometimes, he explained why he could not help and where the person could find assistance, if any. For the most part, this session was about receiving the constituents' requests or petitions. Then from 4 to 7 p.m., he responded to those requests and petitions and resolved their problems. Many residents requested help to buy *gers* (felt tents), provide college tuition, or pay medical bills. I saw Serjee standing nearby and talking with a few people as the crowd flocked mostly to Samdan.

Later, Serjee told me that when she showed up to the meetings for the first few times with Samdan, she became implicated in these requests by default and people expected her, too, to solve their problems. Samdan used most of the party's designated campaign time to attend to the problems of individual constituents. Serjee was left with insufficient time to meet with voters on her own terms during the party-organized voter outreach meetings.

When I saw Samdan's style of campaigning by solving people's problems, and heard more about it from Serjee afterward, I understood why Serjee was receiving almost nonstop SMS messages from residents requesting assistance from her. During one of our lunches, Serjee showed me some of those messages on her phone. As I read several messages, I noticed that they all generally followed the same pattern and composition style. They began by explaining the source of their problems (for example, a family member was sick for an extended time, a family home was lost to fire or flood, someone needed a job or tuition), followed by well-composed pleas for a specified amount of money or other resources. Because I saw Serjee's SMS messages before attending Samdan's campaign, I initially wondered why the voters would write these kinds of SMS requests for money from a candidate. I especially wondered why voters felt it legitimate to request what I thought at that time was personal help from someone they did not know and to use a formal and literary language. For Serjee, sometimes, these messages felt like harassments, especially since she had neither resources to oblige nor did she think it was her work as a candidate to distribute resources to the unfortunate.

But after observing Samdan's campaigning I understood why Serjee might have received such SMSs. The voters who sent the petition messages were neither harassing Serjee nor requesting to be treated as exceptions. They simply saw her as no different from Samdan in terms of the role that she was performing—governing while campaigning. In turn, Samdan, like most incumbents, intertwined his expected services to his constituency with his campaigning as he was aware of the needs of the residents and the district. As was the case in much of Mongolia, most of the constituency was poor, and state services were limited. To some extent, elections had assumed the function of the welfare state and disaster relief agencies.

The voters' petitions to candidates were not only a legitimate way to address difficulties, sometimes they were the only way to receive the services of the state. The state's functions had been transferred to the candidates' campaign activities. As a sociologist in a private research and consulting firm once declared: "People in Mongolia are poor because they are kept poor." She noted that it benefits the politicians to keep the population in relative poverty so they can address those needs in exchange for votes. The politicians, however, are aware that neither poverty nor receiving "help" from them precludes the voters from making independent choices. Thus, they come up with various ways to ensure that their support translates into votes. For a new candidate who has no access to public funds, then, to compete in a parliamentary election means governing a constituency with mostly private resources.

Since Serjee was a challenger, she could not take up the role of the state and had no resources of her own that could match the welfare services of the incumbents. She confronted Samdan for not staging regular voter outreach meetings that consist of the candidates explaining their programs and promises and telling the voters about their broader visions of the country's development. She explained to him that since she was not an incumbent, she could not match the services he was providing to the constituents. In response, Samdan agreed to stage meetings with the incumbents in a "classic" voter outreach style. During the first meeting after the campaign organizers introduced the candidates, Samdan took the stage and spoke for more than twenty minutes, leaving Serjee less than ten minutes before the Q&A with voters.

After that meeting, Serjee, somewhat infuriated, explained to Samdan again that because she was a new candidate, she needed her portion of the time to present at the meetings in its entirety. Samdan got embarrassed, apologized, and said: "You speak the whole time during these meetings. I will just stand. You are right. You need the time." He also argued that Serjee should wear something pleasant and gentle (*ayataihan*) rather than a long structured dark wool coat and a flowing bright scarf. "Too sharp," he commented. Serjee did not budge and continued to wear her outfit without any hesitation.

In moving forward with her campaigning, Serjee used tactics that would enhance her image while revealing the negative aspects of the candidates of the opposing party. For instance, she broadcast a television program that criticized the candidates from the opposing party. As soon as she did so, Samdan,

her cocandidate and party rival, called her to request that she stop broadcasting it. As Samdan explained to her, the voters and the opposition would
blame him for indulging in those sorts of "black" public relations and might
then launch similar attacks against him—they would not attribute the programs to her because she was "clean." Serjee then commissioned a *shtork* (a
short television ad) for voter education that taught voters how to vote, or,
more precisely, how to circle candidates' names on the ballot (*yaj duguilah
yum be*). In the ad, a voter who wants to vote for Serjee's party is positioned
next to an instructor who says, "It is easy to vote. Just circle the two S's, for
Serjee and Samdan, and then all your wishes will come true." Then the advertisement goes on to introduce the two candidates. "It was such a well-made
advertisement," Serjee says. "But as soon as I broadcast the ad, Samdan called
me and told me to stop doing it. . . . I asked why and he said that the advertisement is just too pushy, looks like a requirement. So, I never broadcast it
again."

Based on electoral rules and principles of voter education, political groups
were not allowed to teach the voters how to vote, especially when the instruction was as partisan as Serjee's commercial, which directed voters to circle
Samdan and Serjee. Samdan was right in suggesting that it was against the
rules. However, there was also a double standard being applied. It was acceptable for Samdan to use the resources designated for the district to enhance
his campaign and act as an agent of the state, as "a problem-solver." But Serjee
could not use the voter education framework to enhance her chances of being
elected. For another, Samdan's doling out of state resources for his campaign
activities was framed as doing work for his district. Even if journalists and
investigators revealed his dealings, it would be hard to blame him, as his work
was also humanitarian and appreciated by the poor and disenchanted members of his constituency.

From Samdan's point of view (and those of his advisors and consultants),
Serjee's infomercial and other activities were inappropriate because he was
expected to win. Serjee's activities could either harm his reputation or diminish his standing. As a junior, a challenger, and a woman, especially one
without a great deal of money, Serjee could be expected to win on Samdan's
coattails, but not to win *instead* of him. This was an unstated insider rule I
learned about while conversing with the consultants who were advising both
Serjee and Samdan and who were commenting on who should be winning
in this race.

Moreover, the election was not just a competition among individuals
within political parties. It was also a competition between incumbents as
a group—regardless of their party affiliation—against the challengers. As a

former advisor to various politicians told me, the 2008 Parliament worked hard to get reelected in its entirety (*büreldhüüneeree*). In other words, many incumbents regarded the incumbents of the opposition parties more favorably than they did newcomers from their own parties. That was because the ruling political parties had merged some of their interests and found ways to negotiate deals. Such a political development occurred along with an ongoing discussion of a mining agreement between the Mongolian government and foreign companies. Since 2006, public discourse about mining had transformed from positive and hopeful to critical and cautious. That was due to multiple events and developments, including popular resistance to the pollution of water, pastureland, and soil; a backlash against foreigners owing to Canadian/American mining financier Robert Friedland's international speeches that depicted Mongolia as a place of profitable resources with low taxes and few regulations; and accusations of corruption against high-level officials— just to name a few.[5] Hence, according to people who had access to various political circles, the political parties did not want newcomers who would challenge their anticipated agreement with international mining companies.

As another female candidate, Tsedevdambyn Oyungerel (see Introduction and chapter 5), became convinced based on her own experience, women were frequently used as sacrifices in men's deals over seats, including among men of different parties. While it is impossible to prove such claims in most cases, including that of Serjee, women were often treated as outsiders in politics, especially during crucial decision-making times. Women's marginalization is hardly visible when the parliamentary sessions are aired in public; women politicians look perfectly competent and respected as they speak at formal meetings beside their male colleagues. The issue is that many important decision-making and negotiations take place not in the auditoriums during meetings in Parliament but in saunas, billiard rooms, hunting parties, outdoor outings, and during nighttime drinking meetings that Serjee had to attend. Female candidates like Serjee hoped to transform these politics by gaining enough votes and establishing themselves as new kinds of female politicians.

In the end, the election results showed that among eleven contenders for three seats in that constituency, Serjee ranked fourth with over ten thousand votes. As she lamented to me:

> If I could operate on my own, then I would have ranked higher and I would have won the seat. Only for the last week of the official campaign did I have a chance to meet with the voters on my own. My regret is that I did not have an opportunity to act according to what I thought was the right plan. I could

not utilize my resources and prepared materials, and I felt restrained because I also did not want to get into open discord with Samdan. If only I could have met in person with enough of the women, and with the "impoverished and vulnerable" groups (*nen yaduu bolon emzeg bülginhen*) on my own, then I would have gained many more votes. Instead, I ended up going to the meetings with Samdan, which made me look like a subsidiary to him, not an equal. Even the manager for [the opposition party] noted to me: "You look as if you are meant to enhance Samdan's image." I said no, that was not my intention. The manager replied: "But you do look like someone trying to help Samdan to win the seat. When you are doing the meetings alone, you look far more powerful and you garner a lot of admirers. . . . But when you are in a voter outreach meeting with Samdan, you talk for ten minutes, and then Samdan talks for the rest of the time and it looks like you are trying to gain voters for Samdan." Then the manager said: "If you were doing the voter outreach meetings on your own, then you would have been our biggest competitor and we would have been very concerned. We could not have attacked you in order to bring your rating down because you were so "clean"—there was nothing negative about you to criticize. You made a mistake [in not striking out on your own]. You just helped Samdan win."

Conclusion: Electionization as Force

What does Serjee's story tell us about the electionization of Mongolia? First, it shows that elections suffuse social worlds well before and beyond the official twenty-one days of campaigning. Aspiring candidates campaign for at least two years, with both formal and informal events. The intraparty elections, meetings, logistical adjustments, internal competitions, and workshops are the formal preparations. The candidates' activities in their constituencies that take place during celebrations and holidays, such as self-contained festivals, concerts, free or discounted classes, free medical checkups, public lectures, and gifts and donations, are all designed to enhance the profiles of the candidates and consolidate the voter base and the administrative structure. That nonelection elements of everyday life become a means for unofficial public relations for candidates during nonelection times is an important aspect of electionization in Mongolia and likely elsewhere.

Second, Serjee's story shows how elections themselves are implicated both in everyday life and in the production of gendered persons, old and young. Many services of the state or local governments have fallen into the hands of MPs, thus creating a new set of expectations for incumbents or candidates. Such expectations are higher in areas where people have a harder time securing state services and economic resources. It is thriving partly because the official state, now under neoliberal governance, has limited its services. Most incumbents have managed to appropriate state functions as a part of the electoral apparatus, as a result of their efforts to wage successful campaigns. While the assumption that uneducated voters sell their votes is prevalent in Mongolia, recent anthropological research shows that people are adept at separating their actual votes from what they say they will do for bribes (Bjorkman 2014).

Third, elections fashion female political subjects who combine socialist and democratic elements of identity and forms of agency. In this case, we see the making of electoral subjects through the expansion of women's organizations and the gathering and training of supporters in the practice of campaigning at workshops. Women learn to be part of a group, to stand for a single cause (a particular candidate), to wear matching outfits and follow the same leader; they also consume and embrace dreams of luxury consumption during workshop coffee breaks and restaurant dinners. The activities that Serjee carried out and the subsequent outcomes remind one of the methods and structures of youth organizations from the socialist period. Even the scarves and uniforms recall the LYP and the RYL. However, new workshops on beauty, self-help, consumption, lifestyle, and image-making are significantly updated from the similar yet much more understated and modest versions during socialism. Members of political parties under democracy are being shaped into propaganda workers and an election workforce, even as their skills and interests as market consumers are also developed. New forms of consumption-based femininities, which accentuate upper-class attributes, thus emerge through electoral activities. Elections also shape feminist inclinations by creating aspirations for political agency and group formation, by mobilizing interest groups and women's groups. As we saw in Serjee's case, elections became a platform for activating a particular kind of professional and classed femininity that is distinct from the rest of the gender regime, either traditional, or market-based, or recent socialist. Serjee strives to break away from the existing forms of gendering she finds confining and unsuitable for her goals and instead activates rather risky attributes that do not fit the expected femininity.

An equally rigorous subject formation has been taking place among voters. They have learned to approach elections as a form of state resource to which they gain access through the candidates. Ultimately, for many people, elections constitute an opportunity to get their "problems solved." The elections have substituted for local governments, community support, social services, and even disaster relief agencies. Some voters have expressed indignation at such arrangements. But they also had to obtain what they needed for their families, so they felt competitive and compelled to pester the candidates and could not really resist the campaigns, even if they disagreed with the situation on moral and ethical grounds.

Elections have increased all kinds of mobility and created a sense of constant production of capital, activities, affects, and subjectivities. Gas and fuel companies make their highest profits during the elections. The movement of people—candidates, campaign workers, voters—to meetings contributes to social time and creates the sense of a communal, shared present. The more the people move, meet, gather, and share, the more time seems to be represented as stable and still as opposed to the temporal model of linear progress that socialism tried always to instill. But this sense of shared presence is often fraught with chaos and commotion that generate excesses of emotion—as well as consumer spending.

A massive amount of production ends as the end in itself: Serjee's efforts in the Sukhbaatar constituency before she had to move to Khentii. Her activities, meetings, and festivities for voters, as well as the women's organization she fostered, all came to naught for her electoral purpose. Years before the elections, they became events, either absorbed into the normal flow of social life or as memories by the participants. Similarly, during the actual campaign, the advertisements that Serjee commissioned did not fulfill their intended purposes. Nonetheless, all the television ads, pamphlets, new forms of knowledge, ideas, and money proliferated and circulated, even if not every effort reached its intended audience.

Ultimately, elections have brought a new kind of social stratification into being. Not only are most of the candidates a part of a new elite, but the followers are also learning and reaffirming their positions within a new hierarchy. Especially for the campaign workers and supporters (privately hired and from the district), casting a vote is a very vexed task; months and years of campaigning for the same person often turn them into believers and voters for their employer. The campaign preparation activities are so vast and exhausting that they put a great deal of pressure on the campaign workers, who are also voters. People become more implicated in elections by working for them because they are compensated, or have the promise of being compensated, in money or in favors, and casting their vote can be seen as an outcome of a long-term investment effort. If campaigns can have purpose and generate outcomes as by-products (as opposed to products) of the actual elections, then it means that electionization is a self-serving and self-fulfilling process.

Intellectful: Women against Commercialized Campaigns

"We need some *oyunlag* (intellectful) women in Parliament. I hope that at least a few will be selected," said a male voter in his forties. This was back in 1996, during the country's third parliamentary elections (and long before I conceived of this project). I went to my constituency's voter outreach meeting as a voter, not as a researcher, and was immediately impressed by that male voter's prointellectual women-supporting comment. The voter's emphasis on "intellectful" as a valuable trait for a candidate was not surprising. An amalgam of local and global values and imaginaries, it was associated with authority on knowledge, a lifestyle that privileges intellectual pursuits over material, and adherence to culturally valued moral values. As *oyunlag* is a description of an individual's deeds and achievements, it is separate from the notion of *seheeten* (intellectuals)—although not unrelated—which automatically presupposes belonging to a social class and possessing traits that are beyond intellectual, such as manners, tastes, networks, family background, and some privileges, among others. Instead, *oyunlag* is an emphasis on the individuals' pursuits regardless of those other traits.

By putting forward the notion of *oyunlag*, the voter mentioned above was expressing his disparagement of the candidate then standing for election, who was a businessman in pursuit of profit, which, from the socialist perspective, was amoral and selfish.[1] It is also notable that he emphasized not just the trait of *oyunlag* but specifically *oyunlag* women. According to the popular conviction, women were not only more *oyunlag*, occupied and engaged as they were in the production of cultural and educational wealth, they were also more ethical and less likely to deviate from the laws in place (see chapter 3's discussion of "The Honest Gender").

To the chagrin of many voters, the standing candidate was, of all things, a beer merchant as a part of his entrepreneurship. The voter who hoped for the election of *oyunlag* women was demonstratively repulsed by the candidate's stump speech, which was about the health benefits of beer. The candidate was proposing to pass legislation that would support beer imports. That way, beer would overtake vodka as the dominant alcoholic drink and so, according to the candidate, solve the country's rampant alcoholism.

It is impossible to know how voters made their choices when it came time to cast their ballots. At least in abstract terms, *intellectful* women who pursued professions related to knowledge production were superior to businessmen, who were in pursuit of self-serving profits, especially by selling alcoholic drinks. The voter's remark suggested that he saw women as the guardians of parliamentary integrity. This was partly a fleeting call for women to come to the rescue during times of crisis, or in response to what the voter saw as failures of the parliament in leading the country back then. It is also possible that the voter was supportive of particular women running for seats, since in 1996 eight women won seats, versus only three women in 1992.

Overall, in the 1990s, *uls torch*, or an elected politician, was a new position and a new figure who emerged with democratization. Before that, during socialism, political offices were filled with top-down appointments and were selected from *seheeten* (intelligentsia) with additional leadership training. In that context, the intellect and educational and professional achievements were understood as a precondition for leadership. However, as postsocialist transformation led to further instability and electoral campaigns became quickly commercialized, elected politicians and politics in general became associated with, although not entirely, shrewdness, money, corruption, dishonesty, and a lack of ethical stances and professional skills. These and other circumstances had contributed to the notion of *oyunlag* being framed as a valuable candidate characteristic for women in male-centered politics.

This chapter explores how some of the women candidates resisted commercialization of campaigns by framing themselves as *oyunlag*. Their goal was to transcend commercialized campaigns by presenting themselves as irreproachable and thus electable candidates. Instead of going along with the spending frenzy, they created and used cultural capital to sponsor their campaigns and gain recognition. *Oyunlag* is seen as a characteristic and as an outcome of hard work and self-cultivation and has become a part of a comprehensive preparation for candidacy—self-polishing. These women emphasize their expertise, professional achievements, reputation, and other nonmonetary resources to present themselves as new *oyunlag* candidates with qualities that were lacking in politics. I describe how the campaigning experiences of four women express different ways of being *oyunlag*. Although these women did not explicitly label themselves as *oyunlag*, as doing so would be considered inappropriately conceited—and thus not *oyunlag*—they presented messages, attributes, and actions that would qualify them as such. It was the public, supporting voters, and their campaigns that labeled them as *oyunlag* to different degrees, in different ways, and on various occasions. Their campaigns help us to envision how politics could be less commercialized and not entirely dominated by neoliberal capitalism.

I start the chapter by tracing how the notion of *oyunlag* transformed as a respectable trait and as a marker of a certain claim for power throughout state socialism and democratization. I show how *oyunlag*'s more definitive significance during socialism as a vehicle for becoming a member of the intellectual class and a potential power-holder became fuzzier during postsocialism as it transformed and intersected with other characteristics that became valuable during capitalism. The examples of the women candidates' campaigns illustrate how they directly and indirectly capitalize on the notion of *oyunlag* and shape their candidacy in opposition to commercialization. The reader will meet Sanjaasurengiin Oyun, who was the first person to bring the issue of campaign expenditure to public attention and lobby for laws to limit campaign broadcasting, to her own detriment as a politician. Jurmediin Zanaa challenged expensive campaigns by launching her own clever interventions with limited resources. Tsedevdambyn Oyungerel used her flourishing career as a celebrity writer to help her in the competition. And, most extensively, my main interlocutor, Burmaa Radnaagiin, compiled her expansive symbolic capital in lieu of money.

The Silken Intellect

The word *oyunlag* literally translates as "with intellect" and describes individuals who define themselves by their intellectual pursuit and educational achievement. In addition to the level and quality of higher education, as in academic learning, *oyunlag* refers to one's moral and political stance as a public intellectual as well as to a choice of lifestyle and profession that privileges self-development rather than accumulating material assets, at least not in conspicuous ways. I illustrate how *oyunlag* has been animated by certain actions and professions in a new context and become a way to define new identities. The abstract notion of *oyunlag* is not gendered: people of any gender can be *oyunlag*. However, in practice, as I illustrate throughout this section, the notion becomes gendered, context-specific, and its meaning and usages have transformed through different periods.

Most women who aspire to achieve an electable self and become electoral candidates, embrace the characteristics of being *oyunlag* as a part of
self-polishing—perfecting oneself in a comprehensive way. The notion of having more *oyunlag* people in the national leadership, for most Mongolians, is
related to a sense of the country's political self-determination, security, independence, and ability to modernize. These notions evoke the class of intellectuals or *intelligentsia* (*seheeten*, which literally means "with consciousness" or
"mind-full"), who had been shaped as part of the development of nationalism
and nation-building in Katherine Verdery's (1996) analysis of Romanian and
other Eastern European intellectual classes since the seventeenth century.

While being identified as *oyunlag* implies certain responsibilities to the
community, the notion differs greatly from being an *intellectual* as a distinct
and privileged class, which was already defined in the context of, specifically, state socialism in Mongolia. The presocialist (pre-1921) equivalent of
intellectuals—the educated nobles, clergy, and business owners—occupy little space in the larger social imaginary when it comes to the concept of intellectual, partly due to the suppression of the past. The new socialist state sent
the most promising young people, mostly from upper-class backgrounds, for
further studies to universities in Western Europe in the 1920s and 1930s. During Mongolia's political cleansing in the 1930s, however, the educated groups
were almost entirely purged and gradually replaced by Soviet-educated ones.[2]
Thus the term *seheeten* in Mongolia mostly refers to this newly bred category
of state socialist intellectuals, and thus the term is historically specific. It does
not automatically describe the presocialist intellectuals given the state ideology. Verdery (1991) argues that intellectuals in Romania were the architects
of the national discourse. In a similar way, as Simon Wickhamsmith (2020)
illustrates, the new socialist Mongolian intellectuals worked to convince the
populace of the state rhetoric of equality, progress, and a prosperous future. As
such, in socialist Mongolia, *seheeten* or intelligentsia refers to the successful
people who were initially given the power to create the nation's aspirations.[3]

Despite their privileged position, many individual *seheeten* assumed critical stances toward the state. This happened as a backlash against totalitarianism, the political violence in the 1930s, the persecution of intellectuals in
the 1960s, and the increasingly Sovietized political leadership of the country
(Jamian 2017; Rupen 1979; Shinkarev 2006). In Mongolia, the infiltration of
some Soviet dissident intellectuals' cynicism toward the Soviet system and
more liberal socialist ideology (see Zubok 2019) also impacted some strands
of *seheeten*.[4]

By 1990, some Mongolian *seheeten* saw their job as a critical and construc-
tive engagement with society and leadership and not just as the producers of

ideological content for the state, especially in humanistic fields.[5] The members of *seheeten* led the democratic movement in the late 1980s and early 1990s. The concept of *seheeten* transformed after the collapse of socialism.[6] It became less definitive and lost value because of its association with state socialism, Soviet domination, and the past in general. The *seheeten* also shrank as a class, since the state no longer oversaw the previous state socialist class structure.

The notion of *oyunlag* is no longer confined to the realm of the intelligentsia-as-social-class nor does it imply an *automatic* precondition for political power. Instead, it now applies to anyone who primarily strives to pursue knowledge for self-cultivation and contributes to the production of knowledge. The leadership class, the aspiring upper middle class, and everyone else who can afford higher education beyond basic college degrees has also adopted *oyunlag* as an objective.[7] One could label someone as *oyunlag* (unlike *seheeten*) based on achievements of self-cultivation without knowing their full background.

The gender of the term has also transformed. During socialism, the most successful representatives of the intelligentsia were mostly—although not exclusively—men, similar to higher positions in other areas. The intelligentsia as a social class waned with the end of state sponsorship of cultural production, like literature and theater, and the advent of the market economy and private businesses. An association of *oyunlag* with the male gender also diminished. Business activities (especially trading) became not only desirable but also in some cases necessary for survival. The more visible and successful businesses often belonged to male entrepreneurs. Amid the new and chaotic pursuit of profit, educated women who chose to pursue intellectual activities, while remaining modest in material terms, became the new embodiments of *oyunlag*.

Oyunlag became associated with women's political activities from the early 1990s: in particular, NGO-building and political participation. This was partly the result of some highly educated and politically active women introducing the importance of women in political and social life in the newly democratizing context. At the beginning of democratization, it was women intellectuals who "imported" *oyunlag* as a part of their identity into the newly emerged political space rather than the new knowledge-political space shaping them into *oyunlag* individuals. These women's strategic use of the newer language of international development (for example, "women's empowerment"), as well as the US First Lady Hillary Clinton's language from the Beijing Women's Conference in 1995 (for example, "women's rights are human rights"), highlighted their own *oyunlag* capabilities as being informed, skilled in leadership, and networked with (and thus accepted by) international entities. By earning their reputation at home through international connections, they propelled their messages to the populace. They advocated gender equality, women's empowerment, political participation, and leadership.

One of the NGOs conveyed its *oyunlag* identity by its title: The Liberal Women's Brain Pool.[8] The Mongolian version of the title—*Liberal Emegteichüüdin Oyunii San*—uses the word *oyun* ("intellect") and not *brain* (as in the English translation), as *oyun* directly evokes *oyunlag* and is culturally more suitable. Although critics labeled some of these politically active women as opportunists, overachievers, and power-seekers, many also have come to see them as *oyunlag*.

The Mongolian electorate ranks education (*bolovsrol*) as the number one criterion for voting for a female member of Parliament.[9] Education remains the major characteristic of the *oyunlag*. However, expanding the notion of *oyunlag* to include women's political activities, especially NGO-based activities, was crucial and novel in creating a respectable and powerful feminine identity in opposition to the heightened and openly expressed misogyny evident since the end of socialism. A category of *oyunlag* as a key attribute for a political candidate was an antidote to an expressive focus on material wealth during capitalism and was aimed at transcending the commercialized political campaigns as well as attendant developments in Mongolian society. It was an antidote to the media's obsession with sexualized and objectified images of women like beauty queens and fashion models and, as Waters (2016) argues, the importance of erotic capital as a resource for upward mobility. This new categorization was vital for the overall elevation of the status of women as groundwork for changing legislation, media images, and the perception of women as a diverse and respectable group. It emphasized women's productive capabilities beyond biological reproduction.[10]

Democratization equipped women in politics with a new language and new forms of action. However, women were not new to politics or to leadership positions prior to democratization. As the notion of *oyunlag* as a womanly trait has come to the fore, Mongolians' traditional association of women as having "*torgon uhaan*" ("silken intelligence"), or "*torgon medremj*" ("silken perception"), also reinforced the gendered aspect of the term. *Torgon medremj* is a general term that communicates insightfulness, awareness, an ability to "read" other people's thoughts and emotions. A silk thread is a metaphor for something subtle but strong and resilient. During socialism, women were encouraged to pursue professions that capitalized on their emotional-cognitive abilities associated with female gendered characteristics, such as perceptiveness and subtlety. Men were promoted mostly in industry, engineering, and agriculture, while women were seen as more suitable for ideological and cultural production, education, and social welfare services—fields more associated with being *oyunlag* and especially with the "silken perception."[11]

Although *oyunlag* is a revered trait, it is not a direct substitute for money, power, and networks that are necessary for staging a candidacy. With democratization and a free market economy, men have gradually come to dominate the most lucrative and large-scale businesses, while women tend to dominate small- to medium-scale businesses. Cultural and educational fields, which were funded by the state, have shrunk or become a part of the market. The commercialization of elections disadvantaged newcomers, women, and candidates who were outside the business sphere. Female candidates are at a financial disadvantage as they cannot always fund their campaigns at the same rate as male candidates.

Oyunlag does not particularly denote any levels of wealth; depending on the electorate, too much reliance on *oyunlag*, without demonstrating wealth and power, can therefore hurt a candidate's prospects. Mongolian voters— many of whom are disappointed by the elected leadership—tend to prefer immediate gratification through gifts and services over long-term promises (see chapter 2). Thus an *oyunlag* candidate, who is automatically associated with high education and moral standards, can fall short against someone who distributes money, goods, and other material resources. But while being *oyunlag* does not guarantee votes, *oyunlag* women have used their skills, knowledge, and reputation to garner support and resources, increase popularity, and expand networks in order to become accepted as *electable* for office.

Pulling the Plug on Campaigning

Complete with entertainment, gifts, festivities, and gatherings and parades, campaigns stage ongoing events that lead to a general sense of elation, thrill, and agitation. Televisions blast out concerts, political debates and advertisements, and biographical profiles on behalf of candidates. From the moment the electoral campaigns are announced, quiet clandestine campaigning gives way to an explosion of events that take over the media, streets, and other public and private spaces. The all-consuming debates, competitions, and rumors can easily trap voters into endless watching, listening, and opining.

The 2004 election campaigns felt like they were generated by magical genies who were granting one wish after another in the form of concerts, juicy fights among candidates, and addictive "black PR" that revealed the "dirty laundry" of various contenders. It was yet another evening of reveling in endless entertainment when the head of the Civic Will Party, Sanjaasurengiin Oyun (the only female political party leader), appeared on one of the television channels and turned the campaigns inside out. With an even and firm voice, which also became scratchy from the stresses of being on campaign

FIGURE 5.1. Oyun giving an interview during her campaigning in 2008. Photo by the author.

trails, she critiqued the lavishness of the electoral campaigns and called into question the financial sources for such frivolous spending. Her words seemed to pull the plug on the campaigns:

> Look how much money has been spent on posters, TV programs, individual advertisements, and published materials. Where does all this money come from? Who monitors it? Does the money come from public funds? If so, then who gets access to them, and who does not? Who will be responsible for a potential budget deficit?

Oyun's denunciation came at a time when there were fewer limits imposed on concerts, shows, and other forms of enticement and especially on the campaign's use of broadcast media. The system of monitoring these restrictions was also limited. Oyun was also a committee member on the development of election laws and lobbied for restricting paid political advertisement during the campaign period from 50 percent of airtime to 10 percent. Like other restrictions, this was done in order to limit campaign expenditure and to help bring some equitable participation for candidates. However, several broadcasting stations critiqued this clause as it limited their revenues during the most lucrative time. When they learned that Oyun was the initiator of this law, they banned her from their broadcasts. Oyun's criticism, nevertheless, influenced politics and her reputation in the long term. Laws to regulate the length of campaign periods, the amount of printed material, and broadcast time were implemented in the following years.[12] Although these regulations and laws had different outcomes, the discussions on campaign regulations have become a major part of elections. Unlike all other women candidates I discuss in this book, Oyun was the only incumbent. As a sister of a well-respected late leader of the democratic movement, Sanjaasurengiin Zorig, Oyun had already accumulated the symbolic capital of widespread recognition and a well-established reputation among the public (fig. 5.1). Oyun's reputation has also been further consolidated as an honest and uncorrupt politician. In subsequent elections, some other candidates began adopting Oyun's take on alerting the public to the political parties' unequal access to public resources. Electoral financing became, at least, not a taboo but a part of a larger campaign discourse. It remains murky, however, at a deeper level.

The Charisma of the *Oyunlag*

Jurmediin Zanaa was an independent candidate, a head of an NGO, "Citizen's Alliance," that focused on human rights, and one of the leaders of civil society. Born in the 1950s, she was well recognized and respected by the public (*niigmees hüleen zövshöörögdsön*). Although Zanaa had participated in the democratic movement in the 1990s, she was known as a civil society leader instead of being associated with the Democratic Party (DP). In her introduction to voters during a meeting with volunteer advocates for her campaign, she explained that she firmly decided to run as an independent instead of seeking a DP platform because the DP no longer adhered to democratic principles.

One of the most well-known public figures in the 2000s, she was sharp and direct, always freshly groomed to perfection and clad in impressive attire and accessories, and sported a distinctive look everywhere she appeared. Unlike other women, who received criticism about their looks and age, Zanaa was able to turn her seniority into a charismatic and authoritative self-presentation. She induced admiration in some while intimidating others, including other women candidates, to the point that they avoided attending the same social events, especially smaller ones, in case they would have to encounter her face-to-face. While Zanaa's popularity, looks, and credibility added to her candidacy, her monetary resources were limited even compared to other women as she had no political party platform to boost her rating scores or centralized party-organized campaigning to count on.[13] She was entirely on her own.

Yet Zanaa had turned the difficult situation to her benefit. She harmlessly and skillfully piggybacked on some other candidates' campaigning, often even

boosting her opponents' visibility. For instance, since organizing voter outreach meetings in different parts of a large constituency was costly and labor-
intensive, Zanaa decided to skip it. Instead, she met voters right after wealthy
candidates' campaigns. My research assistant Ariun-Undrah Namsraijav
(Undrah), who accompanied Zanaa during her voter outreach meetings,
shared the following with me:

> Sister Zanaa was about to enter the auditorium of a voter outreach meeting
> of a DP candidate. "Are you allowed to go in?" Zanaa's staff asked her anx-
> iously. "Of course, I am allowed. See if they [the DP candidate and the staff]
> kick me out!" she said. With that, Zanaa entered the room, and when the
> DP meeting was about to end, she walked across the auditorium toward the
> candidate on the podium. The candidate, a younger man surrounded by a
> fleet of bodyguards and staff in dark suits, all looking like "wardrobes" (*shkaf
> shig, shakf shig*) [i.e., strong and menacing], stopped at the sight of Zanaa ap-
> proaching. The candidate blushed upon recognizing her. Each greeted Zanaa
> with a respectful handshake and politely and swiftly left the auditorium. At
> that moment, one of Zanaa's female staff members loudly announced to the
> auditorium: "The meeting will be continued with an independent candidate,
> Jurmediin Zanaa! Everyone, please stay seated!" But about one-third of the
> people left. They were a fake DP "audience" who followed the candidate. As
> soon as only the real voters remained, Zanaa said to them in a personable
> way: "I must tell you something very important." The audience fell into si-
> lence. Zanaa talked about the mining and exploration boom and some of the
> drawbacks of the mining agreement that the government was hoping to pass.

"And listen to this!" Undrah continued:

> Since Zanaa only had a mobile *shtab* (a campaign office) in the form of a van
> (as she had no funds to rent offices), she was always on the move. Thus, in-
> stead of waiting to meet some thirty-plus people per meeting (an average size
> of voters who would gather in most subdistricts, discounting pre-hired "fake"
> attendees), Zanaa simply walked and talked with everyone on the streets most
> days while her team used the van to distribute her campaign's printed materi-
> als. Her favorite spots were the bus stops, which had the densest gatherings
> during rush hours. I counted Zanaa's meetings! Within two days she met at
> least two hundred people that way. This was a bigger number of people than if
> she tried to organize a meeting in an auditorium. And hers was all free!

Zanaa's campaigning did not attract as much attention as other campaigns.
Nevertheless, she had demonstrated to some of the public that she was able
to campaign with a fraction of the resources of most candidates. This was
an achievement, given the fact that she was an independent candidate without a party platform, a newcomer, a nonprofit leader (for example, she could

tap into neither state nor private funds), and a strict opponent of expensive campaigns. In this way, she showed that politics could be done differently compared to most candidates who spent much more money than they had and thus worked to regain it afterward.

Zanaa is *oyunlag* in a variety of ways. For one, her background, reputation, and lifestyle spoke to the notion of *oyunlag*. Zanaa (2005) earned a PhD and wrote her dissertation on gender studies and was one of main architects behind the gender equality law. Her circle of friends consisted of diplomats, professors, and lawyers. Zanaa was a former professor of Russian (during socialism) and then of English (after the fall of socialism) at the State Pedagogical University. But unlike some intellectuals who stayed out of political contests and away from social engagement, she was a public intellectual who was also an activist, a whistleblower, and, when necessary, a protester. What distinguished her from straightforward strikers, and also makes her *oyunlag*, is the breadth and depth of her critical analysis of the social and political life of the country. She was not there to fix one important problem (for example, laws on land privatization), but engaged in a critical analysis of major sociopolitical issues as they rolled in.

Like many intellectuals in the humanities who knew English, Zanaa helped to build a new civil society in the democratic era. She was one of the first women (along with Burmaa, Oidovyin Enkhtuya, and others) to apply for and receive international funding to establish Western-style NGOs, and to promote human rights, women's rights, and other democratic values and programs. During the time of my research (2006–17), Zanaa was directing the Center for Citizens' Alliance, an NGO that focuses on women's rights through awareness and education programs.

In the late 1990s and early 2000s, she was associated with introducing the term "gender" (and an accompanying understanding of gender issues) to Mongolian political and social discourse. The concept helped activists, and society at large, to regain an awareness of the related issues. It helped to enrich if not rebuild a foundation for discussing and lobbying for women's and gender issues, which had been dropped after socialism. Zanaa inspired the new generation of mighty feminist activists. However, the term "gender" generated much dispute at that time. Many people continued to be critical of Zanaa's contributions despite their positive outcomes (which were not immediately visible or valuable to some). Some people opposed the language of gender and women's rights, as well as Zanaa as a person. Many people also conflated the notion of "gender" with "women's rights," and thus "gender" was understood as "feminism" and feminism was understood as "women's empowerment." The term "gender" became associated with "women in politics" and, in general, with high-achieving women (*kar'erist hüühnüüd*). Even men who saw themselves as progressive and modern complained to me: "All these women who talk about gender just want to become bosses. Hence, consider staying away from them." Such a view was not related just to Zanaa's introduction of the term "gender" and associated ideas about gender equality.

It was also related to her uncompromisingly harsh critical standpoint. From the 1990s until the late 2010s, Zanaa sharply and relentlessly critiqued political and social ills and misdeeds, corruption in politics, neoliberal cutting of state services, and protested foreign investment in mining. She asked pointed and specific questions. Her mode of speech was direct and unceremonious. For some people, she garnered a reputation as an agitator and a disruptor; for others, she was a formidable leader and a courageous advocate. Her sharp language, exacting demeanor, and general "iron-lady" look challenged a dominant stereotype of gender and age. But more than that, her piercing language was a form of a weapon; it disputed the "hegemony of representation" (Yurchak 2007) that normalized the power-holders' formulaic and generic language of avoidance, simplification (*böörönhiileh*), and pacification. Pierre Bourdieu (1991) discusses how the ruling class uses language to engage in the symbolic violence of imposing its views to subordinate the populace. In Mongolia, the leaders' formal language tends to be rounded, lacking specificity and details. So Zanaa's sharpness was a destabilization of that dullness and avoidance. Her approach was *oyunlag* as it fit her purpose to take down the politics but did not fit the expected manners of the intellectual class and "cultured" (*soyoltoy*) women.

Once, prior to the 2008 election, a famous television program host, Shagdarsurengiin Gurbazar, was on air with Zanaa discussing the motives behind her resistance to foreign investment laws and mining agreements (see chapter 2). Zanaa's well-informed political engagement challenged the stereotype of middle-aged women as outdated, home-bound, and ignorant about politics. By demonstrating her in-depth knowledge of the laws, politics, and prognosis of the mining under the by-then-current laws, she appeared distinctly *oyunlag*. At the end of the program, Gurbazar thanked Zanaa and said that it was so wonderful to see her as a leader (*lider*), fighter (*daichin*), and *oyunlag*, and that it was great that she was not at all like the women with their skirts dragging on the ground (*hormoigoo chirsen*)—a derogatory stereotyping of an older woman who appears unkempt and outdated.

As the key spokesperson on the concept of gender, Zanaa was, without hesitation, placed on a team of lawyers, activists, scholars, and politicians to develop and pass the long-overdue (and outstanding) Law of Mongolia on Enforcement of the Law on Promotion of Gender Equality, known colloquially

as the gender equality law (*genderin tegsh erhiin tuhai huuli*). However, for
the law to pass, Zanaa would need to be more strategic than she had been before. This meant that the discussion on "gender," which has come to be associated with "overachieving women"—among some of the public—needed to
"cool down" (*namjirah heregtei*). Another feminist, the head of the National
Committee on Gender Equality, Baasankhüügiin Enksaihan, who oversaw
the passing of a law on gender equality, told me the following:

> Sister Zanaa was the backbone of the years of writing, lobbying, and passing
> the law. Like all of us, she was anxious about the potential resistance to this law
> at the legislature. I could tell that she was ready to fight for it with her usual
> sharpness. When we started lobbying at full force, I pleaded with her to sit
> back. I told her, "Please sister Zanaa, let us handle this!" We needed to be ami-
> able; we did not want to anger anyone. And there was no need to re-inflame
> the polemical discourse from the past [she meant the resistance to gender,
> which remained conflated with feminism, and Zanaa].

Being one of the architects of the law on gender equality was one of Zanaa's *oyunlag* achievements. I had participated in several daylong writing and
planning meetings on the gender equality law with Zanaa and many other
lawyers, activists, NGO leaders, and feminists in 2007 and 2008. The women
had studied gender equality laws from all over the world, consulted international experts, and employed their knowledge of the country in order to come
up with the right articles, definitions, and the scope of the law's coverage (for
example, guarantees of equal rights in civil service, health care, and labor relations). Zanaa was the most knowledgeable about the theories of gender and
the structural and institutional nuances that mattered in articulating the pas-
sages of law.

The gender equality law needed to be flawless in a male-dominated Parliament that had little interest in attending to gender-related topics. The law
had to be a work of persuasion and give no excuse for a rejection because
most male politicians, who comprised the overwhelming majority of Parliament, had no incentive to pass it. A slight defect or ambiguity would have
thrown the law in jeopardy. The law-developing working group even solicited
an official letter from the Philology Department of the Academy of Sciences
of Mongolia to explain the word "gender" from a professional linguistic perspective and to examine the ways it could be translated into Mongolian. The
letter, which Enksaihan read aloud to the group during one of the writing
meetings I attended, explained the definition of gender (the idea that gender
is a society's culturally specific perception of male and female characteristics)
and stated that as the word had no equivalent in Mongolian, it was necessary

to adopt the word in its foreign version (which was already in use in the larger society). (A thorough definition of gender was included in the law.)[14] During the discussion of the gender equality law in Parliament, one of the long-term male legislators, Erdeniin Bat-Üül, announced that he had never seen such a perfectly developed law in more than a dozen years in the office and encouraged everyone to read it as a textbook example of law-making expertise.[15]

In the subsequent election of 2012, Zanaa became a member of a newly established Civic Movement Party. Of thirty-eight candidates the party put forward, thirty-six candidates were women. One of them was Zanaa. The new party's campaign was modest, especially compared to that of the two major parties' (DP and MPP) and their domination of the electoral landscape. Yet the act of "jumping in" to this crowded arena as a party that was comprised almost exclusively of women was a feminist message to the society and not just the election (see Fig. 3.10).

An Intellectful Celebrity: Funding with a Novel

Tsedevdambyin Oyungerel refused to pay the "donation" (50 million tugrik) the DP was soliciting from its candidates because she saw this as a way of excluding newcomers.[16] Without the donation, the DP refused to give its mandate for candidacy. Yet Oyungerel did not waver and, in the end, one or more anonymous supporters donated the sum for her. She never discovered who they were. Right after the 2008 election, I contacted Oyungerel, who competed in an election in Khövsgöl Province in northern Mongolia and lost the vote by a small margin. She agreed to an interview and graciously invited me to her house. She was unable to go outside because she had injured her back in a fall from a horse while campaigning in Khövsgöl. She was not in much pain (she said without any hint of self-pity), but she could not sit for long periods and had to lie down or kneel instead.

After Oyungerel and I had tea, we went to her spacious living room, furnished with large sofas and coffee tables, a media center, bookshelves, and at least two work areas complete with computers and other technology. Oyungerel got involved in politics at the beginning of the country's democratization in the 1990s. She contributed to shaping the DP's long-term policies as well as to overseeing its daily activities, helping the party develop into a fully fledged opposition to the seventy-year-old MPRP. Yet as successful as Oyungerel's career had been inside her party, it was still not enough to gain a seat in Parliament. As she noted, "Despite all the work that women do, they tend to become stepping stones for their male colleagues." Therefore, she sought a political office through a public recognition as a person of high achievements and capabilities.

Indeed, back in 2002, Oyungerel made a splash in the Mongolian media. She was accepted to an MA program in International Policy Studies at Stanford University, but she could not afford the fees. She launched a national campaign to raise funds for her tuition. Reaction to this enterprise was mixed: some praised her for perseverance while others accused her of turning her situation into a public relations performance. However, her message was clear: she was in politics not to accumulate money but because she was a politician—and she needed additional training to enhance her credentials (she eventually earned her degree in 2004).

In 2006, Oyungerel arrived at Yale University's World Fellow Program, which prepares public and business leaders. As a strategy for gaining popularity back home, she was instructed by the program to write a book, a combination of memoir and platform statement. Oyungerel's first book, entitled *Notes on my Study in America* (2007a), narrates her experience in being accepted to universities in the United States and shares advice on finding scholarships. The book's readership was limited to students mostly in the city of Ulaanbaatar. It was not helpful in her pursuit of votes in rural Khövsgöl province, where she planned on competing.

In order to attract voters in Khövsgöl, Oyungerel wrote a second book, entitled *Nomadic Dialogues* (2007b). It is a phrasebook for English-speaking tourists; it is also useful for Mongolian families who wish to sell homemade products such as cheese and felt souvenirs and explain their surroundings to tourists (the book contains, for example, a section devoted to explaining that flies in the countryside are not as dirty as those in more urban areas, and do not contaminate food with disease-carrying agents). The book became a bestseller in Mongolia. Still, according to Oyungerel, it did not garner enough fame to enhance her candidacy.

By the following year, Oyungerel had finished her third book, a novel called *The Green-Eyed Lama* (2008), together with her husband Jeffrey Falt. They had been writing it off and on for more than ten years. This was the book that brought Oyungerel nationwide fame and a substantial amount of money to boost her electoral campaign.[17] The novel was based on the political violence of the 1930s and its long-term implications for Oyungerel's family and the community that surrounds Dayan Deerkh, a monastery in Khövsgöl province. The main protagonists are based on Oyungerel's grandmother, fictionalized as Sendmaa (a partial reversal of her real name, Densmaa), and her great-uncle, using his real name, Baasan: a green-eyed Buddhist monk, an artist, and the lead sutra reciter (*unzad*) of the Dayan Deerkh monastery.

Oyungerel's book tour provided an effective opportunity for precampaigning before the official election campaign. She traveled in Khövsgöl Province and gave talks about *The Green-Eyed Lama*. The first print-run sold out immediately:

> I had no idea that people would be so eager to purchase a book, as money is in real short supply in the *taiga* (snowforest). I was so excited and moved that I offered a discount "*taigin tavan maynga*" (taiga's discount—five thousand [*tugrik*]). People stood in line to buy my book and I even had to sell the display copies. The younger readers told me that they had been so engrossed in the book that they stayed up through the night reading it. I keep receiving email requests about the next volume of the novel.

As noted above, sales from *The Green-Eyed Lama* sponsored much of Oyungerel's campaign. In a place where candidates mostly use money and power in order to garner attention, Oyungerel addressed the emotional needs of the populace and thus established a connection with her constituency. When I asked her why she decided to write a novel in the first place, she said that she did so because no one has been writing after the collapse of socialism. "During socialism, the state sponsored writers. After socialism, no one paid writers to write literature, so people stopped writing. There was a space for novels." But this was also only a small part of her answer to my question.

A fuller answer emerged in an impromptu way during our discussion about her campaigning. While Oyungerel and I were looking at some of her campaign pictures—glamorous images of her and three other candidates riding horse carts, emerging from a helicopter, riding on the back of a truck and waving to voters in Khövsgöl—we happened to also look at her other files. In one was a black-and-white photo in which Oyungerel was crying amid a crowd during a large public gathering. The shot was from September 10, 1996—the first day Mongolia commemorated the Victims of Political Repression. "A journalist snapped this picture and it appeared in a newspaper," said Oyungerel.

"Why are you crying?" I asked, even though I thought that the answer was somewhat obvious—she was saddened by the commemoration. "I was sad because I felt sorry for my ancestors," said Oyungerel.

> This was the first time the country commemorated the victims of political repression and it was a true public explosion of grief. There were so many people who brought pictures of their family members and who knew so much about them. It was incredible. I felt sorry for my ancestors because no one was grieving for them because we did not know who they were. "My poor ancestors," I thought, and I felt ashamed. I could not even grieve because I did not even know them.

Since then, Oyungerel has repeatedly returned to her ancestral homeland in Khövsgöl to inquire about family members who fell victim to the political repression. They became the protagonists of her novel.

Oyungerel also realized, unexpectedly, that by revealing her immediate ancestry, she might have protected herself against black and white *hel am* (rumors, curses, and other verbally and ritually inflicted harm) and especially "black public relations." "People kept telling me that I have a really powerful ancestry," Oyungerel said. "Even my opponents mentioned that to me." It is not clear the extent to which knowledge about Oyungerel's powerful ancestry had made her opponents refrain from launching so-called "black public relations"—that is, spreading negative information that would affect voters' opinions. In previous elections, her reputation was tainted by an organized black PR campaign that criticized her marriage to an American man who was considerably older than her. In rural, more traditional, and much less cosmopolitan settlements of Khövsgöl, a woman married to a foreigner was seen as a traitor to her people. In fact, Oyungerel was often asked why she chose to marry an older American instead of choosing from her young and handsome Khalha countrymen. But in 2012, when Oyungerel was running in the urban district, she did not receive the usual questions about her marital choice. When I asked her how she blocked the black PR, she associated the absence of the negative publicity with her new strategy, which was to campaign only with two other DP cocandidates as a "trio" (her constituency could elect multiple members) and to refrain from giving (*gantsaarchilsan toglolt*) "solo performances" or distributing materials only about herself. That way, she reasoned, the attackers would not separate her from the rest of the candidates. And since the other two in the group were men whose family situations were stellar, the opponents did not touch Oyungerel's potentially vulnerable spot: her marriage to an American. It remains unclear, however, who defended Oyungerel from the black PR: her powerful lama ancestor or her influential male colleagues.

Through her authorship, Oyungerel gained nationwide recognition without paying any money (that is, to journalists and producers) but by making some instead. She became a celebrity who was not a beauty queen or a trophy wife, but *oyunlag* (intellectual). Unlike *seheeten* (intelligentsia), which indicates a social class, *oyunlag* emphasizes a person's moral values and capacities without an indication of class membership. By choosing to write a novel that unearthed history suppressed under socialism, Oyungerel displayed herself as a new intellectful politician of the democratic period; the socialist state's patronage and ideological impositions would no longer dictate her choices.

Oyungerel's voice became that of an artistic and creative author but also an unofficial visionary, as the book proved to be bigger and more influential than her voice as a politician (for example, her protest to the repeal of the gender quota for parliamentary members had no impact). She convinced her party to nominate her as a candidate based on the fame she gained primarily as an author. She fulfilled the criteria for being a "cultured" person who was qualitatively "better" than the rest of the ordinary electorate, whether she intended to do so or not.

It is notable that Oyungerel wrote her novel as a serious fiction writer, unlike other politicians, both male and female, who write polemical columns and editorials. Many politicians (mostly male) have written memoirs explaining their moral and political views, essays about current politics and economy, and books explaining the personal and professional "programs" of their intended leadership. Oyungerel's novel carried out the quest of democratic revolution of the early 1990s while also questioning an all-too-often absent history of past violence. But unlike direct political attacks against the MPRP, she used a subtle work of art. Thus, in addition to acquiring recognition (being known or recognized by the electorate) through a literary endeavor, Oyungerel acquired the characteristics that voters sought, such as being *intellectful*.

Campaigning with Symbolic Capital: The New *Oyunlag* in Politics

Strong in math, Radnaagiin Burmaa obtained a degree in electronic engineering at the Technical University in Sofia, Bulgaria, in the 1980s. Upon returning to Mongolia, she worked for the first Mongolian electronics company, MONEL (Mongolian Electronics). There she also met likeminded engineers who shared her concerns about the country's future and a desire to build a more open, free, and prosperous society. Having been addicted to coffee while in Sofia, Burmaa questioned why there was no coffee in Mongolian stores and why she was not allowed to enter Soviet stores that carried coffee beans. "I wondered why we, Mongolians while living in our own country, could not shop in places where Soviets could shop," she told me. She participated in the democratic movement in the late 1980s as MONEL became its underground headquarters. "MONEL was one of few places with Xerox [photocopying] machines. We used to stay up all night and make copies of posters and Baabar's (1990) [polemical] writing for distribution.[18] We were preparing the democratic revolution in our offices," she told me.

Following the democratic revolution in 1990, Burmaa began to build NGOs. For her it came somewhat organically, as a part of her political activities as a DP member:

After founding the DP, we established [its] women's organization [the Democratic Women's Committee] in the early 1990s. We did so because my women
colleagues and I wanted to involve more women in politics and be a part of the
democratization. We ended up modeling our organization after the MPRP's
women's organization, because that is all we knew back then. After traveling to
the United States and European countries, I learned about a thing called "the civil
society" and the importance of citizen-centered participation that was outside
of political parties. So upon coming back I established "Women in Social Progress" [an NGO]. Then I traveled some more and observed elections and learned
that in democratic elections voters need to be informed and knowledgeable.
So, upon my return, I established a "Voter Education Center" [another NGO].

The civil society that Burmaa and other women helped to create was not
only friendly to women but also potentially empowered them.[19] These women
NGO leaders were also ahead of the state (and, in the case of Burmaa, her political party) in determining the steps for building the new society.[20] Building
NGOs also meant transforming selves. Burmaa gained expertise in entirely
new fields of inquiry. From being an electronics engineer, she was now expe-
ditiously learning English, lawmaking, advocacy and public outreach, grant-
writing, and learning about a new world of international organizations. These
activities reshaped Burmaa to become a new *oyunlag* figure in politics.

Burmaa's knowledge of and expertise in democratization was especially
valuable to the DP. Despite its dynamic leadership and enthusiastic member
groups, in the 1990s, the party lacked professionals who were skilled in day-
to-day governing and state-building in contrast to the bigger and more experienced MPRP, which had ruled the country for seven decades and which
had had cadres who received leadership training in the institutes in the Soviet
Union and in Mongolia during socialism. The MPRP remained in full power
and won the first two parliamentary elections (in 1990 and 1992) by a land-
slide, even though the politburo resigned and the country adopted the multiparty system in 1990. In such circumstances, the civil society that Burmaa
helped to develop was beneficial for the democratization of society at large
beyond narrow multiparty competition. The establishment of democracy
among the populace had strengthened the DP and contributed to its victory
in the 2004 election.

Burmaa's activities in building civil society make her uniquely *oyunlag*.
Her *oyunlag* outlook was the product of the new expertise and agency she
acquired in the context of politics. She was not striving to be *oyunlag* for self-
cultivation, or self-expression, or to lead a particular kind of lifestyle. Instead,
her goals to build institutions pushed her to learn new skills and knowledge,
not the other way around.

Yet, despite being a valuable cadre for the DP, Burmaa had to give up her party membership because international grant-making to fund NGOs required the grantees to be free from political affiliation. In addition, Burmaa's party stance also made her realize she needed to be free from politics if she wanted to contribute to the civil society. Back in the early 1990s, Burmaa secured some impressive funding from the UNDP and the Asian Development Bank, among other international organizations. However, the DP's financial officers assumed that because the organizations that Burmaa chaired were established originally as offshoots of the party, the money that Burmaa won would also belong to the DP. Burmaa thus realized that the organizations she had created needed to be separate from politics and she had to leave the political party. Official politics and NGO-building have come to be mutually exclusive in order to insure the NGOs' neutrality.

Burmaa's departure from her political party echoes the experience of other women who received recognition from international organizations but remained marginalized within their respective political parties (excluding the Civic Will Party, led by Mrs. Oyun). Many of these women chose to work within civil society. The stable income that NGOs provided during Mongolia's economic recession in the 1990s, and the relative freedom to chair one's own NGOs, also encouraged some of the most politically active women to leave their political parties and join civil society. In retrospect, this move was disadvantageous to their political careers and to politics, which became even more male-centered than before. Like the women who went on to build highly successful NGOs, Burmaa gained social networks, recognition, and reputation. But she also lost her position and insider ties within her political party.

Social Circles versus Assemblages

Upon deciding to run for a parliamentary seat, Burmaa was able to bring together the fruits of her affiliation with the DP and her leadership in civil society, although asynchronously. She rejoined the DP prior to the election of 2008 (which inevitably upset some members of civil society). The DP gave Burmaa a *mandaat* (mandate) to run as a candidate for election. Burmaa came with a reputation as *oyunlag*, a civil society leader, and a spokeswoman for common citizens. But because she left the DP in the late 1990s to pursue NGO-building, by the time she returned to the party in 2008, she had lost her networks and felt alienated from the more intimate aspects of the party.

Since Burmaa did not have the financial resources to "throw money" (*mongo tsatsakh*) to stage campaigns that would overwhelm those of her opponents, or gain close political allies, she relied on her existing symbolic capital, much of which was based on her background in civil society. In line with Pierre Bourdieu's (1993, 7) characterization, Burmaa's symbolic capital was centered on various "degree[s] of accumulated prestige, celebrity [status], consecration of honour and . . . founded on a dialectic of knowledge (*connaissance*) and recognition (*reconnaissance*)." Prestige, respect, and admiration are coveted properties among politicians, and especially among electoral candidates. Difficult to buy with money or cultivate through campaigns, the abundance of symbolic capital distinguished Burmaa's candidacy.

Unlike many other candidates who established NGOs, networked, and pursued postgraduate education mainly to become electoral candidates, Burmaa's symbolic capital was in existence before her intention to run for a parliamentary seat. In the following, I distill some of Burmaa's symbolic capital into three spheres: she had *social circles* rather than *social assemblages*; relied on *social memories* instead of *promises for the future*; and provided *gigs of honor* instead of *paychecks only*. Most candidates strived to build *social assemblages* (*süljee*) as a part of their voter base during both the campaign and noncampaign period. Most of these assemblages were based on already existing networks, such as kin, classmates, and compatriots (*nutag*) (Sneath 2018) but became activated and streamlined in a context of electoral campaigns. The assemblages that were formed around administrative units such as *khoroo* and *bag* were especially consistent because the local officers oversaw the distribution of aid packages, jobs, and services from the state. Various members of these groups acted as facilitators for maintaining a loyalty to a particular party or politician through encouragement and reminders. Many political aspirants and candidates strived to maintain the loyalty of these groups through *promises for a better future* and by providing services and paid gigs. These were hierarchical, reciprocal, and conditional relationships that were developed by the candidates and aspirants for elections. It is these informal channels that were developed in electoral contexts that have come to filter and channel many aspects of Mongolia's economy and state services (see chapter 2).

Burmaa did not create or animate similar assemblages for the purposes of elections. Instead, she had diverse independent *social circles*, which she had developed in the past at various points of her career as an engineer, NGO builder, and politician. Unlike social *assemblages*, in which candidates were at the top of the hierarchy, Burmaa was a member of her various *social circles*. If *assemblages* were created in anticipation of elections, Burmaa's *circles* existed independently from the candidate and elections, were based on shared experiences and friendships, and were heterogeneous in their motives for existing.

FIGURE 5.2. Burmaa at her campaign in Ulaanbaatar, 2008. Photo by the author.

No one had any distinct obligations to reciprocate, donate, or help the candidate. The connections among the members inside these circles were not associated with elections, or Burmaa, or anticipated exchange, although the members did get together for the purposes of Burmaa's campaign. Of course, social circles can (and they sometimes do) transform into assemblages for the purposes of supporting a candidate who is a member of a circle. But none of Burmaa's circles organized into coherent assemblages based on reciprocal and contingent relationships. Let me describe the opening of Burmaa's electoral campaign, which gives an overview of the *circles* to which she belongs and how they explain and support her as a candidate.

Burmaa's first campaign was launched on June 2, 2008.[21] It took place in a youth resort outside of Ulaanbaatar. About 1,000 voters from Burmaa's constituency were bused to the resort. In addition, there were about 300 people— Burmaa's close supporters—consisting of celebrities like pop singers, comedians, and poets, as well as high-profile lawyers, award-winning teachers, popular intellectuals, plus friends and colleagues. They were there to attract voters and to convey to them the respect, recognition, and prestige that they attributed to Burmaa (fig. 5.2).

Numerous groups of people who had become associated with Burmaa during various points in her multifaceted career emerged on the stage to contribute their praise and sometimes money to her campaign. They identified

her various fields of impact and thus expanded her repertoire as an intellectful and productive candidate. As these different groups took to the stage, one
after another, to introduce themselves, their relation to Burmaa, and their
mutual work history, Burmaa was unfolded in a new light as a person and
as a candidate. It became a work of collective memory—a narrative memoir.

Most electoral candidates tend to bring along well-known individuals,
including their teachers and mentors, to their campaigns to endorse their
candidacy. Burmaa's campaign was special, as each group provided a catchphrase that captured Burmaa's distinctiveness and thus, electability. Each
group played off the previous catchphrase, thus further expanding and sys-
tematizing the distinctions. This was impromptu and worked well with the
voters, many of whom listened only selectively and grasped only memorable
catchphrases.

The first group of supporters were representatives from civil society. "For
most people Burmaa is known as *Irgenii Burmaa* [short for *Irgeni Niigmin
Burmaa* (Civil Society Burmaa)]," they noted. This group was the most heterogeneous in composition and consisted of clusters from media, city dwell-
ers, NGO groups, and the DP. The civil society was a strong voice in the
country in 2008. Consisting of some of the most educated and dedicated individuals, and with a strong voice and sharp opinions, it rivaled major political parties in its impact on the larger society.[22]

The next group to the stage was composed of several young professionals who talked on the subject of *Children's Burmaa*. They spoke about their
experiences in youth and children's programs—UNESCO's One World forum
and the Mini-Parliament Global Citizenship for Youth—which Burmaa had
organized for children in the 1990s and early 2000s. "She is also known as
Education Burmaa," added some people in the audience, thus accentuating
their shared value.

As an alumna of a university in Bulgaria, Burmaa was known as *Bulgaria's
Burmaa* and thus drew supporters from other Bulgarian alumni in Mongolia.
This was a group of middle-aged professionals, mostly women, who also demonstratively presented cash donations to Burmaa's campaign expenses. After this initial meeting, a dozen volunteers from this group came on a regular
basis during her campaign and worked on the most meticulous and daunting
jobs, like checking on the distribution of the campaign material. For the voters, it was important to register that Burmaa got her higher education abroad,
in Eastern Europe, which was the most modern and developed socialist ally
during the Cold War.

"For us, Burmaa is known as *MONEL's Burmaa*," said the next batch of
people, mostly men and women in their forties and fifties. The title came from

her first job at MONEL after she returned from Bulgaria. The friendships she had made there were unique, memorable, and long-lasting. As the first electronics producing company in still-socialist Mongolia in the 1980s, MONEL employed the brightest engineers, most of whom had earned an education abroad. "When in the late 1980s, we turned our company into a secret 'cell' of the fledgling democratic movement, our boss was an awesome man; he pretended not to know our nightly activities. We appreciated that, and never missed our work during the day," Burmaa said to the audience. "And because Burmaa was one of our comrades in shaping the democratic movement," said one of the supporters, "she is also *Democracy's Burmaa.*"

In addition to the above titles—civic, children's, education's, Bulgarian, MONEL's, and democracy's—more titles emerged, such as "52s" (referring to Burmaa's secondary school), *darga* (chairwoman), *seheeten* (a member of intelligentsia), and *shudarga* (honest). The launching of the campaign, among other things, revealed Burmaa's personal histories and her skills and achievements on a single platform. It was an event that spoke to the ways in which Mongolians refer to candidacy: *ner devshih*, which means elevating one's name. In this case, Burmaa's name was not just elevated but also expanded to match her past and present activities, identities, and social belongings.

Gatherers, Warmer-Uppers, and Movers

One of the most demanding aspects of electoral campaigns are voter outreach meetings. These vary greatly: while some can be as simple as the candidates walking into the local market to speak with interested voters, others are staged as the most extravagant entertainments that money can buy. Campaigns strive to employ skilled poets, rock stars, and popular movie stars to boost voter attendance. They rent large concert auditoriums, use fireworks, and dry ice, release countless balloons, employ uniformed cheerleaders, and display their presentations on multiple LCD screens. In addition to campaigners who distributed candidate materials and provided on-street live advertisement for the candidates, campaigns also employed paid or "fake" voters who attended voter outreach meetings to create an illusion of a crowd, which, in turn, would attract others.

The campaigns that were staged by the DP local branch staff for Burmaa and her other two corunners (Elbegdorj and Bayarsaikhan) employed a young female lead speaker, an MC. Clad in a slim white pantsuit and platform heels, with long hair and sparkly makeup, she eulogized charismatically, sometimes enhancing one candidate over others. She disappeared half-way through the campaign period, however, and we learned that she had accepted

a similar gig elsewhere for more pay. The DP branch's attempts to find a re-
placement for the young MC proved to be futile and the candidates had to
do without such a role. Their group campaign felt a bit depleted thereafter
also because each candidate began investing a bit more in their individual
"*toglolt*" ("performances").

Every candidate had his or her personal *shtab* (campaign center) and a set
of campaigners. Campaigners were usually recruited from college students
and other young people, who followed the candidate to the voter outreach
meetings. They gathered voters from the neighborhoods, staged parades, distributed campaign materials, and spread good words about the candidate.
Finding enough campaigners was not easy as the work required prolonged
time commitment, discipline, and dedication. Much of the campaign period
also overlapped with the college exam period.

Many of Burmaa's campaigners were the students of and acquaintances
of the alumni of UNESCO's One World forum and the Mini-Parliament—the
programs that Burmaa ran back in the 1990s. Now successful professionals,
several of them reminisced to me excitedly about their experiences in these
programs—the best times of their lives. They came to help Burmaa out of
gratitude, a sense of camaraderie, and to reminisce fondly. Like these young
people, Burmaa's immediate supporters sought little or no direct personal
gain from contributing to her campaign, either financially or in kind. Their
motivation to help her was different from the workers of most other candidates I have known, who saw their contribution as a favor to be returned after
the candidate wins the seat or as a paid gig. Such giggers constantly compared
the campaigns of different candidates by appearing and disappearing during
meetings, workshops, and lunches. They were often on their phones talking
to their friends who were working in other candidates' campaigns. They also
eagerly told their peers in Burmaa's campaign (and me) about other candidates and their campaign activities, handouts, and promises. The people who
sought to benefit from Burmaa's campaign, though, quickly learned to seek
out a different candidate who would pay them more. Yet many of Burmaa's
supporters were convinced that she deserved a place in Parliament owing to
her skills, intellect, and moral values. Volunteering or working for her, they
said, was an honor.

Burmaa, meanwhile, treated the campaigners with kindness and generosity. She diverted funds for better lunches, toiletries, extra bottles of water,
chocolates, and even raincoats for the campaigners, thus causing worries
among her staff about her already overstretched funds. Several times she was
late to her own meetings because she was preparing snacks for her campaigners or hanging out with them in the parking area. Some of her staff cautioned

that she was paying too much attention to the campaigners and not enough attention to herself or to her other duties. But Burmaa worked diligently so that the campaigners had the best experience she could provide.

In turn, the campaigners became attached to their roles and found ways to enhance their input. They divided into groups and created an efficient and imaginative system of "gatherers" (*tsugluulagch*), "warmer-uppers" (*biye halaagch*), and "followers" (*dagaldagch*). During the 2008 election, the constituencies had been expanded threefold compared to the previous elections. Candidates struggled to meet voters in person and often covered up to five subdistrict meetings per day. (As discussed in chapter 3, the campaign media had exploded that year.) The biggest challenge was to gather enough voters before the meeting. It was the work of the campaign office to prearrange the local meetings, which became increasingly difficult in areas dominated by temporary summer cabins and in dispersed suburbs. Most gatherings were done through word of mouth from one resident to another and usually by campaigners announcing the upcoming event through loudspeakers while driving or walking along the streets. Many candidates were accompanied by movie stars and performers to attract voters, but, short of money, Burmaa had to rely on the campaigners alone.

In this situation, the "gatherers" went ahead of time to a neighborhood to announce the upcoming voter outreach meetings in markets, streets, and community water wells and plead for residents to congregate. As the voters trickled to the meeting area (a street or a hill), the second group would entertain them as they arrived by staging a "warm-up" show. This was done to prevent the gathered voters from dispersing while Burmaa was campaigning in another area or was on her way. The "warmer-uppers" turned into stage actors. They performed Burmaa's campaign program by taking turns articulating the points in a form of a conversation and adding humor and excitement along the way.[23] The "gatherers" would then move on to the new neighborhoods to announce the meetings, and the "warmer-uppers" would "transfer" the ready-to-engage voters to the third group, the "followers," who would arrive with Burmaa. By the time Burmaa and the "followers" arrived from her previous meetings, the voters would be "warmed up" and ready for an in-depth question-and-answer session. Through careful coordination, imagination, and camaraderie, the campaigners practiced their performing and organizational skills and demonstrated their own intellectful-ness. It was Burmaa who, through seemingly "pointless hanging outs" that so unnerved some of her staff members, had created a memorable, educational, and exciting experience for the new generation of students. In retrospect, Burmaa recreated a similar experience for these youth as she did for their predecessors, the alumni of the UNESCO's One World forum and the Mini-Parliament for Youth a decade earlier in the 1990s and who originally sent these new students and acquaintances to her.

Financing: The Guide against Chaos

Besides her symbolic capital, Burmaa still needed cash to sponsor her campaign in two ways: her *individual candidate campaign* and a part of the *group campaign* organized by the DP's campaign office in her constituency for Burmaa, Bayarsaikhan, and Elbegdorj. Bills streamed in one after another for print media, posters, T-shirts with her portraits, volunteers' lunches, and even stackable plastic chairs for voter outreach meetings in suburban districts. Photographs and posters, billboards, banquets, and airtime and print coverage also needed funds.

The expenses of Burmaa's individual campaign were clear and straightforward. Yet the bills she received from the DP's campaign offices (the main headquarters and the district office) were not always broken down and thus unclear. Most important, despite her diligent payments, rumors circulated that Burmaa had not paid her portion of the salaries of the campaigners the district hired for the group. Burmaa speculated that some of her payments toward the salaries of district campaigners did not reach their destination. When Burmaa inquired about the breakdown of financial statements from the district's campaign office, she received no answer. Only long after the elections and after the campaign offices ceased to exist did she receive a reply that her financial contributions could not be tracked down because the district office had ceased to operate.

This was especially troublesome for Burmaa. As an expert on elections, she worked hard to eradicate this type of uncertainty among many others and to establish legal frameworks for financial transparency. In an ironic twist of fate, the money she paid toward the salaries of the campaign workers came from the election manuals that she had authored for the organizers of the election campaign specifically in order to avoid this type of murkiness. She was undermined by the very system she was working to fix and the people she, as the head of the Voter Education Center, was trying to train in ethical conduct.

Burmaa's experience with this irregularity was indicative of the larger and different types of contestations that have taken place following most elections, with the 2008 election culminating in violence and tragedies. It showed that her unparalleled expertise in elections, which she actualized in her manuals for conducting elections, was especially useful in preventing fraud and confusion. As such, it could potentially save not only time and resources in legal battles but, more importantly, people's lives, as the most tragic aspect of the election meddling was the murder of five citizens during the postelection uprising on July 1, 2008.

Every election year since the late 1990s, Burmaa and her staff produced a number of manuals and brochures. The most significant ones were two voluminous handouts for parliamentary elections, one a *Manual for Organizing Elections* and another a *Manual for Election Observers* (both by Burmaa 2008, 2012). The 2008 *Manuals* were particularly extensive. These were mainly for use in campaigns and especially by their managerial staff.

The *Parliamentary Election of 2008: Manual for Organizing Elections* (Burmaa 2008) for example, maps out the election in a comprehensive way for every possible stakeholder: candidates, campaign workers, managers, organizers, political parties, and others. In its eighteen chapters, it covers every aspect of elections: the organizations of administrative bodies; campaigns by candidates and political parties; the role of observers and media monitoring; voter registration lists; Election Day; and ballot counting. The manual's detailed guidelines were designed to limit election fraud and to prevent mistakes. It made transparent the laws and restrictions and even illustrated how seemingly taken-for-granted and blameless events and actions in everyday life were interpreted differently in legal contexts. The manual included fraud prevention strategies at every step of the election process, from voter registration to the organization of the voting center to vote counting. For instance, the manual discussed the nineteen different misdeeds that could occur during voter registration. Some of these were as egregious as registering voters in several districts or omitting an entire neighborhood from the registration.

This and other manuals were necessary guides for the campaign staff to electoral laws, campaign rules, constituency size, media law, and other aspects that changed with every parliamentary election. Aware of the extreme stress and chaos campaign staff experience every election, Burmaa designed her manuals as large calendar workbooks with deadlines, reminders, and "to do" lists for each day of a campaign. Many of Burmaa's party colleagues commissioned the manual ahead of time. It was important for the DP to be vigilant, said Burma, as it had a track record of losing votes owing to fraud. "No one expects that he or she will be a victim of a fraud," Burmaa noted. "It is only right before the votes are cast that candidates realize that fraud is unpredictable and can be snuck in at every step of the way." The first batch of people who bought Burmaa's manual were some of her party colleagues who were running for seats and who had been victims of electoral fraud in previous elections. Then, other political parties, especially the MPRP, also purchased the manual in bulk. As Burmaa kept explaining the importance of the manual to her party, the DP bought multiple copies of it to distribute to all election staff throughout the country. Altogether, 10,000 copies were produced and sold. The money that Burmaa earned with the book became the core for her campaign financing and she was proud that she was able to get through the election without a lucrative business of her own or becoming indebted to a business magnate.

From Revealing the Fraud of 2008 to the 2012 Election

The 2008 election was unlike any other. On June 30, demonstrators protesting the victory of the MPRP gathered in front of the party's headquarters, which is adjacent to Ulaanbaatar's main Sukhbaatar Square. The protesters accused the MPRP of electoral fraud. Burmaa did not win a seat and was convinced that her votes were stolen (which she was able to prove afterward, although indirectly). Upon hearing about the demonstrations, she went there with her staff to gather signatures from the protesters in order to back up her argument. Since almost every election was followed by a protest and allegations of fraud, the demonstrations at Sukhbaatar Square were far from unusual. After Burmaa talked to some of the leaders of the Civic Movement who were at the demonstrations, her staff urged her to go home. The demonstration was expanding.

By the next day, the demonstrations had turned into riots and plundering. The police failed to disperse the crowd and by midnight of July 1, the president of Mongolia, Nambaryn Enkhbayar, declared a four-day-long state of emergency, with the military on the city streets and curfews for public activities (fig. 5.3). That night five people were murdered as the government brought in the armed forces and began persecuting the demonstrators. About 800 people were detained, half of whom where later tried and sentenced up to seven years in prison (Delaplache, Kaplonski, and Sneath 2008). Unfortunately, most cases were filed not as politically motivated but as vandalism and burglary. Both President Enkhbayar and Elbegdorj issued a pardon and released most of the detainees. There was, however, no rehabilitation, which would have been suitable for political prosecution. In order to erase the records of human rights violation and police clashes, major television stations were shut down during the crackdown by government forces on the rioters. Discussions about the causes and nature of the riots, the failure of the government and the police to respond to the riots in a timely manner, and the violation of human rights during and after the riots became a major concern following the elections (Oleinik 2012; Undarya 2009). In the aftermath,

FIGURE 5.3. The military on the streets during the curfew on July 2, 2008, in Ulaanbaatar. Photo by the author.

the persecution of the detainees instilled fear and silence among the populace almost immediately.

During the riots in the first few days of July, Burmaa visited the headquarters of the DP. Elbegdorj and the other DP executives were busy giving speeches on television. Burmaa mentioned to Elbegdorj (Bayarsaikhan and Elbegdorj won for the DP and Burmaa lost) that her votes were stolen. In response, Elbegdorj told her that instead of complaining about her electoral losses, she should be on the streets helping the victims of the state detention and false accusation. This was her job, he said, as a leader of civil society, a human rights specialist, and as a woman. When Burmaa said that she planned to file a lawsuit to recover her lost votes, Elbegdorj warned her that she would not go very far with her claims and investigations.

Burmaa was disconcerted that the DP administration pushed her aside without any attempt to help her to retrieve her stolen votes. She immediately began work to prove the election fraud. Ultimately, Burmaa told me, that was the best way to demonstrate the innocence of the falsely accused rioters, whose motives were to alert the public about the election fraud.

The revelation of the fraud was fraught because the barriers came not only from the opposition (the MPRP) but also from Burmaa's own party, the DP. In multiple-mandate districts, candidates competed not only against other parties but also against cocandidates from their own party. Burmaa's case was especially tricky since her cocandidates Elbegdorj (the DP chairman) and Bayarsaikhan won the seats. If her investigation revealed any irregularities related to her own party members (and not just the MPRP), then it would have been harmful for her on multiple levels. It would damage the DP's reputation even further, sever her affiliation with it, and some members of her party might even retaliate.

Moreover, after the election, the MPRP and the DP had come to an agreement to build a coalition government. Essentially, this meant that the DP, especially the chairman, Elbegdorj, had no incentive to support Burmaa's attempts to recount the votes. Even if the DP was going to remain fair, it was no longer interested in revealing any electoral fraud by the MPRP. The two parties were no longer competitors: they were allies. When Burmaa contacted the relevant authorities to have her district's votes recounted in the archives, after some delay, she was told that the requested material was no longer available in the archives.

Nevertheless, Burmaa was able to prove that there was a significant fraud in the election at large even though she could not prove that there had been *sanal zöösön* (a migration of her votes to another candidate). Several candidates from different political parties, in addition to Burmaa, and separately, also requested the recounting of ballots in the same constituency, but received no response.[24] Burmaa went further in her endeavor and started finding and piecing together evidences.

Through meticulous tracing, Burmaa revealed numerous cases of misconduct during ballot counting and reporting in her (Chingeltei) district, including 1,114 miscounted ballots in eight precincts, the fixing of ballot counting summary sheets with whiting out and pencils and erasers, and the "disappearance" of at least two precincts for a day prior to submitting the counted results. Overall, each of the five candidates who competed in the constituency had anywhere from 152 to 10,597 miscounted ballots.[25] Burmaa also argued that much miscounting occurred because the chairman of the GEC, Bataagiin Battulga, illegally announced that unregistered voters without voter IDs still could vote with their citizenship IDs on Election Day on June 29, 2008. Burmaa argued that the chairman's announcement was a breach of the law as his position did not include the right to make such changes during the election. Moreover, the resulting increase in the number of unregistered voters "had impacted the results of the elections in large urban areas."[26]

With these and other materials, Burmaa eschewed the country's court system as her charges often were not accepted by any existing branches of the court, thus challenging the entire legal structure, consisting of different courts and their administrative tiers. Throughout the fall of 2008, each legal body either rejected her charges or sent her to a different court. First, Burmaa went through various administrative courts. Seeing no results, she then appealed to the Constitutional Court (*Ündsen Huulin Tsets*). At that point, the Constitutional Court instructed Burmaa to go to the Supreme Court (*Deed Shüüh*). When Burmaa went to the Supreme Court, it instructed her to go back to the Constitutional Court. After months of bouncing Burmaa's claims back and forth, mostly between the Supreme Court and Constitutional Court, the former replied to Burmaa that her case could not be taken by either of the courts and that she needed to stop her endeavor. At that point, Burmaa again declared that as a citizen she had a constitutional right to seek protection from a legal entity, and if there were no courts to oversee her case, then the legal system must supply one for her.[27] The only place left for her to submit her charges was the civil court. After about two months, she won her case there. The civil court decreed that Battulga had breached the law (allowing unregistered people to vote), which had impacted the election results.[28] The next morning (January 5, 2009), Battulga summoned a press conference to declare his resignation from the General Election Commission.

With this victory, Burmaa was able to prove that the election of 2008 was fraudulent (even though she could not prove that her votes were stolen). This was important to her because she wanted to show that the postelection riots of July 1 were not unfounded, and neither were the rioters' claims that the election was rigged. The government crushed the riot, and many innocent people were arrested and tried. Burmaa hoped that her achievements in this court battle would also help the prosecuted rioters to contest their charges.

However, Burmaa's verification of the fraudulence of the 2008 election was beneficial for the two big parties in their own way. The DP and its chairman, Elbegdorj, were now freed from any potential charges for enticing the crowd to riot. In accordance with the existing legislation, however, the results of the elections could not be revoked once MPs had been sworn in. Elbegdorj, who now was a part of the coalition government, had little interest in challenging this legislation and fighting with the opposition in order to gain more leverage for his party or to recount the ballots in order to bring the election results closer to the truth.

The MPRP had lost its reputation due to the human rights abuses in suppressing the riots and the tragic murder of five citizens by the armed squad skirmishing with the rioters. But by collaborating with the DP, the MPRP also eschewed any forces that would contest its power and keep it accountable for the violence against the demonstrators. "Now, in the next election, the DP will have a green light," people frequently claimed. Overall, Burmaa's confirmation of election fraud in 2008 helped the DP's candidate, Elbegdorj, to win the

2009 presidential election. Freed from any potential allegations, Elbegdorj had more leverage than his opponents, especially the MPRP candidate. As a new president, Elbegdorj initiated an act of amnesty, and most people who were arrested during the riots have been released from the prison (Oleinik 2012).

Burmaa's work on contesting the electoral fraud enhanced her reputation inside her party, which she previously lacked owing to the nonpartisan status that her commitment to civil society forced upon her. Prior to the 2012 election, she worked to transform the legal structure of the elections in order to make it more favorable to newcomers, women, and people outside of business spheres. She worked as a member of the working group drafting electoral law. In 2012, this law was changed to allow mixed-member proportional representation: voters had two votes to cast, one for a single-seat constituency and another for a party. Burmaa was given one of the top slots on the party list and first among women (the placement instructed by Elbegdorj). The election of 2012 was favorable for women as nine women won parliamentary seats, which was a drastic improvement compared to only three women having won in 2008.

Conclusion: *Oyunlag* as a Disruptive Force

This chapter illustrates how *oyunlag* as a respectable gendered trait has been activated in a new context of democratic politics and commercialized campaigning. Although partially rooted in the concept of *seheeten* (intellectuals) as a social class, *oyunlag* has been separated from it and has become democratized, individualized, gendered, and in some cases even fragmented. Even though there are many people who could be called intellectuals, such as poets, writers, academics, and artists, intellectuals no longer constitute a circumscribed class in neoliberalizing Mongolia. The power and presence of *seheeten* as a class, with its embodied and distinguishable traits, manners, and tastes from the period of socialism, has largely waned. But the continuity of *oyunlag*—in a variety of ways—reveals the nuances of the transformations that took place in Mongolia.

The intellectuals and the socialist state were mutually enhancing entities, with the former creating the content of the MPRP's ideology to influence the populace. The intellectuals helped to maintain the tight connection between the party-state (with its lofty ideals) and the populace. As Wickhamsmith (2020) shows, the intellectuals were tasked to produce the content of the state ideology and thus were central during socialism. Through their work, they kept the gap between the rhetoric of ideals and the actual circumstances invisible and, by doing so, helped to control potential discontent.

Thus, it was ironic but not unexpected that Mongolia's democratization in the late 1980s began with the acknowledgment of that gap by discontented intellectuals. Like Burmaa, who was denied entry to Soviet shops to buy coffee and who chose to stop pretending to believe in the rhetoric of prosperity and happiness, many people who came of age in the 1980s began criticizing the party-state. Indeed, what happens when a pretense for privilege, superiority, and class exclusivity disappears? The women candidates I followed in this chapter are illustrative of the nuanced and multifaceted changes in the Mongolian state. The experiences of these women illustrate that electionization is not just a matter of proliferation and perpetuation of campaigns in their own right. It is also about reworking the fundamentals of the country, its core institutions, values, relations, and economy.

By proving election fraud in 2008, Burmaa demonstrated her unparalleled expertise in the legal sphere. Through her meticulous work, she exposed the inadequacy of the nation's legal and court system, acting like an "X-ray" machine. Her work showed that the July 1 demonstrations had a basis and that the demonstrators were politically motivated. Burmaa showed that the state's prosecution of the demonstrators' actions as burglary or the demonstrators as mere criminals as opposed to justifiable political unrest was a misclassification.

Zanaa's piggybacking on wealthy candidates' campaigns, her use of offensive language to rupture the politics that often shields itself in formulaic language, and especially her outstanding self-presentation, were a repudiation of the campaign system that served mostly select groups in business and politics. By campaigning on foot in the streets and at bus stops, Zanaa was especially adept at "engaging the communities of despair and promoting moral citizenship" (Klumbyte 2014, 474) through sharing the space that was rarely visited by the candidates.

She acted as a loudspeaker and a whistleblower and revealed the internal workings of politics as a part of her campaign. She used her emotions—such as anger—as a political message to alert others about what she thought went wrong in the society and to share her awareness of the despair of others.[29] During her constituency visits she encountered many abandoned and sick people. Upon seeing them, she harshly scolded the local administration, thus, literally extending the voice of the people whose words and pleas were no longer being heard or considered. With her language and performance of emotions, she purposefully breached the courteousness and self-possessed manners that were the characteristics of the upper class to which she belonged. Her edgy haircuts and sharp outfits were also political statements: she was in control of herself and ready to get things streamlined elsewhere—in politics.

Although there is no applicable definition of charisma and its descriptions take many different forms (Seale-Collazo 2012), Zanaa's charisma is based on her ability to induce action and affect in others. She did it through an overt expression of the feelings and conditions of others while demonstrating a control over her posture, gesture, and looks.

The new *oyunlag* are independent individuals who use their expertise and motivation not only to maneuver within the space to gain power but to build new spaces and awareness to propel Mongolian society into what they envision as a more just, humane, and democratic place. As Burmaa revealed the inadequacies of the country's court system and demanded a new kind of court for her case, she helped us understand how elections are far bigger phenomena than we might think. These women use their skills and values to deal with the encroaching demands of neoliberalism and to negotiate spaces, identities, belongings, and power to fight against commercialized campaigns. Electability for these women, thus, is not about adhering to the system, but transforming and disrupting it. In some ways then, these women are electable for a system they are envisioning and seek to create.

Self-Polishing: Styling the Candidate from Inside and Outside

A Makeover

I began the Introduction of this book with a description of my conversation with Legtsegiin Ariuna, whose enthusiasm for the 30 percent women candidate quota for parliamentary elections encouraged me to pursue the study of women candidates' experiences in running for Parliament seats. In this last chapter, I present another vignette about Ariuna that was also formative, but in a different way. The following encounter with Ariuna illustrates the importance of a particular beauty and bodily makeover on the part of women candidates as well as women in general. Although notions of beauty and what is considered appropriately feminine in the realm of politics are vague, unstable, and are constantly debated with little consensus, Ariuna demonstrates some of the effects of the femininity that she chose to embody.

Speaking with Ariuna, I found that I could not quite place her historically, generationally: I could not tell how old she was—not confidently, at any rate. I could not tell whether she had come of age before or after the fall of socialism. At home, in her robe and slippers, she looked like she was in her late forties. Outside, with a salon coiffure, a slimming black pencil skirt, and stiletto heels, she transformed into a woman in her early to midthirties. In fact, when I saw her in public for the first time, I did not recognize her for a good fifteen minutes. I was with a friend who stopped to talk to her. Since I did not recognize Ariuna, I said "hello" in a formal way and gave the two women some space to converse while I noted the campaign activities taking place around me. I felt like I had heard her voice before, but I could not recognize it. But when my friend said, "Goodbye, sister Ariuna," I was shocked to realize that it was *the* Ariuna whom I had visited a few weeks ago in her home.

Ariuna was one of the trustees of the DP and the Head of the Women's Organization of her party. She told me much about the importance of the candidate quota for women (see Introduction) and why she was planning on competing in the election. Ariuna's impressive political career, however, seemed ordinary compared to her skills in transforming her looks when she went out in public. I take Ariuna's almost magical makeover as a point of entry to another domain of electable selves—a sphere of negotiating femininity, style, and beauty as necessary attributes of successful candidacy.

The Benders of Neoliberalism

"She works so hard, I do not know when she sleeps," claimed our mutual acquaintances regarding Duuya (pseudonym), who was the head of a recently established television broadcasting station. Duuya was coveted by other broadcasting stations. "The television station was successful because all the brightest people who worked with me at my previous post followed me," Duuya said modestly while she ate a small assortment of beet, cucumber, and cabbage salads at the Italian restaurant in downtown Ulaanbaatar. Duuya's reporters might have been the best, but her gifts for leadership were exceptional too. According to her colleagues, she was *changa* (strong), *mundag* (awesome), and *sürhii* (capable) and was able to accomplish what many others did not even dare to try.

Instead of continuing as director of the station, Duuya wanted to run for a seat in the Parliament. Directing a broadcasting station, however, she thought, was an insufficient qualification for a successful candidacy. "I need to prepare myself (*biiyee beldeh heregtei*) for the candidacy. I need to recharge my brain (*togloigoo tsenegleh*) and master my English," she said to me. "Otherwise, my international relations will suffer because I will have to rely on someone else to translate for me. I need to develop myself (*ooriigoo hogjuuleh*) and to do so I need to earn a doctorate from abroad." In her meetings with me, Duuya emphasized her interest in enhancing herself as an *oyunlag* (intellectful) person.

In addition to her *oyunlag* pursuits, Duuya was keen on refashioning her looks. "Duuya is very thin now, looks great, and changed her wardrobe," a mutual friend commented. "She is now beautiful (*goyo bolchihson*)." I recalled that during our lunch in the Italian restaurant, Duuya told me that she was on a Japanese diet and that a salad fit the diet's requirements. Duuya was undertaking a comprehensive improvement of her body, brain, and everything else about her. Duuya was not alone. Many female candidates developed new and existing attributes associated with femininity in order to create genres of womanhood they thought strategic to their plans as electable candidates.

The above vignettes about Ariuna and Duuya convey some recent developments in Mongolian notions about what it means to be a person of a particular class, status, lifestyle, and gender. One, is the expectation to present one's most attractive self in public: *hamgiin höörhön deeree tavih* (to dial up on the beauty). Another development is the practice of constant and comprehensive renovation of one's body and looks with the latest fashions, beautification techniques, and health discoveries, as well as charging one's brain with new knowledge and skills, preferably by studying abroad. Although these are not entirely new practices, globalization and travel, import of consumer goods, economic prosperity among certain groups, diversification of the economy, and the emergence of lifestyle industries made them more routine. The renovation of the self resonates with the updates in the material environment such as renovation of homes and kitchens and remaking of school curriculums, which have been going on in Mongolia since the beginning of the market economy in 1990s. The ethos of renovation encompasses bodies, minds, and the surroundings.

In chapter 5, *Intellectful*, I explored how candidates emphasize their intellectual pursuits to achieve *electable* selves and overcome commercialized campaigns. In this chapter I continue to explore the making of electable selves and turn to the candidates' strategies of campaigning and precampaigning that are geared toward crafting and styling appropriate looks and inner selves. The goal of the women candidates is to gain and present electable selves: educated, beautiful, and charismatic. I call the comprehensive activities that these women employ in updating, improving, and shaping themselves into electable candidates *self-polishing* (*biyee beldekh*, literally "preparing one's body"). It refers not just to preparing one's physical body but also to cultivating the perfect self. In Mongolian, *biye* means body, but it also means a person, especially when the word is used in phrases such as "*minii biye*" or "*tuuni biye*" ("I" or "he/she").

I argue that democratic elections in Mongolia—with their perpetual campaigning and unrestricted expenditures—have influenced the emergence of new postsocialist political subjects who embody new consumption-based femininities, attributes of upper-class professionalism, and gendered values. Female candidates and their self-polishing are an especially vivid example of how *electionization* impacts subjects and activates existing as well as new forms of techniques for remaking selves. The female candidates' practices of consumption and the globally informed updating and reframing of their selves as electable candidates constitute a larger rearticulation of class identity and an attempt to be a part of a global leadership class. Elections emerge as sites for the remaking of upper-middle-class women and, therefore, of gender more broadly. What it means to be a Mongolian woman is a notion that is perpetually transformed within the arena of democratic elections in Mongolia.

Far from being influenced by neoliberalism in an overall way, these women candidates strategically employ some of the aspects of neoliberalism in order to refute the parts that they disagree with. Scholars, such as Aihwa Ong (2006), have urged attention be paid to the unevenness of neoliberalism by distinguishing the facets of neoliberalism that are beneficial to certain populations but harmful for others. Christina Schwenkel and Ann Marie Leshkowich (2012) note that neoliberalism has come to assume diverse meanings and forms. These insights are helpful to discern the ways in which the Mongolian women candidates navigate the new challenges associated with neoliberalism. The transformation of electoral campaigns into electionization was partly due to neoliberalization. Campaigning in elections now means sponsoring a perpetual governing mechanism, which has further marginalized women candidates within politics.[1] At the same time, in their attempt to transcend this type of campaigning, these women engage in a comprehensive practice of self-polishing by perfecting their minds and bodies in order to make irrefutable selves. They do so by taking advantage of the proliferating industry of beauty, health, and fashion.

The women candidates' attempts to reach electable selves also resemble the flexible selves of neoliberalism who undergo constant reconstruction in order to meet the demands of an unstable market (Freeman 2014; Rose 1999). However, electable selves are not just neoliberal selves whose purpose is to succeed in the given system. By striving to achieve electable selves, these women strive to transcend the commercialized electoral campaigns and male-dominated politics at large. By rejecting the neoliberalization of politics by using self-polishing through consumption, they bend neoliberalism: they use one aspect of it to deal with another.

These women use fashion, beauty and health products, and lifestyle strategies to connect their minds and bodies in order to mold themselves into beautiful (see also Edmonds 2010; Miller 2006) and charismatic beings. Attention to self-polishing among candidates is especially important when we consider the meaning of beauty for women voters. Anthropologist Hedwig Waters (2016, 8) argues that in order to protect their social and economic standing, women from a variety of backgrounds subscribe to a belief in beauty as a socioeconomic elevator and, thus, pursue standards of beauty associated with modernity and the upper class. Waters's (2016) research among women in the nomadic countryside is especially telling in a context of electoral campaigns.

Women voters, especially in economically challenged regions, tend to judge women political candidates by looking for signs of well-being, prosperity, and beauty. Voters expect to see the promises of the candidates through embodiment. The logic is that the women candidates must display their power and prosperity, which immediately translates into beauty, before they can promise a comparable future to others. The *imij* (image) that the women candidates project is especially important because it is a primary mode of connecting with voters. Since most of these women candidates do not have sufficient funds to provide a continuous stream of gifts, gigs, and infrastructure developments to their constituents in order to offer them opportunities to evaluate their capabilities, they sometimes end up being judged by their image and the impressions that they make during meetings. The voters interpret, judge, and evaluate the impressions that the candidates make in myriad ways.

In what follows, I will sketch some of the competing demands that women candidates confront and must negotiate. Further, I will situate women's self-polishing practices in a broader history of self-development and analyze various self-polishing strategies as exemplified by three particular candidates, Oyungerel, Zanaa, and Odontuya, in the 2008 and 2012 elections.[2] While their personal stories may be exceptional, these women are representative of larger dynamics and demographics. For many women, the idea of "campaigning" or even precampaigning extended well beyond their formal stump speeches, media appearances, and scheduled meetings with voters. It was a process of self-polishing, both inside and outside, and updating looks as well as "brains."

Super Secretaries and Parliamentary Candidates

The women's comprehensive striving toward self-perfection through education, professional achievements, and a display of attractive and charismatic selves was partly enhanced, for better and worse, by the vagueness about what being *electable* meant, and how *electability* could be measured. While no one could explain to me exactly what *electable* actually meant, over time I came to understand that candidates were expected to present impressive personae to attract voters and to possess additional symbolic (reputation, prestige, and fame) and cultural capital (knowledge and expertise) with which they could support their party and its members.[3]

The major political parties structurally replicate the gendered values of a more traditional household in which the division of labor parallels the patriarchal "public" versus "private" divide. The men mostly perform on the front stage or in public and women take care of the infrastructure or the back stage of campaign preparations. In the parliamentary elections, it was mostly women who carried out the many managerial and organizational campaign tasks for male candidates. The idea that in a political party (at least of the Democratic Party in the 2000s) men not only had more power and prestige but were expected to be more successful than women was apparent in a comment that Oyungerel, a candidate in 2008, made in an interview on television right after the repeal of the women candidate quota in 2007.[4] "I said in my interview that the Parliament's decision felt as if I had been slapped in my face after doing all the hard work in the kitchen . . . for seventeen years," she told me. Party politics are a part of gender politics in which men were expected to lead and succeed and women were expected to support them: "Men see us [women in political parties] as their stepping stones," Oyungerel said.

My friend and feminist writer Baatarsurengiin Shuudertsetseg frequently complained to me about the "patriarchal" nature of the political parties: "There is little opportunity for women's advancement [as a politician]," she noted. "The most educated women become super-secretaries or, if good looking, romantic mates," she said. "It is not only male party members who see women as caretakers, supporters, and servants, though," she explained. From the beginning, the DP was not limited to people who had political interests; it was also a de facto public (*olon niitiin*) organization and a place to socialize, attend events, network, find eligible mates, and find "clean" and nice office jobs as secretaries and managers. (In contrast, MPRP was a closed organization with a strict membership policy that required entrance exams and background checks until 2000s.) Many young people, including single women, who were active in the DP in the 1990s fostered the notion that they came to the DP spaces not just for political reasons but also to socialize with their peers. Thus, the day-to-day interactions of male and female party members (for example, women dropping by and taking up the roles of office workers, whether officially or just to help on a temporary basis, or for casual flirtations and friendships) reinforced the gendered division of labor and expectations of what it means to be a woman or a man in the context of a political party, explained Shuudertsetseg. The view of women as being less suited to candidacy thus became embedded in the gendered assumptions and built into everyday interactions and expectations.[5] Women's roles in the party, thus, had been reinforced by patriarchal structures that steer women into low-ranking and less serious roles.

Thus, many female candidates had to disrupt this established perception of women's political allegiance and roles. They consciously strove to create an image of themselves as equally qualified relative to men but also as separate and distinct from other women who joined the party for reasons other than theirs. They tried to do so by creating perfect selves with the best possible education, the most attractive looks, and the most righteous messages to appeal to the electorate. Shaping electable candidates also entailed a breaking away from everyday femininity and scripting of formal selves to make the surrounding people take seriously the women planning on running for elections. These women needed to achieve a delicate balance: being too distant and haughty could destroy their networks and breed foes, but being too friendly would deny them the necessary respect.

Although many women have the know-how to run a campaign, for the most part the parties did not expect them to run for office themselves. Because female candidates have limited paths and prescribed models for self-conduct, they must chart their trajectories on their own. In the process they are sometimes caught between multiple, conflicting demands imposed on them by party leadership, voters, election managers, and their own perceptions based on media, gossip, and the advice of friends.

Electability as a Shifting Target

The qualities that the public expects parliamentary members to possess—mainly, but not limited to, integrity, honesty, and competency—do not necessarily coincide, and sometimes even conflict, with the qualities sought by the party leaders and the internal electoral management. If the qualities do converge, the various players' opinions about the same characteristics can differ.

For instance, a former advisor to several political leaders noted: "The party leadership [referring to the two major parties] does not care about qualities like individuals' intelligence, independent thinking, or outspokenness. What they care about the most is the candidate's ability to be a team member, maintaining loyalty to the party and taking their part in the game. In fact, independent thinking and the ability to speak one's mind can be considered a nuisance and works against the person." Outspoken persons are not welcomed into the close-knit network that holds most of the party's power. To be considered seriously, this advisor told me, a candidate needed to comply with the party's tactics and work according to the plan; a person with a mind of her own is not such a candidate. "No party leadership tolerates an independent and outspoken woman who challenges the leadership."

The qualities that are shunned by party politics, however, tend to be sought after by voters. A female voter who went to a campaign meeting for a new female candidate came back disappointed:

> She did not talk much, and her speech lacked persuasion and passion. She looked weak next to her male colleagues. We need women who can represent and advocate for us. For that they need to be able to stand on their own, speak up, and be equal to men. Otherwise, why vote for them? Plus, her outfit was

too mundane and her shoulder bag was hanging from her, which made her look sloppy! Her frumpiness bothered me. She could look neat and polished at the very least!

Moreover, women candidates are expected to outperform the populace's expectation and be models of success. They must possess "a wow factor." During a focus group interview of different segments of the population from throughout the country, I asked a group of twenty voters what criteria they had in mind when evaluating the female MPs. The answers were vague, but they generally were things like "being well-prepared," "being educated," and "ready to take on the tasks." The constituency, which had several women candidates, could have chosen to vote for at least one female candidate. For instance, Manjaagiin Ichinnorov (Nora), a human rights lawyer, was one of their candidates. I asked the group if anyone had voted or considered voting for her. All twenty said "No." When I asked why not, most people remained quiet. Some men explained that she needed to do much more to impress them and that staging parades as a part of her campaign and conducting voter outreach meetings was not enough.

One of the men, familiar with Nora's background, said: "She is not doing enough as a human rights lawyer!" I asked what they thought she should have done in order to gain their votes. After brief silence, the man replied: "She should have gone to Malaysia and defended Altantuya's case!" At this point several people joined the man and started shouting out that that is exactly what Nora should be doing. In fact, they went further, suggesting that as a human rights lawyer, she should *not* even be thinking about running for office but rather should defend those people who need her services the most.

The legal case that the interviewees referred to was difficult and lasted for more than ten years, involving national and international courts and human rights organizations (Ellis-Petersen 2018). According to the extensive media coverage and the staff members at the Mongolian National Center Against Violence, Altantuya was a young Mongolian woman who was murdered in Malaysia in 2006. She worked as a translator for Abdul Razak Baginda, a defense analyst from the Malaysian Strategic Research Centre think-tank, during his negotiations to purchase Scorpene submarines from France for the Malaysian government. Altantuya staged a protest in front of Baginda's house after he refused to pay the commission he had promised her upon receiving the submarines from France. Shortly after the scandal, Altantuya's mutilated body was found near Kuala Lumpur. Many Mongolians were distraught that neither the Malaysian court nor Mongolian officials put sufficient effort into dealing with the case in a timely way (Lhagva 2015). Thus, it was understandable that Mongolians wanted to help the victim's family. However, the fact that Nora, as a female candidate, was expected to rectify a situation that even the Mongolian government and international organizations found too complicated spoke to the voters' unlimited expectations of the female candidates and to the morphing of the campaigns into governing as a part of electionization.

Some voters expected female candidates to be equal, or at least to look equal, to their male cocandidates in the same constituency. At the same time, many other voters—especially male voters—were repelled by more outspoken and assertive female candidates. Once, an adult son of a female candidate called on her phone right after the candidate's television appearance. During the television interview, that candidate spoke with a bit more assertiveness than her usual soft-spoken and gentle self. Yet her son instructed her on the phone that she needed to be "nice" and that she need not behave "like a man." In almost every step of their campaigns, from local-level nominations to running for parliamentary seats, female candidates faced conflicting and ambiguous demands from multiple audiences and evaluators.

By the time female candidates were set to run, most had their own understanding of what they would be doing to improve their electability and what would work best for their campaigning. Their self-polishing practices are diverse and speak to their identities, interests, and to the specific social and cultural resources they commanded. With the help of new consumer and media technologies, self-styling practices, and beauty and health enhancing technologies, women campaigning for Parliament in Mongolia have treated their bodies and minds as editable materials to be molded into perfect selves—selves that might be *oyunlag* (intellectful), attractive, and *khorezmtei* (charismatic). It was by presenting these and other similar traits that most of these women strove to convince voters and party leadership that they were *prepared* to run for and win parliamentary seats.

Self-Polishing: Change Yourself, Change Your Home, and Then Change Your Country

I use the term *self-polishing* to describe practices for maximizing and refining a gendered self with the aim of becoming an electable candidate. These practices echo with the neoliberal ideas of self-governing and self-responsibility. A free-market ethos, media images of fashion, beautification ads, lifestyle centers, and abundant shopping opportunities also motivate people to shape their bodies through consumption practices (Edmonds 2010). However, a deeper and more important personal development strategy started in early twentieth-century Russia, the vestiges of which have influenced the political ambitions of contemporary electoral candidates. Indeed, the idea of self-development or self-cultivation (*ööriigoo hogjuuleh*) was a part of the socialist state's grand project of making the new socialist person and the core of the socialist construction (for example, Shirendev 1969). It was more complex than is recognized by the Foucaultian (1977) notion that the state molds its citizens into "docile bodies" and subjects through centrally controlled institutions such as schools, police, internal affairs organizations, collective and state farms, as well as through recreation. The early Soviets believed that through the appropriate personal development, individuals would shape themselves into builders of the new society (and not just selves).

This idea emerged after the October Revolution in 1917, during the 1920s and early 1930s, which was a period of liminality in the Soviet Union, when the old institutions were destroyed or dismissed and new directions and designs for daily structuring of life were not yet in place (for example, Fitzpatrick 1978, 1979). Serguei Oushakine (2004) argues that during this period, which saw an ideological and governing vacuum, prominent writers, pedagogues, and intellectuals became convinced that human activity could rule nature. They saw culture as a "second nature" and the production of selves as part of the project of Soviet modernity. Socialist selves constructed themselves in the absence of framework or basis but also rebelled against the disorder and obliteration of the everyday from the previous regime. The rupture created a condition of absence that required the expedited creation of something new—and, indeed, of newness itself—a sense of the necessity of goals yet to be determined, of action as a way of "overcoming the existing order of things" (in the words of Maxim Gorky) and building everything anew (Oushakine 2004, 399). "The 'fresh' people were reinventing the world for everybody in order to build the substance of their own life" (396).

Oushakine's study is useful in understanding selves beyond Foucault (1977, 1988), who does not question the stability and distribution of the institutions of domination. Throughout Mongolian history, the institutions and systems of domination transformed and overruled the previous ones, thereby bringing in repeated use of ruptures (Højer and Pedersen 2019), which are periods of uncertainty, and a sense of newness that allowed people to imagine new beginnings, both for good and bad ends. However, self-development was not the final goal but the means to build the society both as a social body and a philosophical and moral framework. It is for that reason, the display of a polished self—neat, well-groomed, and radiating health and energy (known as *hiimori* wind horse)—was indicative of the right energies and skills for governing. This ethos cuts against the neoliberal emphasis on individuality and

self-renovation for succeeding in capitalism. Self-development was meaningful, as seen in the Mongolian proverb "Change Yourself, Change Your Home,
and Then Change Your State." The proverb has often been used to criticize a
candidate who supposedly lacked self-development and thus was not fit for
the Parliament.[6]

Self-Styling: Power Suits and Updated *Deel*

The image of the ideal Mongolian woman shifted from the mothers and workers of the socialist period to fashion models and trophy wives.[7] The sexualization of women in global media and a more general eroticization of culture
have influenced ideas about proper womanhood. Women came to be judged
not just by how educated they were or by what positions they held profes-
sionally but also by how well they emulated the figure of the modern woman,
as embodied in advertisements (cf. Collier 2009). Thus, being and becoming part of an emerging middle class entails displaying outfits that resemble
those featured in Western fashion magazines such as *Vogue* and *Cosmopolitan*. Makeup, expensive jewelry, and high heels have become de rigueur.

The public obsession with women's bodies and discourses about sexualized and commercialized femininity denigrate female candidates and MPs no
less than other middle-class women. During campaigns, I often heard people
ask, "What is a woman politician supposed to look like? What is the right
image for a woman in a parliamentary seat? Is she feminine or not feminine
(*emegteileg uu*)?" If women become vulnerable when they are objectified in
this way, that vulnerability does not disappear when they win seats in Parliament. While denigrated as moral and social beings, women have been exalted
as beauty queens, movie and pop stars, fashion models, and trophy wives.

Given the threats of denigration and even harassment on the one hand,
and the populace's obsession with women's bodies on the other, it is understandable why female candidates have consistently made "safe" and formal
wardrobe choices. These women's self-styling practices are directed toward
preventing possible belittlement and harassment and, instead, toward gar-
nering respect. I borrow the term "self-styling" from Lily Chumley's (2016)
study of arts students in China, who learn to assume a "creative personality"
in their exams. The Chinese art students Chumley studied were being trained
in a fast-changing art scene informed by new liberal and commodity aesthetics, yet they still confronted, often indirectly, the rigors of realism and the
socialist state's enduring impact on art. Female politicians in Mongolia are
immersed in new and previously unavailable commodities of femininity, but
they must navigate a misogynist environment of male politicians, invasive

media, and a critical electorate. Both Chinese art students and Mongolian female political candidates are intensely scrutinized and perform under extreme pressure. Chumley uses "self-styling" to indicate an individual's way of being and performing on a test; I use it to emphasize the candidates' shaping of their appearance, primarily through clothing and cosmetics, to set safe boundaries and to set themselves above others. In other words, these women use self-styling through consumption—one aspect of neoliberalism—to overcome electionization, a different outcome of neoliberalism.

The candidates' self-styling is a form of symbolic distancing through clothing and is meant to elevate the candidate above her surroundings but bring her closer to the evocative images that the campaign promises might generate. Candidates are supposed to be somewhat lofty with dignified styles and status-making accessories and look superior to mainstream women. In making themselves political subjects, the candidates use bureaucratized and corporate styles of suits and dresses. Most tend to wear a version of a Chanel-inspired, perfectly tailored, buttoned-up suits, sometimes complete with boutonnieres and high-heeled pumps. These are not just coveted items that project wealth and status; through them, the women command respect in order to keep denigration at bay, to convey their equal status with men, and to project glamour but without an explicit sexualization of themselves. Roland Barthes writes that

> the man's suit and the woman's suit by Chanel have one ideal in common: "distinction." In the nineteenth century "distinction" was a social value; in a society which had recently been democratized and in which men from the upper classes were not now permitted to advertise their wealth—but which their wives were allowed to do for them by proxy—it allowed them to "distinguish" themselves all the same by using a discreet detail. The Chanel style picks up on this historical heritage in a filtered, feminized way. (1995, 107)

Barthes's idea explains the dress code not only of female politicians but of anyone trying to set herself apart from the crowd in a society that is reconfiguring its social stratification. The political and bureaucratic style changed little since the days of socialism when intellectuals, professors, and political cadres also wore business-style suits to distinguish themselves from herders and workers. However, Barthes's (1995, 107–18) further comments also speak to the female candidates' striving to distinguish themselves as *intellectful* and as political elites, now from the nouveau riche who tend to prefer dresses and jewelry that are more suited for cocktail-style occasions:

> Of all the fashions, Chanel style is . . . the most social, because what it fights, what it rejects, are . . . the vulgarities of petty bourgeois clothing; so it is in

societies confronted with a newly arisen need for aesthetic self-promotion, in Moscow—where she often goes—that Chanel has the best chance of being the most successful. (Barthes 1995, 107)

In the following I will analyze the deployment of two different outfits: a Western-style power suit worn by Oyungerel and a traditional *deel* worn by Zanaa. Each outfit has a distinct meaning. The traditional deel conveys nationalism and adherence to one's heritage, whereas the Western-style power suit was originally designed by female designers to emulate male suits and make space for women in careers and the public space. However, Zanaa and Oyungerel have appropriated these outfits to convey their individual political messages, which extend these connotations. Their outfits are doubly meaningful in the political and cultural contexts of changing gender politics that already frame them as particular kinds of women. Through each outfit, these two women communicate with multiple audiences at the same time, and they remake, update, and reconfirm the identities that they strive to convey. At the same time, their outfits also gesture to the ambiguities and uncertain changes in gender notions in Mongolian postsocialist society.

NATURAL LOOKS AND THE WESTERN POWER SUIT

Before I met Oyungerel in person, I met a young woman from rural Khövsgöl (Oyungerel's native province as well as her election constituency in 2008). The young woman, Jagaa, told me that she knew Oyungerel well, and that she was planning to work for Oyungerel's campaign in the upcoming election, even though she had been diagnosed with uterine cancer. Jagaa could not refuse Oyungerel's request to work for her campaign, she told me, because "Oyungerel invested so much in her electoral campaigns during previous [years] and even made some sacrifices." "Oyungerel cut her beautiful long hair," she said. "She had the rarest and longest hair. She was a real *miss*."

The word *miss* in Mongolia means a beautiful woman akin to a beauty queen in a beauty pageant, and it is derived from the phrases "Miss Mongolia" or "Miss Universe." Mongolians began to use "miss" as shorthand to signal physically attractive women. (It is common to hear phrases like, "So-and-so has a truly miss wife.") But Oyungerel wanted to eschew her image as a miss. In her images in the media and in public she hardly used any signals or attributes—eye-catching jewelry, a complicated hairdo, revealing clothes—that conveyed an intention to be seen as a miss. With a straight, short bob hairstyle, a dark power suit, and no visible make-up, Oyungerel was far from the decorous young women vying for validation of their looks by spectators.

By modifying her looks, she made it clear that she sought acknowledgment of characteristics other than her physical attractiveness, such as her power and professionalism. It was as if she were blunting her beauty in order to put forward her other traits that were necessary for her to become a political figure. Oyungerel was still "a naturally good-looking" (*ugaasaa saihan*) woman according to most people. She just stopped framing herself as feminine in a dominant style that is influenced by a conspicuous consumption of beauty products.[8]

In the context of the country's obsession with beauty practices, Oyungerel is unique in her choice to forgo the feminine beauty so often associated with long hair, plentiful makeup, frilly dresses, and accessories, and instead to use less feminine accessories in order to command power and attention. While she was in Ulaanbaatar as well as in other more urban areas of the country, Oyungerel chose to wear mostly white button-down shirts with darker business suits and matching shoes. She also carried a briefcase, which created a particularly gender-neutral look—if not masculine in style—that Oyungerel often sought (fig. 6.1).

In addition, while campaigning in the countryside in Khövsgöl, she wore knee-high riding boots and a dark-colored, pattern-free traditional Mongolian robe called a *deel*, just like her three male cocandidates (figs. 6.2 and 6.3).[9] According to Oyungerel, the defeminization of her image in both city and country was necessary for her political career. She even got into the habit of giving a prolonged handshake with a forceful squeeze. This would not distinguish her from her male colleagues and would not send any confusing messages, as she put it.

Oyungerel received consultations on presenting an appropriate image as a political candidate in the United States during her term as a Yale World Fellow. Accordingly, it was at that time that she cut her long braids into a contemporary bob and opted for natural and minimal makeup (although she kept brighter lipstick, better suiting Mongolian tastes). She was instructed to wear clothes of a uniform style in order to be easily recognizable to the voters. She created a sleek and streamlined image resembling lawyers in US television shows. She also had her campaign picture taken in a professional photo studio that served high-profile politicians, including Hillary Clinton, who is particularly symbolically linked with the pant suit. There, she also received instructions on smiling and posing.

Despite all these transformations, however, Oyungerel noted that more feminine clothing and accessories might have been a useful tool for gaining sympathy and attracting voters in Mongolia. Once, after an especially hot day of campaigning in June 2008, she changed her campaign *deel* and boots

FIGURE 6.1. Oyungerel, with her campaign helicopter in the background, in Khövsgöl Province. Photo courtesy of Oyungerel.

FIGURE 6.2. Oyungerel and the other three candidates dressed in *deels* and boots at a voter outreach meeting in Khövsgöl Province. Photo courtesy of Oyungerel.

FIGURE 6.3. From power suit to traditional *deel*: Oyungerel gives an interview on horseback for the local broadcasting station during her campaign in Khövsgöl Province. Photo courtesy of Oyungerel.

for a sundress and strappy sandals. As she went about the streets, she could not help but notice how people looked at her interestedly and approvingly. "I sensed that I was more welcome in a dress than when I was wearing suits and *deel*," she said. Although the idea of campaigning in a dress crossed her mind, she decided to stay true to her chosen campaign image.

Most female candidates and politicians whom I met seemed to forgo what could be considered more daring attributes of femininity, at least in terms of dominant Western fashion standards. For instance, women showed very little skin beyond their faces and neck, wore no loose, long hair or bold makeup, and kept their suits and dresses free of adornment like frills or lace—all of which are liberally used by Mongolian women in other settings. Only some wore jewelry—standard pearl necklaces, brooches, and earrings that demonstrated professionalism and success. Oyungerel's decision to forgo campaigning in a summer dress and sandals, choosing instead to stick to her wardrobe of dark *deel* and knee-high boots or business suits, can be understood as a strategic image-making technique amid the discourses and images that circulate in Mongolia's popular imagination, media, and political arena. Even among other female candidates, who continued to wear colorful suits and more jewelry, Oyungerel's consistent dark-colored suits made her stand out.

The color and the style of her suits were Oyungerel's further distinction from the rest of the female candidates. Overall, her outfits were doubly distinct: first, they stood apart from the increasingly posh, feminine, and often sexualized clothing of some of the populace; second, they differentiated her from the other female candidates who usually wore more colorful suits and dresses.

But Oyungerel transformed herself beyond her exterior as well. She was told that her voice—one of the most important tools of a politician—was too "thin" and high-pitched and therefore not suitable for prolonged and pleasant listening. She took lessons from professional singers and practiced speaking in a low, substantive, and "thick" voice that was both authoritative and charismatic. It took her two years of practice to acquire the kind of voice she considered appropriate for a politician. Indeed, when I was visiting Oyungerel at work, she made use of her different voice registers. She spoke in a thick, somewhat monotonous tone to her assistants. And then she spoke to me in a high-pitched, dynamic tone. I was perplexed about the subtle but noticeable shift until she explained her voice training sessions to me.

Charisma and the Up-to-Date *Deel*

Although the Mongolian fashion industry has interpreted and reimagined the traditional *deel* in bold and creative ways, politicians' use of the *deel* does not involve such modifications. Instead, as one female candidate illustrates below, the traditional *deel* can be used to underscore a candidate's adherence to public ideas about proper femininity.

One of the first feminist and activist politicians of the contemporary era, Zanaa ran as an independent during the 2008 election. She chose to wear a *deel* made of blue jacquard silk and a long, flowing scarf that draped over her shoulder all the way down to her ankles (fig. 6.4). In urban Mongolia, *deel*s are not worn as regularly as in the countryside. Most women in urban areas, especially educated, middle-class women, wear Western-style clothing on a regular basis. They wear *deel*s occasionally, usually for special events such as award ceremonies, national holidays, or when invited to give speeches to large audiences. Shawls are not a part of the *deel* and are not a traditional piece of clothing. Thus Zanaa's combination of *deel* plus shawl was new and unexpected, adding to her noticeability in a way that her Western-style clothes (though fashionable) never would have. In Western clothes, Zanaa would have blended into the urban crowd. But during the election of 2008, one could spot Zanaa's silk shawl in various parts of Ulaanbaatar, especially because the length of the flowing shawl extended her charismatic presence as she walked through the space.

FIGURE 6.4. Zanaa at her fund-raising campaign in Ulaanbaatar in 2008. Photo by the author.

One time, I was in a car with another female candidate, waiting for a traffic light to turn. Zanaa crossed the street in her bright blue *deel* and a wide-brimmed hat with her nearly transparent shawl floating gently a few feet behind her. The candidate I was riding with knew Zanaa well and told me that a well-known oracle (a person who foretells the future or connects with a higher power) had suggested the outfit to her. (The oracle suggested blue *deels* and shawls to Zanaa but suggested sharp business suits worn over light shirts to another woman.) When I inquired what the oracle was trying to suggest, the candidate explained to me that the oracle was tailoring these women's images to make them noticeable and acceptable to the public. Apparently, the candidate to whom the oracle suggested sharp, dark business suits was soft-spoken, quiet, and modest. By suggesting that she wear Western-style dark suits, he was sharpening her image, making her appear powerful and persuasive. It was meant to give force. I later found out that the "gentle" woman who was instructed to wear sharp suits was Büdeegiin Mönkhtuya (see figs. 3.2 and 3.7).

The situation was different for Zanaa; hence the outfit of a *deel* with a shawl. Zanaa was a feminist, an activist, and a leader in civil society in Mongolia. She was uncompromising and direct in her claims, and she never shied away from critiquing male chauvinism, corruption, and other wrongdoings. Some people found her utterly intimidating; others found her too direct and thus uncomfortable to be around. Everyone who knew Zanaa found her to be full of charisma. I attended several women's meetings of different political parties. Whenever a discussion arose about female candidacy, women mentioned that some very charismatic women from civil society, such as Zanaa, were powerful competitors who diminished their chances of winning.

Zanaa's *deel* and shawl enhanced her existing charisma and added other characteristics that Western-style clothing could not have. Zanaa began her career in civil society by building coalitions as a feminist and advocate for gender equality. When she introduced the concept of gender equality in the early 1990s, it was misunderstood as a call for women to fight to become *darga* (bosses). Because both gender and feminism are seen as Euro-American concepts, Zanaa was associated with Western values more than with Mongolian ones. As one young woman in rural Mongolia noted to me, many Western-educated candidates do not seem to "descend on the Mongolian soil"; they are "removed" (*höndii*), and that is their problem. It was not clear to me if the oracle whom Zanaa consulted saw her as not quite fitting the Mongolian "soil." To be sure, by wearing a Mongolian *deel* throughout the election campaign, Zanaa successfully reminded the populace that she was indeed embedded in the country's "soil" and traditions. Moreover, with a distinctly feminine accessory like a shawl (a *deel* is more gender neutral), the oracle intended to soften her image and make her appear less harsh. The shawl enhanced Zanaa's femininity but without any invitation to intimacy, since it was worn over the *deel*, which usually covers the entire body to the lower calves. And while the shawl extended Zanaa's presence in physical terms, it did so without the body; the long, flowing silk was there to represent Zanaa, but it was not her body. Of course, with *deel* and shawl, Zanaa was not remade anew. She was still the cosmopolitan, feminist, and Westernized urban woman. Thus, the flowing shawl, the memorable accessories, the power suits, briefcases, and the *deel*—worn in specific contexts and by distinct individuals—all comprise important self-styling tools that increase charisma and power while fending off sexist and sexualized denigration and insults by some media and public.

Inner Cultivation: Care of a Candidate

Candidates' self-polishing goes much deeper than choosing a clothing style. It was not enough to present the appropriate items on the body; it was also necessary to demonstrate preoccupation with the body itself as well as its interior—to cultivate mental and bodily health. Odontuya, a candidate in

Ulaanbaatar whom I met in spring of 2008, focused her efforts on cultivating and presenting a refined inner self in addition to her attractive and polished exterior. Odontuya was the owner of an office furniture retail chain, Sentoza, which imported its goods from Singapore and other Asian countries. "She has money and her husband is influential, so she is taken seriously by the DP," noted one of my interlocutors.

I invited Odontuya to lunch and we agreed to meet in front of one of many Western-style restaurants serving rather ordinary steaks and stewed meats in downtown Ulaanbaatar. She got to the meeting before me, even though I had arrived early. We sat and Odontuya lost no time in introducing me to some of the preparations for her campaign, pulling out and explaining campaign brochures she had brought with her. Throughout our meeting she conveyed to me clearly that our meeting was a part of her work (that is, campaign preparation) and that she was presenting herself to me as a diligent, organized, and competent candidate. She told me that she had expanded her NGO, *Irgen Ta Bayalag* (Citizen, You Are the Wealth), in order to reach out to her constituency.[10] She had been sending greetings and birthday cards to the people who lived in her constituency, organizing arts and crafts parties for children, putting together a free exhibit of the 400 souvenir dolls she had collected since childhood, and much more. We quickly agreed that it was necessary for me to visit her NGO and get to know her everyday work.

We next met at the office of Odontuya's NGO in a large four-story building on one of the main streets in Ulaanbaatar. As we walked through the facility, Odontuya introduced me to her staff members and their responsibilities. The last room we entered was dark, and two young people were operating an old-fashioned film projector that was playing a black-and-white film. It was footage of Odontuya's family that her father shot back in the 1960s or 1970s. The scene was in the countryside, on the edge of a forest and the bank of a stream. "It must have been our family vacation trip," Odontuya remarked. It showed a little girl of about five or six years squatting in front of a little tub and intensely kneading and rubbing a piece of clothing in some sudsy water. Everyone in the room was glued to the screen. Odontuya remarked, "Hmm . . . not sure what I was washing, perhaps my clothes. I have always been a workaholic." As we left the darkened room, Odontuya told me that she planned to use these films to make a documentary about herself to show during the campaign.

Perseverance and a work ethic would become one of the implicit messages in the image Odontuya projected to the public. For instance, in both her handouts to voters and on her personal website, Odontuya mentions she learned to play the piano, which was a rare thing to do during socialism, when instrument playing was mostly limited to the professional music school students. In 1978 she won first prize in a piano competition with Mozart's "Turkish March" and was awarded a vacation voucher to Bulgaria.[11] Although she never told me explicitly how many work hours she puts in each day, throughout our conversations and her interactions with others I noticed her emphasis on work as her top priority. Her work ethic was a source of pride.

Among the many activities and projects that Odontuya introduced me to, "Healthy Citizens Are the Country's Wealth" spoke directly to her attempt to turn the notion of wealth away from material possessions and frame citizens as the wealth of the country. Odontuya advocated *self-help*—a new trend that was a part of Westernization and neoliberalism. She advised her constituency members to practice self-care and adopt healthy lifestyles, healthy eating, and exercise. She also told me about her personal fasting habits and how, by structuring her lifestyle around fasting, she gained limitless energy, abundant time to work, a glowing complexion, and a beautiful, slim physique. She invited me to a lecture she was giving to railway workers, as the national railway station was a part of her constituency.

I met Odontuya, a couple of her assistants, and someone arranging her lecture at the entrance to the national railway depot. It was a beautiful summer morning and we walked through the railway building. Odontuya changed her wardrobe daily but kept on her favorite strappy midheel sandals, which looked far too delicate to walk on gravel and loose dirt. We were early and the lecture room was not open. While we waited, Odontuya told me why she decided to fast.

> A few years ago I met an old male friend in a Beijing airport. It was winter and I was wearing layers of sweaters under my down coat. I was busy setting up my business and paid little attention to myself. The friend of mine greeted me and half-way through the conversation he said: "Hmm . . . it is that age, you know, when women begin to stop paying attention to their bodies and appearances (*biye hayadag*). Many women begin to gain weight, age, and ignore their make-up and clothing." So I really did not want that to happen to me. I decided to take matters into my own hands.

After Odontuya told me of her fasting, exercising, and dieting activities, we walked to the lecture hall. Approximately 150 female railway workers came to Odontuya's talk (fig. 6.5). She gave a lengthy introduction about learning to be happy without depending on the opinions of others and without attachment to material possessions. Then she continued:

> Mongolian women are strong and able and they succeed in all professions. However we all, even the most successful ones, share a common drawback.

FIGURE 6.5. Odontuya giving a lecture to railway workers in 2008 in Ulaanbaatar. Photo by the author.

We know little about healthy lifestyles and we do not consider health to be a prime foundation for beauty. While most women strive to acquire diamond jewelry and designer clothing, they do not know and are not interested in knowing about healthy foods and the culture of healthy eating.

I, too, about five years ago, used to eat fatty dumplings, and blamed others for my weight gain. Back then, a Russian friend of mine gave me a book about healthy lifestyle, health foods, and disciplined and regimented eating habits. I changed my lifestyle a hundred percent. I understood that beauty is directly linked to a healthy body and a calm mind. Thus, expensive cosmetics, skin care, and fashionable clothes are only limited tools for achieving beauty. I understood that with patience, discipline, and self-management, one may exercise, take care of one's body, and refrain from harmful substances, and use only what leads to a youthful appearance and healthy body. For instance, diet pills and creams that promise rapid weight loss will not stop aging; they will only contribute to self-consciousness about body image.

In contrast, Odontuya suggested, fasting helps achieve a desired weight loss, cleanses the internal organs, and helps one gain energy and vitality. She suggested a 24-hour fast—eating only once a day. She was lecturing to female railway workers, predominantly conductors who serve domestic trains and the Trans-Siberian trains between Moscow, Ulaanbaatar, and Beijing. Since their schedules prevented them from eating during regular meal times, Odontuya suggested that the conductors could turn their inconvenience into an opportunity to fast.

Next, she talked about the properties of some common foods. Rice is nutritionally poor, she said. It has saved numerous Asian populations from hunger and starvation. It has fulfilled its historical function. However, now it is time to lessen our consumption of rice and eat more nutritious foods, like homegrown vegetables and wild berries. Among foods to avoid, Odontuya mentioned clear ("cellophane") noodles made of potato starch. Instead, she suggested, carrots would be a much better option. "My daughter is too busy to sit down and eat. She plays outside all the time. So we bought a juicer," she says. "We juice the carrots and my daughter drinks the juice in an instant, and can run out and play. We do not have to make her sit and eat carrots." Further, "Every evening I go home and walk on a treadmill for an hour. I sweat and cleanse all the pollution from my body . . ."

The idea that one can achieve beauty and health through nutritional and caloric modifications and exercise was not new. Odontuya's lectures were useful, however, because of the ways in which she tailored specific information to the current Mongolian market and lifestyles. With the expansion of the market economy, new, previously little known foods became available to consumers. Traditionally, the Mongolian urban and semiurban diet consisted of meat, wheat, dairy, and cold-weather grown vegetables. When Odontuya asked the railway workers what they wanted to know about health and beauty, several women expressed their desire to learn about the nutritional qualities of various foods.

Odontuya's lectures reconnected the domineering notion of beauty as an innate or purely visual phenomenon back to health, lifestyle, and nutrition. She reminded the women that beauty was something modifiable, with deeper roots in the body and the results were dependent on individual perseverance. (She did not mention plastic surgeries and the Botox treatments as options, which was deliberate and a change from the context of beauty propaganda that were centered around those more invasive bodily modifications.) Odontuya's approach centered on the idea that bodies can be shaped, maintained, and polished by human action, scientific knowledge, and will. This was reminiscent of the idea that bodies do not belong only to nature but also to culture. She further implied that healthy bodies constitute capital to beget other kinds of capital—namely, beauty and energy, which can be further used to beget other capital.

During the campaigns in 2008, 2012, 2016, and 2020, Odontuya's tailored suits and dresses accentuated her trim body but without revealing any skin.

FIGURE 6.6. Odontuya's campaign poster. Ulaanbaatar, 2012. Photo by the author.

She chose either dark business colors, or gold and silver silk suits that made her look polished and dignified (fig. 6.6). With minimal adornment except rather conventional jewelry sets and brooches, the clothes emphasized her perfected and polished body and character. They reflected self-censorship, distinction, and compliance with expectations. Her body-molding techniques "from within," through fasting, exercising, and dieting, were a celebration of her freedom, wealth, prestige, access to knowledge, and self-control. Odontuya's making of her beauty and health was private but not secret. It was beyond the gaze of her male colleagues and beyond journalistic intervention, not because she hid her "recipe" but because her rate of economic and personal investment in self-care is above the capacity of most people.

Conclusion: Beauty as a Political Project

Here I have discussed some of the self-polishing pursued by women candidates in preparing and running for parliamentary election. By self-styling through their wardrobe and make-up choices, or by adopting a healthy lifestyle in order to improve their looks and much else (or through a combination of these things), these women treated their bodies and minds as pliable and infinite. Their exhaustive efforts at self-polishing went beyond their immediate goals of becoming candidates and winning seats in Parliament and extended into their way of life and the structuring of their values, sentiments, and choices.

I have examined the strategies of women in relation to the marginalization of women in politics and in relation to the commoditization of elections that has developed in Mongolia as part of its neoliberal transformation. The campaigns have become perpetual engines for economic production and for shaping and creating practices that spill over beyond elections. Through multiple tactics for improving themselves as moral subjects, professionals, and leaders, these women go well beyond the stereotypes (entertained by their male party colleagues and the media) of women as sex objects or super-secretaries unfit for real politics. They recreate classed, professional femininities that offer alternatives to the existing media images of women as beauty pageant contestants or trophy wives. Thus, the formation of female political subjectivities combines Pierre Bourdieu's notion that the external world is durably internalized as *habitus* and Sherry Ortner's (2001) argument that subjects are always knowing and tactical. Ortner argues that subjectivity is a basis for agency. So, while female candidates are in a subordinate and subaltern position in relation to dominant male leaders, they are agentive in a culturally constituted way and are shaped by a context in which direct access to political power is not always available (see Ortner 2001).

Further, the female candidates use the shifting gender expectations to their advantage and shape not only their tactics but also the cultural and political environments in which they operate. I emphasize that these women's campaigning strategies consist not only of navigating existing politics but also of creating new resources, images, and knowledge that help them claim, at least to some degree, their own political spaces and situate themselves as subjects within it. In that sense, I argue that female candidates are not just incorporating themselves into the existing male-dominated arena but are also creating new spaces and arenas of influence.

As mentioned, I was first able to learn about various aspects of self-polishing—as a form of long-term campaign preparation—by getting to know about a dozen female candidates long before the actual elections in the summers of 2006 and 2007 and then by shadowing many of them on a regular basis prior to and during the elections of 2008 and 2012. Because I was able to continue to be in touch with many of these women (from 2006 to 2019), I came to understand how their investments in long-term campaign preparations shaped them into kinds of politicians—and, indeed, kinds of political subjects. I argue that the democratic elections in Mongolia constitute an arena in which what it means to be a Mongolian woman is often revised, reconfigured, and reinvented. Elections are sites for the remaking of upper-middle-class women and, therefore, of gender more broadly.

Most of these women see themselves as self-possessed, self-regulating persons—autonomous subjects—and have a sense that they have the capacity, the agency, to control their lives (see Ortner 2006, 143). At the same time, in a political hierarchy dominated by men, their experiences of seeking power have in many cases been undermined, both explicitly and implicitly, by legal codes, cultural expectations, and economic structures. In the process of becoming prepared (*beltgegdesen*) for elections or creating *electable selves*, with the help of new technologies, practices, knowledge, and resources, these women have come to treat their bodies and minds as materials that can be molded into selves that both transform *and* accommodate gender hierarchies. The female candidates' agencies are situated within relationships of power, but they also challenge the authorities above them, the political parties, the electoral politics, and one another.

Some of these women's strategies entail dramatic transformations in lifestyle and body image. They discipline their minds and bodies, engaging in such activities as dieting, exercising, transforming their voices, practicing public speaking, networking, writing bestsellers, and getting advanced degrees from the world's top universities. Many of these strategies are drawn from various arenas of current and historical experience, including international and transnational circuits of feminism, socialist propaganda practice, and especially the expansion of capacity-building workshops and training programs overseen by international organizations like the UNDP, Euro-American NGOs, as well as by governmental, private, and political entities. Upper-class Mongolian femininity is entrenched in a mutually constitutive political and economic pursuit and is becoming an editable code, operating in global circuits of exchange.

CONCLUSION

The Glass Ceiling as a Looking Glass

"Has the world hit some sort of 'glass ceiling' in securing a greater presence for women in national parliaments?" This question appeared in a report by the Inter-Parliamentary Union, which observed that progress in women's representation in national parliaments worldwide has been excruciatingly slow (Sengupta 2015). *A Thousand Steps to Parliament* has offered a partial answer to the Union's question. I have done so by showing how women candidates' paths to Parliament are intertwined with the larger politics of neoliberal capitalism and gender as well as with global and local feminist politics. In the course of their struggles, these women have influenced the state, politics, and elections, while being shaped by them as well. Their official legal battles as well as smaller scale individual tactics and strategies have shown the ways the "glass ceiling" is constructed and, simultaneously, how these women can be a "looking glass" to illuminate the role of elections in a society that has been rapidly neoliberalizing while also striving to advance in building democracy.

I hope this book will open a path for thinking about the transformation of elections in the era of neoliberalism—a transformation from elections to electionization—and that this new formation will allow us to critically assess our conceptual apparatuses and language. I have traced the impact of neoliberalism on formal politics and political life as a way to balance the current academic focus on neoliberalism largely in economic spheres of life. As presented here, the selves, subjects, and subjectivities are being transformed not just through neoliberalism directly but also through an additional filtering through a political sphere, which in turn, has been adopting and adapting to neoliberal changes. The neoliberal changes imposed on Mongolia starting in the early 1990s were meant to liberalize trade and finance, privatize state assets, and shrink the welfare state. While these changes have been implemented and repeated (often at the expense of rampant inequality), many other changes, both expected and unforeseen, also occurred during the past thirty years. The democratic elections have taken over the spaces that had emerged due to the reduced role of the state and expanded due to the liberalization of financial and trade sectors.

Mongolia is an intriguing example for thinking about how Western institutions and concepts find their realization in places not built on the basis of liberalism, rational choice, and free markets. Mongolia has been enthusiastic about democratization, while its political leaders have been assertive about neoliberalization. This conceptual divide in the country has created tension, competition, and economic frothing or bubbling (*höösrölt*), even plunging Mongolia into near bankruptcy. Mongolia's gender politics became intertwined in the outcome of it all, which illustrates that gender and politics are unstable but mutually constitutive entities.

Throughout I have shown that the Mongolian parliamentary elections, although similar to elections in Euro-American democracies, are also very different. The formal institutions in Mongolia carry out the elections in relatively expected ways, through designing the electoral system, ballots, and campaigns. However, there is a vast unofficial realm of everyday life where campaigns continue outside of electoral structures and seasons, and the Mongolian populace has appropriated them to deal with the uncertainties of neoliberalism. In other words, elections in Mongolia are much more than what they were intended to be. As such, sometimes existing concepts that have been developed in other places do not fit the new sprawling practices.

Thus it is inaccurate to approach Mongolian society on the basis of rational choice theory or on the assumption that individuals and their choices are fully autonomous, as in idealized Western liberal societies, or by expecting that the communities will suddenly switch to following the rules of law to the detriment of their safety nets embedded in kinship and locality. However, some of the preconditions that had led electoral campaigns to become embedded in everyday life and to strengthen kinship and community networks were due to neoliberalism. Much of the populace has appropriated electoral campaigns, both during the campaign periods and after, as a way to deal with the uncertainties that emerged with the shrinking of the state, fluctuations in the market, and the irregular nature of opportunities for employment and education. Both the campaigns and the populace strengthened various social assemblages and kinship relationships, and created new ones, with different motives. Similar to how neoliberalism enhanced the traditional networks in Mongolia, in Colombia, as anthropologist Maria Vidart-Delgado (2017) illustrates, the modern political campaigning reinforced the traditional "patron-client" relationships instead of eradicating them as intended. Elections are not isolated events restricted to formal institutions.

As discussed, electionization means that campaigns, to be successful, have come to substitute for actual governing, for the welfare state, and even for the private sector, organizing social life and providing disaster relief funds. Candidates act like charities by donating money to voters' medical expenses, like local governments by fixing roads and schools, and like the private sector by supplying communal parties and celebrations. As Elizabeth Dunn (2008) and other anthropologists have shown, the state during neoliberalism has expanded into other entities by outsourcing itself to new actors and institutions. In Mongolia, electoral campaigns have become one such institution, and much more. Operating beyond the formal campaign periods, electoral campaigns have blurred the boundaries between public and private spheres by organizing time, rearranging livelihoods, and redirecting economic and social resources.

In addition, electionization means that campaigning lasts, in clandestine forms, for almost all the entire four-year period between elections in addition to the extravagant campaign events during election seasons. This constitutes added obstacles for aspirants and candidates, including women, who strive to find a place in politics and in parliaments in particular. Sponsoring the activities of governing and charity as a part of campaigning is a financial challenge for most women. Campaign financing remains largely a private and closed arena, and various legal attempts to make it transparent have met with little success. Nevertheless, elections are vastly popular, among both candidates and voters. This book explains how the multiple significances of elections make them attractive to participants in a number of ways, which has made elections acquire a life of their own.

In retrospect, the ubiquitous portrait posters on Mongolia's streets were the physical versions of the digital facial images on social media that came to dominate the 2016 and 2020 elections in Mongolia (and elsewhere). In addition to the privatization and commercialization of electoral campaigns, the personalization of campaigns on Facebook, Twitter, and other social media in 2016 and 2020 has transformed the space of politics into even more ubiquitous virtual presences. Mongolians' drive for technological modernization (see Buyandelger 2014) and cheap electronics from China support this trend. It is not just the candidates, political parties, and the sponsors and supporters that are preoccupied with upcoming elections well ahead of their arrival, as happens in the United States and in other places. The politicization of everyday life has set the country on a rotating clock: every four years most government positions get taken over by the members of the winning party. The hype around elections, high voter participation, and consolidation of various social assemblages is understandable in the context of the elections' immediate impact.

In addition to the almost insurmountable financial obstacles, the current period of post–#MeToo, with its widespread misogyny and new forms of patriarchy and authoritarianism, also presents obstacles to women candidates. The jettisoning of the women candidate quota in 2007 and its diminishing upon reinstitution in 2012 (from 30 percent to 20 percent) was not only discouraging but also left women with limited official routes for candidacy. In addition, everyday small-scale obstacles require women to use tactics of maneuvering from the ground-up as opposed to acting from a perspective that affords a view from above and makes opponents' moves visible or predictable (de Certeau 1984). Different political formations have presented varying opportunities and limitations for women politicians, who continue to self-develop and shape themselves into electable selves. Political ambitions and organizing skills, along with the power of abstract principles of gender equality, renewed from the legacies of the socialist state, aided women as the society has transformed from more centralized and collective-based to individualistic and centered on private resources. Many women who came of age during socialism and who were able to envision themselves in powerful roles also transferred their aspirations, *habitus*, and ethos to the newer generation. They, in turn, helped to build democratic institutions, lobby for legal changes, and take advantage of new opportunities.

Therefore, despite their economic limitations and political marginalization, women candidates' clever and alternative ways of campaigning show how politics can be conducted differently. In an attempt to become *electable*, the women candidates work on self-improvement by "charging their brains" (*tolgoigoo tsenegleh*) and polishing their bodies. I have emphasized how women frame themselves as *oyunlag* (intellectful), finance their campaigns by writing books, and use their scholarly and political expertise to intervene in legal matters. They treat their minds and bodies as flexible and renewable by constantly improving on their education and skills, by collecting academic degrees, and by updating their looks through new wardrobes, face-lifts, and body sculpting. These women candidates strive to eclipse the commercialized campaigns with their perfect irrefutable selves. They put the best versions of themselves, electable selves, which are also a partial product of neoliberalism, up against another neoliberal outcome—commercialized political campaigns.

For that, electoral campaigns are stages for refashioning forms of gender and class identities. In democracy, as Joan Scott (2019) argues, uncertainty about rulership reinforces a preference for male leaders—a normative figure associated with power—and thus men dominate political leadership despite feminist efforts to gain equality. Scott's argument finds culturally specific and technologically mediated materialization in Mongolia in the form of the panorama of candidate posters during electoral campaigns, as discussed in chapter 3. Electoral campaigns and images reveal how particular kinds of gender identities (upper class, polished, groomed in certain styles), for both men and women, shape what it means to be an *electable* candidate. Because ideas of electability for women are contested and shifting, women carefully and rigorously negotiate their representations. While Scott's (2019) argument about democracy's tendency to naturalize gender holds largely true for masculine identities in Mongolia, it resonates little with the experiences of women, whose association with culture gets enhanced in the context of making *electable* candidates.

Gender and politics, as social institutions, are therefore in constant flux and interdependent. Practices of campaigning and gaining power have become legible as influential "technologies of gender," to borrow Teresa de Lauretis's (1987) formulation. However, the fact that expectations for women are only intensifying, pressing them to display forms of femininity in order to be counted as properly electable women, speaks to the persistent, even growing, disparity in power between genders.

To return to the acknowledgment of multiple feminisms with which I started the book, it is worth recalling the power of solidarity among feminist organizations internationally during the less neoliberalized late twentieth century. There is much to learn from women's movements that have helped women gain footing in national parliaments. Various interparliamentary organizations, from the EU to the UN and others, can become platforms for more progressive transnational influences on national legislatures that are now influenced by neoliberalism. The dispersed but still (ac)cumulative gains, as well as the travails and tribulations and the official and unofficial strategies of Mongolian women, can serve as an instructive looking glass to understand the making—and, perhaps, the path toward the breaking—of glass ceilings.

Acknowledgments

I thank friends, colleagues, and family in Mongolia, the United States, and all over the world for assisting me in numerous ways with this project. While teaching and parenting, mostly solo, it felt nearly impossible to fulfill MIT's tenure requirement to complete two book projects with the second book covering a brand-new research subject unrelated to the first one. Since parliamentary elections only occur every four years, I postponed my job at MIT for a year to start the new research in Mongolia while also continuing to work on my first book, *Tragic Spirits* (2013). The research spanned three parliamentary elections in 2008, 2012, and 2016, and I am brimming with gratitude toward everyone who made this book possible and helped me to keep my child, my mind, and job intact.

In Mongolia, my closest friends, and interlocutors, Yadamsurengiin Khishigsuren and Molomiin Otgonbayar and their respective families and friends, have provided all-around inspiration and assistance. Khishigsuren generously offered the resources at her Maxima Research and Consulting firm in Ulaanbaatar and assisted with trips, interviews, media research, and transcriptions. My colleague and friend, Mongolia's prominent feminist writer Baatarsurengiin Shuudertsetseg, has been instrumental in this research by tirelessly introducing me to many of my key informants, women political candidates. Over the years I have been fortunate to have the amazing Nerguigiin Baasanhuu as my main research assistant. I thank my other research assistants, Bayasgalangiin Naranzul, Namsraijavyn Ariun-Undrakh, Boldyn Gerel, Bolormaa, and Okhidoin Otgonjargal, whose contributions deeply enriched this book.

I am grateful to Sumiyagiin Oyuntuya, the director of the Voter Education Center in Ulaanbaatar and thank the center's staff for kindness and generosity.

I thank my colleagues in civil society and feminist engagements, Tumursukh-iin Undarya, advisor at MONFEMNET National Network; Davaasurengiin Enkhjargal, director of the National Center Against Violence; Baasankhuu-giin Enksaikhan, former director of the National Committee for Gender Equality; and Naidangiin Chinchuluun, chairwoman of MONES. I thank Baasanjaviin Oyunbilig, Zagasbaldangiin Enkhjargal, Jamsrangiin Bulgan, Andrei Vagayev, Valyagin Burenjargal, Dondogdulamyn Tungalag, Jamsran-giin Bulgan, Tuvsanaagiin Bekhtsetseg, and Tsedevdambyn Oyunchimeg for providing valuable interviews, information, and other assistance. This book would not have been possible without their input. I thank Professor Seden-javyn Dulam, whose experiences of running for a parliamentary seat helped me to conceive of the possibility of an ethnographic research on elections. I thank Mongolia's first PR consultant, who chose to remain anonymous.

I thank all my interlocutors, especially women candidates and aspirants as well as journalists, public relations specialists, campaign workers and man-agers, and staff members of various election districts, who generously and thoroughly shared their experience, knowledge, and opinions. I especially thank Radnaagiin Burmaa, Tsedevdambyn Oyungerel, Davaasambuugiin Oyuntsetseg, Sanjaasurengiin Oyun, Chimediin Bazar, Jurmediin Zanaa, Saldangiin Odontuya, Manjaagiin Ichinnorov, Legtsegiin Ariuna, Shagda-ryn Battsetseg, Tögsjargalyn Gandi, Natsagiin Udval, Natsagiin Dulamsuren, Dugersurengiin Sukhjargalmaa, and other women and men in politics who chose to remain anonymous.

The global community of Mongolianists and Mongolia anthropologists provided much help by exchanging ideas and sharing resources. I thank Christopher Atwood, Lauren Bonilla, Nicola Di Cosmo, Rebecca Empson, Lars Højer, Christopher Kaplonski, Jessica Madison, Myagmariin Saruul-Erdene, Marissa Smith, Urtnastiin Erdenetuya, Jargalsaikhanii Sanchir, Gan-tulgiin Tüvshinzaya, Uyangiin Daribum, Lhamsurengiin Munkh-Erdene, and Tsültemiin Uranchimeg (Orna).

I gave talks on different sections of the book at various institutions, all of which helped me gain greater insight and deepened my analysis. My sincere thanks to the following people and institutions for hosting my presentations: Julian Dierkes at the University of British Columbia, the Institute of Asian Research and Anthropology Department, and a Workshop on Mongolia; Dr. Franck Bille at the Institute of East Asian Studies, Mongolia Initiative at the University of California, Berkeley; Christopher Kaplonski, at the Anthropol-ogy Department at the University of Cambridge in the United Kingdom, and Hildegard Diemberger, Caroline Humphrey, and Nikolai Ssorrin-Chaikov for comments and conversations; Netina Tan at McMaster University in Hamilton,

Ontario, Canada; Zhanara Nauruzbayeva at Columbia University Harriman Institute; Elizabeth Woods for inviting me to present at the Davis Center for Russian and Eurasian Studies at Harvard University; Jamie Bue at the Association for Central Eurasian Students at Indiana University in Bloomington; Brandeis Anthropology Department in Massachusetts; Morten Pedersen at Aarhus University in Denmark; Ivan Sablin and Jargal Badagarav at the University of Heidelberg, Germany; Tomas Matza during Soyuz Postsocialist Cultural Studies at University of Pittsburgh in Pennsylvania; Burenjargal Tangudai, Nasun Bayar, Chimeddorji, and other colleagues at the School for Mongol Studies at the Inner Mongolia National University in China. I wrote the first draft of the book during my fellowship at the Institute for Advanced Study in Princeton, New Jersey. I thank Serguei Oushakine, Didier Fassin, Hugh Gusterson, Jill Locke, John Holmwood, Sharun M. Mukand, and Joan Scott for their careful and in-depth engagement with my work.

I am deeply grateful to several amazing editors at the University of Chicago Press. I thank David Brent for his enthusiasm and interest in the early stages of this project and Priya Nelson for moving the book through the Press's pipeline. Alan G. Thomas keenly helped with the book during an especially busy and stressful time due to COVID-19 and a reorganization at the Press. I am excited and grateful to Mary Al-Sayed for her enthusiasm and support and Tristan Bates for thoughtful and steadfast help for the duration of this project. The comments of the three anonymous manuscript reviewers were crucial in strengthening the book in various ways.

My deepest gratitude goes to my colleagues at MIT Anthropology, Stefan Helmreich and Heather Paxson, who tirelessly read numerous drafts of the book and offered their careful and thorough comments each time. My gratitude to Heather extends far beyond her help on the book as her all-around support has kept me going during some of the most challenging times during the writing process. I thank Christine Walley for reading drafts of the chapters and Graham Jones and Michael Fischer for helpful and exciting conversations.

Erika Evasdottir's reading of the entire manuscript was essential. I thank my writing group members, Elizabeth Ferry, Janet McIntosh, Smita Lahiri, Ann-Marie Leshkowich, and Karen Strassler for comments on various drafts. I thank the community of anthropologists (and sister disciplines) for friendship, insights on drafts and presentations, intellectual nourishment, and practical support in researching and writing the book. I thank Alexia Bloch, Anya Bernstein, Melissa Caldwell, Xenia Cherkaev, Michael Herzfeld, Lilith Mahmood, Felicity Aulino, Andrea Muehlebach, Chang-Ling Huang, Larissa Kurtovich, David Nugent, Alexei Yurchak, Maria Vidart, Larisa Kurtovic, Tatiana Chudakova, Sonja Plesset, Maple Rasza, Vanessa Fong, Michael Puett, Kristen

Ghodsee, and Elizabeth Wood. A social media-based writing group was a life-saver during some of the dark times during 2016 and COVID-19, and I thank Greg Beckett, Bea Jauregui, and my friend Justine Buck Quijada for their inspiration and help during lockdowns, writing blocks, and most important, for being there on an everyday basis. Michelle Beckett, Justin Dyer, Molly Mullin, Thalia Rubio, Amanda Sobel, and Pamela Siska generously helped with editing various drafts of the manuscript. All shortcomings in the book are mine.

I must mention that although I am a native of Mongolia, I belong to none of the political parties in the country, and I am not personally related to any of the political candidates I study in this book. I was never interested in pursuing politics as my career, just as I was never interested in being initiated as a shaman, although I wrote an ethnography about people who were. Some might see this book as a public relations piece for the female politicians I represent here; they might even ask if I received compensation for the pictures and descriptions in the book. I affirm that I received nothing from the people I discuss. I chose the candidates in this book, and their stories, based solely on my anthropological inquiries. My interlocutors might find their representations in the book insufficient, and some candidates whom I studied or interviewed are simply absent. While every single interview helped me better understand the topic, it is simply impossible, and unnecessary, to include everything. Their depiction in here is quite different from more usual journalistic representations.

My research was generously supported by grants from the Wenner-Gren Foundation, the National Science Foundation, MIT SHASS Research Funds, the Levitan Prize, and MIT Class of 1956 Career Development Chair funds. I thank these organizations for giving me an opportunity to carry out long-term, in-depth anthropological research in Mongolia.

I thank my beloved daughter Eevee for her boundless joy, warmth, and empathy. Hilarious, she makes me laugh every day. Since her toddlerhood she has developed a resilience for change and travel and a deep love for Mongolia. I am grateful for her patience, as I have worked on the book for almost all her life by now; her love and support; and a powerful sense of justice and aspiration for equality. As always, I thank my mother for helping me raise my daughter, for supporting my endeavors, and for being so patient with me holing up to complete this book. She filled her apartment in Mongolia with sacks and boxes of periodicals from the 1990s and 2000s for me and collected new books in Mongolia, sometimes even requesting them from the authors and publishers directly. A retired journalist, she kept me updated on the social and political developments in the country. Her help and enthusiasm have been fundamental to this project.

Notes

Preface

1. Two additional women gained seats after Election Day (June 28, 2012) through reelection in their individual districts, thus increasing the number of women elected to Parliament to eleven.

2. Among the reasons behind retaining the MPRP at the end of socialism in the 1990s was a geopolitical consideration. Obliterating the party, in a sharp divergence from China and Soviet Union, could have been considered a provocation. In 1989 and the 1990s, after learning about the country's choice of democratic transformation, the Soviet Union declared an embargo on Mongolia by stopping all subsidies, which constituted 30 percent of Mongolia's revenue and cut off the oil supply, leaving Mongolia without fuel and at a standstill for months in early 1990s.

3. The Mongolian People's Party (MPP) was founded in 1920, then renamed the Mongolian People's Revolutionary Party (MPRP) in 1924. It returned to its original MPP name by dropping "Revolutionary" in 2010, upon which, a faction that retained the name MPRP had seceded to form a separate political party.

4. The attempts to support women's advancement to leadership have been encountering numerous difficulties. In 2005 the UN Millennium Development Foundation was formed and Mongolia signed an agreement that included improving its women's leadership percentage as one of the preconditions for receiving the grant (see Undarya 2009, 147). In 2006, Mongolia adopted a 30 percent candidate quota for women in light of the agreement, but the quota was revoked in 2007 (discussed in the Introduction). During the fall plenary session, when the Parliament was discussing the quota repeal, MP Erdeniin Bat-Uull argued (although to no avail) that the quota must be kept because revoking it would undermine Mongolia's reliability in the eyes of the international community ("2007 Fall Plenary Session Minutes," January 10, 2008, Parliament Archive). The 2013 report entitled "Achieving the Millennium Development Goals," issued by the government of Mongolia, states that the target of increasing women in politics and decision-making has been marked as "difficult to achieve," which is the lowest rating in the report's evaluative scheme.

5. Although quotas for women in leadership during socialism were not termed as "quotas" (adopted as a *kvot* in Mongolian after democratization in the 1990s), as I discuss in chapter 1, the laws and the appointing of 25 percent of women to leadership began in 1950s and 1960s.

6. In 1973, in a 336-seat parliament, women had 77 seats; "Mongolia," http://www.ipu.org/parline-e/reports/arc/MONGOLIA_1973_E.PDF. In 1977, in a 354-seat parliament, women had 82 seats; "Mongolia," http://www.ipu.org/parline-e/reports/arc/MONGOLIA_1977_E.PDF. In 1981, in a 370-seat parliament, women had 90 seats; "Mongolia," http://archive.ipu.org/parline-e/reports/arc/MONGOLIA_1981_E.PDF.

Introduction

1. Unless specified, all public figures, including women candidates, appear under their real names. I used pseudonyms for nonpublic figures and figures who chose to remain anonymous in order to protect their identities. In cases when the public figures were recognizable even with the use of pseudonyms, I did not provide any identity markers by limiting my reference with generic terms (for example, "someone told me" or "an interlocutor").

2. The terms *candidate* (*ner devshigch*) and *aspirant* (*gorilogch*) demarcate official stages of a candidacy. Technically, everyone is only an aspirant until they are nominated and receive a mandate from the General Election Committee.

3. Gerelt-Od Bayantur (2008) discusses that some fraud and misdeeds are quite common in Mongolian elections and the laws and regulations are constantly rewritten in order to address them for the following elections. Yet, it has been impossible to distinguish massive fraud from irregularities and errors (also see Tuya 2005). The case of the Mexican election discussed by Lomnitz, Adler, and Adler (1993) illuminates how the ritualized and inclusive campaign events makes it nearly impossible to disaggregate misdeeds and corruptions from what can be seen as a system that accommodates both the elites and the underprivileged, thus making it difficult to change.

4. Between 1990 and 2004, the proportion of women hovered between 2 and 10 percent.

5. The country's first constitution in 1924 states that both men and women have equal rights to vote and be elected. See *The Constitutions of Mongolia* (Part One) (2009). See Sablin, Badagarov, and Sodnomova 2021 for details about geopolitical constraints during the adoption of the first constitution.

6. The quota was both new and old. From the perspective of the women who lobbied for it, the approval of the quota in 2006 was a fresh victory. From a long-term perspective, however, women were merely regaining what they had previously lost. In the 1960s under socialism, women had constituted 25 percent of the Parliament at that time. Still, the adoption of the women candidate quota was, nevertheless, a new achievement because the circumstances during democratization were entirely different from those during socialism.

7. Tumursukh Undarya writes that according to law (the Constitution of Mongolia [1992] Article 33, Section 1), the presidential veto would stand if one-third of Parliament accepted it (which it did) (2009, 148). http://www.ilo.org/wcmsp5/groups/public/@ed_protect/@protrav/@ilo_aids/documents/legaldocument/wcms_117392.pdf.

8. The minutes from January 10, 2007, indicate that the parliamentary session approved the president's veto. However, as one MP maintained (Sangajavyn Bayartsogt, who was also the Head of the Standing Committee of Justice), Parliament's approval of the president's veto constituted a breach of election law, according to which, as stated in Article 58, no changes can be made six months before the election. The last day to make any amendments to the election law was December 29, 2007—the day when Parliament repealed the 30 percent quota. The conversation turned then to the issue of whether Parliament did or did not breach constitutional law rather than focusing on the quota. Some male MPs continued to argue that the president's veto

and Parliament's vote on January 10 were illegal ("2007 Fall Plenary Session Minutes," January 10, 2008, Parliament Archive).

9. The women also encountered a verbal attack from the groups that aimed to eradicate the 30 percent women candidate quota. The male leadership and their protectors used the neoliberal ideology of free competition, self-sufficiency, and meritocracy to defend Parliament's repeal of the quota. For instance, a major Mongolian news site, *olloo.mn.*, had published an article by a well-known columnist named Tsenddoo (2008) from the DP, who argued that supplying women candidates with a quota was no different than providing "crutches" to a handicapped person. Support in the form of the quota was, according to Tsenddoo, only a form of belittlement.

10. For the political outcomes of the 2008 election, see Uyanga (2017), who was a candidate in the election, and Ganhuyag 2019. One of the key consequences of the 2008 election has been the collaboration between the key players of the two dominant parties MPP (MAN) and DP (AN), resulting in MANAN—the acronym for the two parties and the word *manan*, which means fog.

11. According to at least one female MP (Arvin Dashjamtsyn, who voiced her opinion during the parliamentary session on January 10, 2008), the revocation of the quota was a way for male MPs to limit the access to Parliament of especially powerful and well-respected women who were equipped to challenge the political leadership.

12. See, for example, the works of many political scientists: for instance, Mona Lena Krook (2009), Monique Leyenaar (2004), and Netina Tan (2016) evaluate electoral structures and propose strategies for improving women's participation.

13. The survey was administered by the Government of Mongolia, National Committee for Gender Equality, and was carried out by researchers affiliated with the International Republican Institute (IRI).

14. Survey results were published as a brochure titled "Women's Participation in Political Leadership: Research on the Populace's Opinion" (Government of Mongolia, National Committee for Gender Equality 2012). The first round of study was published in 2011 and then the second round of study in 2012. Oyungerel, who was an aspiring candidate for the DP in 2008 and in 2012 and then an MP (2012–16), told me that the survey became a landmark document that influenced gender politics and women's participation in elections in 2012. She used the survey results to convince the chairman of the DP, Elebegdorj, to approve the 20 percent quota. In particular, she showed him the following numbers: 55.7 percent of respondents indicated that they would vote for female candidates (2012, 38) and 62.1 percent of the respondents indicated that "qualified women should be elected to office" (2012, 10).

15. Electionization is different from an electioneering, which is an established term in politics that refers to the activities by campaigners within the time and space of campaigns. With the former, I describe a process of campaigns taking over everyday lives and the affective states of citizens beyond official electoral times and spaces.

16. Chari and Verdery (2009, 11) define postsocialism broadly by treating it as a critical standpoint that describes critiques of the socialist past (often entangled with the Cold War), postcolonialism and present-day imperialisms, as well as present-day neoliberal transformations in some previously socialist polities. They animate a debate that has lately emerged about whether postsocialism and postcolonialism might be merged into a compound analytic (Appiah 1991; Hladík 2011).

17. Dunn (2008) and others have shown how nonstate actors have come to act as state agents, thus expanding the state.

18. The usage of the word feminism in twentieth-century Mongolia mirrored the developments in the Soviet Union. It was in usage until the early socialist period in the 1930s, before the

Soviets began to curb its usage and ideology and shrank its national women's organization. By that time, feminism was considered a bourgeois ideology. Yet, among select educated groups, feminism was respected as a philosophical trend and as an expression of individual freedom, sophistication, and cultural value.

19. A basic search on Google for "women in leadership programs" brought up 245,000,000 entries (conducted September 29, 2015). On November 2, 2021, the same search brought up 3,850,000,000 entries. Several training programs within academic institutions appear first on that list. For example, in the Boston area there is the Women's Institute for Leadership Development at Northeastern University, the Women's Executive Leadership Program at Bentley University, and MIT Sloan School of Management.

20. Reports of all four UN conferences on women can be accessed from the UN WOMEN website: https://www.un.org/en/conferences/women. The most recent appraisal of the Beijing declaration states that new challenges have emerged and there is a need to tackle these challenges in order to tackle all areas of concern, including in the area of "women in power and decision-making" (United Nations 2020, 8).

21. Anthropological accounts of NGO practices, and especially the developments of bureaucratic categories and practices, tend to be critical of the organizations' power dynamics, formality, prescriptive approaches to established norms, and the fact that the programs primarily facilitate the existence of organizations more than outcomes in practice (see, for example, Riles 2000 on women's NGOs; Coles 2007 on international NGOs implementing democratization in Eastern Europe). While such critical analyses are useful for understanding internal dynamics and power structures, my concern also extends to the ways the language of these organizations that promote women influence national politics, gender issues, and policy-making.

22. "Achieving the Millennium Development Goals" (Government of Mongolia 2012, 69–79).

23. According to Mongolian law, MPs cannot hold other positions and have to renounce NGO directorships, though many remain consultants as opposed to staff members. I discuss the dilemma of women candidates in chapter 5.

24. There have been at least three aspects to the women's movement in 2000s: women's artistic engagements in literature and cinema; the production of research and reports by women's NGOs on the state of gender and women's issues; and the impact on the media and the general public of the lobby to pass the law on gender equality.

25. For instance, in the United States, the closed-list electoral system tends to be more beneficial for women as it limits in-party competition and gives power to the party leader, which, if that leader supports women, works to their advantage. Yet if party leaders care little about women's representation, as in Mongolia, then the closed-list electoral system is of no more help to women than an open-list system.

26. In Mongolia, women outnumber and outperform men in education while being underrepresented at all political and decision-making levels. See Batmunkh, Altanhuyag, and Osorjav 2013; and Schmillen and Weimann-Sandig 2018 for a quantitative assessment of gender distribution in Mongolian education.

27. Some female candidates had participated in the democratic transformation in the early 1990s, but then they had retreated from national politics, partly due to being marginalized in male-centered circles. International funding organizations also impacted women's withdrawal from politics since many required that their grant recipients give up their political affiliations as part of recipient qualifications (see chap. 5). In her study of women's NGO work in Russia in the 1990s, political scientist Valerie Sperling (1999) argues that international donor requirements

that recipients be free from political affiliation have impeded female politicians from gaining national leadership positions.

28. During the 2008 election, Burmaa campaigned, whereas in the 2012 election, she was on a party list and thus provided a unique set of insights on party politics.

29. About a dozen political parties operated in Mongolia in the early 2000s. The two major parties were the Mongolian People's Revolutionary Party (until the MPRP split into the MPRP and the MPP, or Mongolian People's Party, in 2010) and the Democratic Party (DP). The third most visible party was the Civil Will Party. See Smith 2020 regarding the development and succession of the MPRP and the emergence of the new parties after 1990.

30. The Democratic Party. http://www.demparty.mn.

31. "The Values that the Mongolian People's Party is Striving For." http://mpp.mn.

32. There were 366 candidates registered to compete for seventy-six seats in the 2008 election. The number of registered candidates throughout the elections so far ranges anywhere between 293 (in 1992) and 602 (in 2000). See *The Results of Parliamentary Elections in Mongolia* (2017).

33. The lawmakers I interviewed told me that the shortening of the campaign period was done in order to decrease electoral campaign expenditure. They admitted, however, that the scheme did not work as the campaigns had concentrated their expenditure within the shortened time. More significantly, the shortened campaign period favored incumbents over newcomers, who did not have sufficient time to become recognized among the voters.

34. Julian Dierkes, "Clarification on Electoral Law," *Mongolia Today*, December 15, 2011; see also Julian Dierkes, "New Electoral Law Passed by Ikh Khural," *Mongolia Today*, December 15, 2011. In a mixed-member voting system, voters cast votes for two separate entities on one ballot: they vote for individual candidates competing in their districts and they also vote for the political parties of their choice. In turn, political parties furnish their lists of candidates to be elected, depending on the number of votes garnered. Of seventy-six overall MPs, forty-eight individual MPs were chosen from the individual candidates competing in districts, and twenty-eight MPs came from the political parties' lists chosen proportionally in relation to their garnered votes. In such a system, a political party must obtain 5 percent of the total national vote in order to secure a parliamentary seat. http://www.loc.gov/lawweb/servlet/lloc_news?disp3_l205402958_text.

With the proportional system allotting twenty-eight seats, it is unlikely that a party can win more than a dozen seats. The two leading parties—the DP and the MPP—have nine and eleven women, respectively, on their twenty-eight-member lists. But the DP's first woman is placed at number seven; the MPP's at number ten. See also Pearly Jacob 2012.

Chapter One

1. Women in Mongolia constitute a more educated group than men (Schmillen and Weimann-Sandig 2018). Although women dominate the overall workforce (57 percent), they are concentrated in small and medium enterprises, which comprise 98 percent of all enterprises, and their contribution to GDP is only 25 percent (in SME [small and medium enterprises] and women-owned SMEs in Mongolia 2014: 7). Women also tend to concentrate in state-salaried low-paying positions. In contrast, men tend to be in entrepreneurship and dominate in large-scale businesses in mining, construction, transportation, commerce, and banking (Begzsuren and Aldar 2014, 24).

2. In the context of the United States, political scientists Jennifer Lawless and Richard L. Fox (2010) argue that women tend to refrain from political careers due to a lack of ambition to

run for office. The male-centered politics and the ways in which women are socialized, among many other issues, restrict women's social imaginaries to entertain political ambitions. Lawless and Fox's study focuses more on women's individual choice-making and gives insufficient analysis of the larger structures that restrict women's sphere of actions.

3. My book does not extend to the earlier historical roles of women in Mongolia. Diaz (2019) gives an overview of the women leaders before socialism.

4. The name of the women's organization changed many times: it was the *Women's Section* from 1924 to 1925 and again from 1932 to 1947; the *Women's Department* from 1925 to 1932; the *Mongolian Women's Union* from 1947 to 1958; and finally, the *Mongolian Women's Committee* from 1958 to 1990. These names reflect subtle differences in the power and resources the organization commanded as well as in its formal institutional identity.

5. With democratization since the 1990s, numerous new independent women's organizations emerged. The MWC redefined itself yet again and began addressing issues of women's employment during the market economy along with other organizations.

6. I thank Joan Scott for these insights (personal communication, January 19, 2015).

7. Examples in the literature that demonstrate women's mobilization in time of crises followed by their abandonment in the aftermath include Good 1999; and in the United States, an oral history project *The Real Rosie the Riveter* provides excellent examples of firsthand experiences of women's contribution during WWII: https://rosie.dlib.nyu.edu/about/ [accessed December 13, 2020]. Recently, Michael Knapp, Anja Flach, and Ercan Ayboğa (2016) explore an example of women's prominent roles in the revolution and in the new political system that is based on gender equality and democratic confederalism in northern Syria.

8. Since 2000s, writing historical fiction on elite women from the past has been prevalent among women writers.

9. These propagandistic images were abundant in literature and the visual arts, especially cinema, but scarcely represented in research.

10. Cited in Kaplonski 2014; Uranguya and Bayarsaihan 2004.

11. For instance, women were restricted from spending much time in the north side of the *ger*, which was designated for guests and male family members. The *ger* is also conceptually divided between men's (right) and women's (left) sides, which is also related to gendered responsibilities. Women are responsible for the household and men for obtaining, traveling, and exchanging.

12. One of these women was Badamjav Sedenova, an ethnic Buryat and a wife (from 1926) of Tseveen Jamtsarano (the first head of the Mongolian Scientific Committee) (Rupen 1956, 136; Gerelsuren and Erdenechimeg 2014, 5).

13. Dolgoryn Nima (2009) argues that Padamdulam was "much ahead of her time," too radical and knowledgeable, and thus a threat to MPRP's power.

14. As Kaplonski (2014) writes, women's behavior in public, and the moral and political choices they made, became a matter of contention. Women's hairstyles, clothing, and education, their physical mobility in and around settlements or on the grasslands, and their socialization were hotly debated and often constrained by their families.

15. Founded in 1927 as The *Central Council of Mongolian Trade Unions*.

16. See, for example, B. Lhamsuren and others (1985, 154–60) on the loosening of the leftist politics.

17. This economic development was not a simple improvement in production: from a Marxist-Leninist point of view, it also involved Mongolia jumping directly from feudalism to

socialism, bypassing an entire socioeconomic stage, capitalism, in the process. According to Lenin, "The Mongolian revolutionaries have much work ahead of them in political, economic, and cultural development before the pastoral population can be called proletarian masses." Lenin proposed a new theory whereby, with sufficient help from a more industrialized country like Soviet Russia, "there will finally emerge a new and noncapitalist economic system of the Mongolian *arats* (common people)" (Eudin and Fisher 1957, 207).

18. Ghodsee (2019) also writes that from the Western liberal feminist perspective, which is positioned against and outside the state, the socialist women's collaboration with the state would be considered antifeminist.

19. Women were also mobilized to give their support to Soviet and Mongolian troops prior to World War II when war broke out on Mongolian territory in 1939 between Japan and the Soviet Union/Mongolia, in what is known as the battle of Khalkhin Gol.

20. It is approximately 2,796 miles between the center of the Dundgobi Province in Mongolia and Sverdlovks [Yekaterinburg] in Soviet Union.

21. The number of people who died in World War II in Mongolia remains unknown still, although the battle of Khalkin Gol alone saw 20,000 casualties.

22. This increase seems dramatic and appears to be a consequence of the state's push to shift industry from small craft shops to state factories in the 1950s (Bawden 1968, 394–95).

23. The flip side of the situation, as argued by Gal and Kligman (2000), is that families were fragile and men felt emasculated.

24. See, for instance, de Haan 2012; Gerelsuren and Erdenechimeg 2014; and Ghodsee 2019 for details about the WIDF.

25. For instance, these conferences included the World Congress for Mothers in 1958, the UN Conference on Women in 1975, and the World Congress for Women that took place in Moscow in 1987. The MWC also participated in various movements and projects proposed by the WIDF, such as organizing aid to the victims of the Vietnam War in 1969 (Gerelsuren and Erdenechimeg 2014).

26. During socialism, Saturday was a half-working day.

27. Much more detail could be given about financial and other challenges of the MWC. Sometimes the MPRP Central Committee would approve a budget for MWC operations, such as rewards for appointed activists, sometimes not. In 1973, the MWC successfully negotiated with the Central Committee salaries for all the heads of its branches in eighteen provinces and re-quested money to reward its most productive appointed activists (mostly through international trips and vacation packages) (Gerelsuren and Erdenechimeg 2014).

28. See Ghodsee 2012 on the UN Decade for Women.

29. Regarding the pronatal policy, the state legally prohibited all forms of birth control, including abortion, in order to populate its vast territory. The population grew from just over a million in 1970 to two million within twenty years. See Turmunkh Odontuya 2016 for a discussion on the implementation, circumstances, and diverse opinions regarding the pronatal policy.

30. Films include *Tuvdengiin Bor, Talin Tsuurai* [The Echoes of the Steppes], *Ene Huuhnuud uu!* [These Women!], *Manai Ayalguu* [Our Melody], and *Serelt* [Awakening]. Novels include *Ih Huvi Zaya* [Great Destiny] and *Odgerel. Tsag Torin Uimeen* [The Turbulence of Time and State]. Television shows include *Gazar Shoroo* [The Land] and *Tungalag Tamir* [Tamir the Clear].

31. Since for liberal feminism and many other feminisms, one of the goals is to be an explicit ideology, these kinds of invisible actions are not acceptable. Nevertheless, for the socialist women's organizations in Mongolia and in other places, the goal was to improve women's well-being within the framework of the state.

32. The Revolutionary Youth League was launched in 1921, and the Young Pioneers Organization in 1925.

33. For instance, Dashjamtsyn Arvin, MP (2000–2012), began her political career as the head of the Youth League in the People's Army (Section 231) and was then a staff member of Ulaanbaatar's Youth League. Tögsjargalyn Gandi, MP (1992–2008), was the head of the Youth League in Ulaanbaatar (Gerelsuren and Altai 2008, 24 and 52). Nordovyn Bolormaa, MP (2000–2004), was the national head of the League of Young Pioneers (Gerelsuren and Altai 2008, 40).

Chapter Two

1. Both names are pseudonyms.

2. Local elections take place the fall after the parliamentary elections and presidential elections take place the year following parliamentary ones. There was an exception in both 2016 and 2020 in that province and city elections took place together with the parliamentary elections (unlike previous years when such elections were held separately).

3. In November 1989, I was a student at the National University and participated in the Second National Congress of the Young Artists and Authors (*Zaluu Uran Büteelchdiin Ulsin 2r Chuulgan*) where the attendees discussed the country's political and economic status and its relationship with the Soviet Union and China. Several coalitions were formed at the congress. In a few weeks several prodemocracy groups emerged as a movement against the one-party rule.

4. Also see Dulamyn Bum-Ochir (2018, 2019), who argues that Mongolia embraced capitalism for political reasons in order to secure independence rather than to develop capitalism. With the development of mining, however, the political relationships with Western democracies have transformed into complex economic deals. The Russians, on the other hand, did not fully disappear from the radar. After withdrawing its troops from Mongolia in the early 1990s, Russian involvement in Mongolia was restricted until the 2000s, although it continued through trade, military exercises, and other venues. The Russian government openly resumed its interest in the politics and economy of Mongolia with the development of mining and began "a new Great Game [with] China to control the direction and route of Mongolia's railway lines" (Bulag 2009, 99–103).

5. Hillary Appel and Mitchell A. Orenstein (2018) argue that postcommunist countries have adopted neoliberal reforms without any resistance in order to receive Western aid money and become integrated in the international economy. In Mongolia, the embargos by the Soviet Union also led to accepting structural adjustment policies (also see Bum-Ochir 2020).

6. Milton Friedman's book *Free to Choose* (1980) was translated into Mongolian (Friedman 2001) at the beginning of the neoliberal policies.

7. Some of the democratic leaders during earlier democratization in the 1990s had attempted to follow a Scandinavian social and political model and to build a democratic socialist society, but the direction was quickly changed in favor of the United States' neoliberal model.

8. Michal Klima (2019) argues that in parts of East-Central Europe, the rapid neoliberalization and subsequent impoverishment opened opportunities for new political parties to build followings and expect loyalty in exchange for favors.

9. Elisa Kohl-Garrity (2019, 125) gives a useful historicizing of gifting as patronage. The colonial Qing government institutionalized respect, which was also consolidated through gifting and tributary relations and was rooted in the hierarchical expectation of loyalty. "The "goods" and "financial support" rendered by the Qing emperor or Mongolian aristocracy were part and

parcel of the complex of *kesig* "grace," and therefore, masked in terms of relational exchange within (for example) a filial relation."

10. In the 1990s, the administrative units (namely, precincts, towns, and municipalities) were responsible for furnishing the voter lists. The unit staff members, who were residents in the area, compiled lists from scratch by going door-to-door. Since 2007, the General Election Commission (GEC), an independent body, became responsible for making the voter lists (Chimid 2008, 100–110). The State Registration of Citizens Office provided the initial list to the GEC, which the latter was then supposed to update. However, the GEC relies on local administrative units for help with updating those lists.

11. Several corruption cases involving high-profile politicians have rattled the Mongolian public since 2010. See https://country.eiu.com/article.aspx?articleid=617373245&Country=Mongolia&topic=Politics. Accessed on January 1, 2020.

Among many additional resistances to corruption, there was also a more recent large-scale demonstration on December 27, 2018. "There has been rising anger over a long-running corruption case related to allegations that Enkhbold and other political figures had looked to raise 60 billion tugrik (US$23 million) by selling off government positions" (Mönkhchimeg 2018).

12. Although some political parties have provided their election campaign expenditure reports to the General Election Commission (GEC), I was told by people in the GEC, as well as by members of the NGOs that monitor and observe the elections, that these reports are not fully reliable. Overall, campaign financing remains largely inaccessible for research.

13. General Election Commission of Mongolia 2017. Per the website of the GEC: https://www.gec.gov.mn/. Accessed March 8, 2021.

14. The protests and riots after the 2008 parliamentary elections in downtown Ulaanbaatar were an extreme example of discontent due to the allegations of fraud in the results of the elections (see also Branigan 2008; Delaplache, Kaplonski, and Sneath 2008).

15. *Results of Parliamentary Elections in Mongolia* (2017). Retrieved on March 15, 2021, from https://www.gec.gov.mn/.

16. Some of the populace tend to ignore the official purpose of the Parliament as a lawmaking body and focus more on the works that are relegated to local government. But even if the electorate acknowledges the purpose of Parliament, campaigns fill in for the services of the local administration.

17. Anthropologist Marissa Smith, who studies Mongolia's copper deposit mining company Erdenet, notes that many mining professionals who consider themselves beyond politics still get frustrated if a winning candidate was not one of their expected candidates (personal communication, January 2021).

18. The exchange rate in 2008 was approximately 1,200 tugriks per US$1.00.

19. Benedict Anderson (1998, 266–67) also argues that elections in postcolonial South Asia turned, in the hands of the elite, into electoralism—a form of domesticating participation preventing more intense forms of civic participation like demonstrations and strikes. In Mongolia, however, the populace uses other forms of participation in addition to elections.

20. A good example is the Civil Movement Party, which was officially registered in 2007. Before becoming a party, it was a civil movement (hence the name), inspired by the color revolutions of Central Asia: The Rose Revolution in Georgia (Manning 2007), Ukraine's Orange Revolution (Phillips 2014), the Tulip/Pink Revolution in Kyrgyzstan, and the Jeans Revolution in Belarus. Political gatherings in the streets have produced many members of the Mongolian Parliament, including Batzandan and Magnai (former leaders of the Civil Movement).

21. See Mary Steedly (2000) on the ability of television news to mediate experiences by evoking memories of the past while also creating a sense of connectedness within nations and across national boundaries.

Chapter Three

1. The poster-style visual media diminished slightly in 2012 and 2016 elections due to the election design and economic changes; it compensated with an aggressive use of social media.

2. The number of constituencies changed from seventy-six in 2004 to twenty-six in 2008 and then returned to seventy-six in 2012.

3. Alexei Yurchak (2015) argues that Lefort's assessment of the Soviet Union is mistaken because the totalitarian rulers could themselves fill in the space left by the sovereign, but they had to be mediated by the figure of "Leninism," which was not in the body of the current leader but in the Leninist Party and in the body of Lenin, which was constantly regenerated.

4. During socialism, in 1962, a celebration of the 800th anniversary of Chinggis Khan in Khentii province was denounced by the Soviets (Bulag 1998).

5. More recent campaign images on social media, in contrast to street posters in Mongolia, are more communicative as voters and viewers started altering the images in order to ridicule or alert the public about unethical deeds.

6. The image style also applies to previous elections, even though these are not studied in this book.

7. The poster that featured the two men who let the woman candidate take the front space was problematic in its own way. As one can see on the poster, the names of the candidates are absent, which automatically puts the woman in a disadvantageous position vis-à-vis the two male candidates. The two men have been the most famous politicians since democratization in 1990s. The candidate on the left is Sanjaagiin Bayar—prime minister of Mongolia in 2008 as well as the general secretary of the Mongolian People's Party. The candidate in the middle is Sukhbaataryn Batbold—a former MP and a minister of foreign affairs. He succeeded Sanjaagiin Bayar in 2009 in his posts as Mongolia's prime minister and the MPP's general secretary. In contrast to these two popular candidates, the woman was almost entirely new to politics.

8. Some of the civil society independent members were unhappy that Burmaa was running as a DP member. Although Burmaa was also hesitant about whether to run as a DP candidate, she decided that the party platform was important for her candidacy.

9. In 2008, the candidates and political parties were restricted to four print pages of campaign material in total. One print page equals eight letter-size pages or its equivalent; a candidate or a political party could issue thirty-two pages of material (including a poster) in total. In 2012, the rules changed to separate political parties from candidates: political parties had forty print pages or 320 letter-size pages of material, while the pages for individual candidates remained the same: thirty-two pages of material.

10. Subsequent elections did not decrease the expenditure even though the economic situation has worsened.

Chapter Four

1. Serjee is a pseudonym, which I use at my interlocutor's request. To protect her privacy, I also disguise other relevant details, such as names of places (including towns and constituencies),

names of political parties, and names of related individuals. In addition, I use "her/Serjee's party" instead of the name of the political party.

2. This does not include donations to her party.

3. The intraparty competition for desirable constituencies (determined based on the identities and strengths of candidates) is fierce, and contests can go back and forth depending on various deals and competitions. While officially a candidate's residency in a constituency is required in order to be nominated there, candidates do not always reside in or come from their constituencies. It is common, however, to campaign in one's parents' constituency. Several candidates (for example, Ms. Natsagiin Udval from the Mongolian People's Party) have used the memories of their parents among locals and networks developed by previous generations as establishing points for their campaigns.

4. As mentioned previously, place names have been substituted to maintain anonymity.

5. See Bonilla 2017 for further mining-related discourses.

Chapter Five

1. See Mandel and Humphrey 2002 on the complicated transformation of the view of the market economy after socialism.

2. For further references, see Baabar [Bat-Erdene Batbayar] 1999; Buyandelger 2020; Dashpurev and Soni 1992; Saruul-Erdene 2000.

3. Definitions of "intellectual" as Zygmunt Bauman (1987) notes, are mostly self-definitions to create status groups, social spaces, and separate privileged spaces for knowledge (Bauman 1987). Katherine Verdery (1996, 17) follows Bauman by emphasizing the "site" intellectuals occupy, which is "distinguished from other sites within that space by its coordinates: recognized specialist claims to knowledge of symbolic capital, as opposed, . . . to occupancy of formal political positions."

4. The Soviet Union persecuted many of its presocialist intellectuals while also producing a new intellectual class that served the state. The intellectual class is heterogeneous, from resisting dissidents who had survived persecutions to those favored by the political leadership (see also Elfimov 2003; Shlapentokh 2014).

5. See Shalin 2012 for a detailed history of the Russian intelligentsia and their transformation after socialism.

6. In a similar way to all other categories of class identities, which had been undergoing rapid transformations (Gessen 1997; Humphrey 2002; Mandel and Humphrey 2002).

7. Similarly, during the post-Soviet period, for instance, as Michele Rivkin-Fish (2009, 81) argues, many Russians endorsed the "symbolic capital of *kul'turnost'* and high education long associated with the intelligentsia" as a way to claim a middle-class identity in the new capitalist formation in order to become recipients of newly available economic resources.

8. See Undarya 2018 on this NGO.

9. In "Women's Participation in Decision-Making," a report issued by the National Committee on Gender Equality (Government of Mongolia, National Committee for Gender Equality 2011, 34), 61.5 percent of study participants ranked "education" as the first criterion with which they evaluate the electability of female candidates out of eleven evaluative criteria. The candidates' viewpoints (56.4 percent) were the second most important criterion for selecting female candidates, and experience (49.6 percent) was the third. The least important criteria for electing the candidates were their "image" (7.8 percent) and wealth (5.6 percent). In a 2007 report titled

"Baseline Survey Women Participation in Electoral Process" (2007) furnished by a private research company (MEC LLC Research and Advisory), "education" was also the most important criteria (27 percent), followed by expertise (24 percent) and "popular recognition" (19 percent).

10. As a reminder, the structures and legislature of the former socialist state, which incorporated women at all levels of leadership and instituted a 25–30 percent quota for women in all leadership positions, had been abandoned during the early democratic restructuring in the 1990s (see chap. 1). As a result, women's representation in Parliament, and in other leadership positions, decreased, especially in proportion to their larger representation as a higher educated group at middle and upper professional levels.

11. Alexia Bloch (2003) discusses a similar gendering of professions in the Russian Far East.

12. For instance, a 2008 election law restricted a candidate's (and a political party or a group's) campaign print material (to two newspapers, one flier, and one brochure or magazine), all of which should amount to no more than sixty-four pages of letter-size paper (by Mongolian newspaper printing standards, that equals four "printed pages") (see Burmaa, with Oyuntuya and Mönkhnaran 2008). Even though the posters were restricted only to certain areas, this restriction was completely overlooked. In 2012, the amount of printed material was increased, but posters and other display materials were more strictly regulated by individual districts' Assembly of Citizen Representatives (see Burmaa, with Oyuntuya and Mönkhnaran 2012). Even with these laws and regulations, as numerous media monitoring groups have noted, discreet campaigning (*dald*) on various TV stations continued in subsequent elections while paid advertisements reflected the power of the wealthier candidates. Despite attempts to monitor campaign financing, it has remained opaque (Oyuntuya 2013c).

13. About 20–30 percent of votes come from a political party platform, according to political candidates.

14. Law of Mongolia on Enforcement of the Law on Promotion of Gender Equality: https://www.legislationline.org/download/id/4518/file/Mongolia_law_gender_equality_2011_en.pdf. Accessed on January 12, 2020.

15. The waves of advocacy for lobbying the passing of the gender equality law had helped to promote women in politics for the 2012 election as a side-outcome. The promotion of the understanding of gender equality in the public arena was, among many other aspects, a necessary step in promoting women to candidacy as well. (In the 2012 election, eleven women became legislators.)

16. 1 USD = 1,267.51 MNT as of December 31, 2008; 50 million MNT was 39,000 USD.

17. Although the book is coauthored, it is usually Oyungerel who promotes the book in public.

18. Baabar had written his book in Moscow ca. 1988, although it was not published until 1990 (Kaplonski 2004).

19. See Tumursukh Undarya 2018 for a nuanced analysis and a history of the development of civil society in Mongolia after socialism. I share Undarya's criticism about many of these NGOs being spaces for elitism or at least for the most educated parts of the society. Undarya, as an activist, had larger goals and expectations. I saw the NGOs as a new sociocultural phenomenon, as forms of self-expression, and as ways to consolidate new groups at least as much as entities to serve society.

20. There is an intriguing parallel between Burmaa's relentless initiatives in building the necessary institutions for the new democratizing society and the strategies of women leaders of the Mongolian Women's Committee (MWC) in getting their work done during socialism as discussed in chapter 1.

21. In addition to the 2008 election, Burmaa competed in the 2012 and 2016 parliamentary elections.

22. As an activist, Undarya (2018) argues that the civil society in Mongolia is weak because of their precarious financial situation and a lack of support from the government. As an outsider to the NGO world, I argue that despite such difficulties, the achievements of the civil society have been rich and long-lasting.

23. Among many things, Burmaa's campaign program was concentrated on enhancing higher education, distributing shares to citizens from mining revenue, and developing a more efficient parliamentary system based on the rule of law that could combat nepotism, corruption, and inefficiency.

24. A Petition to the Constitutional Court of Mongolia. Odonchimed L., Ganhuyag Ts., Burmaa R., July 18, 2008 (Personal Archive, Radnaagiin Burmaa).

25. A Petition to the General Election Commission. July 21, 2008, by Burmaa Radnaagiin (Personal Archive, Radnaagiin Burmaa).

26. Supreme Court of Mongolia Final Hearing for a Civil Case #188, April 14, 2009 (Personal Archive, Radnaagiin Burmaa).

27. Declaration of the Constitutional Court of Mongolia: A Hearing Concerning a Classification of Citizen Burmaa's Legal Case, which Has Been Rejected by All Courts. (Personal Archive, Radnaagiin Burmaa).

28. Supreme Court of Mongolia Final Hearing for a Civil Case #188, April 14, 2009 (Personal Archive, Radnaagiin Burmaa).

29. For despair as a multifaceted experience among the marginalized in Russia and Eastern Europe, see Humphrey 2002, Klumbyte 2014, Ries 1997.

Chapter Six

1. The extension of governing to nonstate actors is widespread in other places (see Dunn 2008; Ong and Collier 2004).

2. I do not gauge the efficacy of these strategies or make a direct correlation between these strategies and how these women fared in the elections.

3. The notion of symbolic capital especially applies to the electoral candidates as they strive to impress voters and enter a chain of exchange with the powerful members of their parties. Thorstein Veblen (2007) emphasizes the importance of conspicuous consumption for the new rich trying to break into the previously exclusive, in this case political, leadership. In a similar way, Marcel Mauss (2006) notes the importance of consumption in upward mobility. Pierre Bourdieu's (1984) notion of social capital is also useful here but in a highly specific sense: individuals who possess symbolic capital can exchange it for social capital, if necessary. However, in the electoral context, social capital hardly brings a sense of community or trust.

4. Oyungerel informed me that she was the only politician who was able to squeeze in an interview after calling more than a dozen TV stations and asking for brief airtime. Because the Parliament announced the repeal on December 25, right before the New Year celebration, all TV stations were booked with holiday concerts and programs.

5. The more open and casual atmosphere at DP contrasted with the formal, closed-off, and hierarchical atmosphere at the Mongolian People's Revolutionary Party (MPRP).

6. I see many parallels between *self-perfection* and the Confucian notion of *self-cultivation*. There are Confucian roots to various concepts and values that were adopted by the Mongolians

during the Qing rule in the eighteenth through nineteenth centuries. See Kohl-Garrity 2019 for a discussion on Qing influence on Mongolian philosophical tradition. The Mongolians' Sino-phobia and cultural borders (see Bille 2014), however, make it hard to point at direct connections without going into an extensive discussion. In Mongolia, Chinese linguistic influence is limited; there is little Chinese (or any other Asian) philosophical influence on Mongolia other than Buddhist, and cultural connections are limited to consumption.

7. Such a trend was partly due to shifts in Mongolian newspapers and magazines from state-sponsored to private ownership and to a proliferation of independent media. In order to compete for the largest pool of readership, the media creation of materials that would qualify as "sensational" included the lives of the famous. It is not only that competitive media favors cultures of the sexualization of women but it also mimics to some extent everyday life as well. Since the 1990s, beauty events (for example, beauty pageants, fashion shows, and the contests by body-builders) have become popular.

8. After 2016, Oyungerel changed her self-polishing tactics. She changed to a more feminine style by wearing dresses and clothing of pastel colors and adopting various beautification tech-niques. She also posed as a cosmetics and clothing model while disseminating her beautified images through social media. This change also illustrates the ways in which beauty is a force and an attribute for upward mobility.

9. The *deel* is a traditional robe that is largely ungendered. Certain elements such as the color of the material, the style of buttons and trim, and the shape of the sleeves can be made to mark genders, but this is not required. A *deel* can be left as neutral as one wishes.

10. The NGO's name was a reaction to chasing after material wealth, which has been a dominant preoccupation of many people after socialism. By proclaiming that citizens are also the wealth of the country, Odontuya brought in neoliberal values that see humans as capital-generating products that have measurable and improvable values.

11. "A Biographical Portrait." http://odontuya.com/content.php?id=99&rid=39.

References

Abélès, Marc. 1988. "Modern Political Ritual." *Current Anthropology* 29 (3): 391–405.

Abrahms-Kavunenko, Saskia. 2018. *Enlightenment and the Gasping City: Mongolian Buddhism at a Time of Environmental Disarray*. Ithaca, NY: Cornell University Press.

Ahearn, Laura. 2001. *Invitations to Love: Literacy, Love Letters, and Social Change in Nepal*. Ann Arbor, MI: University of Michigan Press.

Ahmed, Amel. 2013. *Democracy and the Politics of Electoral System Choice: Engineering Electoral Dominance*. Cambridge: Cambridge University Press.

Alphen, E. J. van. 2013. "Explosions of Information, Implosions of Meaning, and the Release of Affects." In *Images on the Move*, edited by P. Spyer and M. Steedly, 219–36. Santa Fe, NM: School for Advanced Research Press.

Anderson, Benedict. 1998. *The Spectre of Comparisons: Nationalism, Southeast Asia and the World*. New York: Verso.

Andors, Phyllis. 1983. *The Unfinished Liberation of Chinese Women*. Bloomington, IN: Indiana University Press.

Appel, Hillary and Mitchell A. Orenstein. 2018. *From Triumph to Crisis: Neoliberal Economic Reform in Postcommunist Countries*. Cambridge: Cambridge University Press.

Appiah, Kwame Anthony. 1991. "Is the Post- in Postmodernism the Post- in Postcolonial?" *Critical Inquiry* 17 (2): 336–57.

Ardener, Edwin. 1975. "Belief and the Problem of Women and The 'Problem' Revisited." In *Perceiving Women*, edited by Shirley Ardener, 1–27. London: Malaby.

Atwood, Christopher. 2004. *Encyclopedia of Mongolia and the Mongol Empire*. New York: Facts on File.

Baabar. [Bat-Erdene Batbayar]. 1990. *Buu Mart! Horin Nedgügeer Zuuny Bosgon Deer* [Don't Forget! On the Threshold of the Twenty-First Century]. Ulaanbaatar, Mongolia: Social Democratic Movement [Ardchilsan Sotsialist Hödölgöön].

———. 1999. *Twentieth Century Mongolia*. Cambridge. White Horse Press.

Ballis, William B., and Robert A. Rupen. 1956. Mongolian People's Republic (Outer Mongolia). New Haven, CT: Human Relations Area Files.

Banerjee, Mukulika. 2007. "Sacred Elections." *Economic and Political Weekly* 42 (17): 1556–62.

———. 2011. "Elections as Communitas." *Social Research* 78 (1): 75–98.

———. 2014. *Why India Votes?* New Delhi: Routledge.

Barthes, Roland. 1995. *The Language of Fashion*. London: Bloomsbury.

Bat, Ö. 2008. "The Ecologist Bayarsaikhan Is Caught." *Century News* [Zuunii Medee], June 20.

Batchuluun, Ch. 1982. *Monkhiin aldar* [Eternal glory]. Ulaanbaatar, Mongolia: Ulsyn Khevleliin Gazar [State Publishing Agency].

Batmunkh, Batsukh, Gereltuya Altanhuyag, and Idshinrenjin Osorjav. 2013. "Achieving the Millennium Development Goals, Fifth National Progress Report." Ulaanbatar: Ministry of Economic Development of Mongolia.

Bauman, Zygmunt. 1987. *Legislators and Interpreters: On Modernity, Post-Modernity, and Intellectuals*. Ithaca, NY: Cornell University Press.

Bawden, Charles. 1968. *The Modern History of Mongolia*. New York: Praeger.

Bayantur, Gerelt-Od. 2008. "Democratic Transition and The Electoral Process in Mongolia." PhD diss. University of Saskatchewan, Canada.

Begzsuren, Tsolomon, and Dolgion Aldar. 2014. "Gender Overview in Mongolia—A Desk Study." Ulaanbaatar, Mongolia: Swiss Agency for Development and Cooperation and IRIM.

Bille, Franck. 2014. *Sinophobia: Anxiety, Violence, and the Making of Mongolian Identity*. Honolulu: University of Hawaii Press.

Bira, Sh., ed. 1984. *The History of the Mongolian People's Republic* [Bugd Nairamdah Mongol Ard Ulsiin Tuuh]. Ulaanbaatar, Mongolia: State Publishing House. [In Mongolian.]

Bjorkman, Lisa. 2014. "'You Can't Buy a Vote': Meanings of Money in a Mumbai Election." *American Ethnologist* 41 (4): 617–34.

Bloch, Alexia. 2003. "Longing for the Kollektiv: Gender, Power, and Residential Schools in Central Siberia." *Cultural Anthropology* 20 (4): 534–69.

Bonilla, Lauren. 2017. "Extractive Infrastructures: Social, Environmental and Institutional. Transformations in Mongolia's Emergent Extraction-Based Economy." PhD diss. Clark University, Worcester, MA.

Bonilla, Lauren, and Tuya Shagdar. 2018. "Electoral Gifting and Personal Politics in Mongolia's Parliamentary Election Season." *Central Asian Survey* 37 (3): 457–74. https://doi.org/10.108 0/02634937.2018.1442319.

Bodoo, D. 2008. "The Movie Narrated by Elbegdorj." *Century News* [Zuunii Medee], March 26.

Borneman, John. 2011. *Political Crime and the Memory of Loss*. Bloomington, IN: Indiana University Press.

Bourdieu, Pierre. 1977. *Outline of a Theory of Practice*. Cambridge: Cambridge University Press.

———. 1984. *Distinction: A Social Critique of the Judgment of Taste*. Cambridge, MA: Harvard University Press.

———. 1991. *Language and Symbolic Power*. Cambridge, MA: Harvard University Press

———. 1993. *The Field of Cultural Production: Essays on Art and Literature*. New York, NY: Columbia University Press.

Bowie, Katherine A. 2008. "Vote Buying and Village Outrage in an Election in Northern Thailand: Recent Legal Reforms in Historical Context." *Journal of Asian Studies* 67 (2): 469–511.

Boyer, Dominic. 2013. "Simply the Best: Parody and Political Sincerity in Iceland." *American Ethnologist* 40 (2): 276–87.

Boyer, Dominic, and Yurchak Alexei. 2010. "American Stiob: Or, What Late-Socialist Aesthetics of Parody Reveal about Contemporary Political Culture in the West." *Cultural Anthropology* 25 (2): 179–221.

Branigan, Tania. 2008. "State of Emergency in Mongolia after Post Election Violence." *The Guardian*, July 2. http://www.guardian.co.uk/world/2008/jul/03/1.

Brenner, Susan. 1998. *The Domestication of Desire: Women, Wealth, and Modernity in Java*. Princeton, NJ: Princeton University Press.

Brink-Danan, Marcy. 2009. "'I Vote, Therefore I Am': Rituals of Democracy and the Turkish Chief Rabbi." *PoLAR: Political and Legal Anthropology Review* 32 (1): 5–27.

Bulag, Uradyn. 1998. *Nationalism and Hybridity in Mongolia*. Oxford, UK: Oxford University Press.

———. 2009. "Mongolia in 2008: From Mongolia to Mine-golia." *Asian Survey* 49 (1): 129–34.

Bum-Ochir, Dulam. 2020. *The State, Popular Mobilisation and Gold Mining in Mongolia: Shaping 'Neoliberal' Policies*. London: UCL Press. https://doi.org/10.14324/111.9781787351837.

———. 2019. "Nationalist Sentiments Obscured by 'Pejorative Labels' Birthplace, Homeland and Mobilisation against Mining in Mongolia." *Inner Asia* 21 (2019): 162–79.

———. 2018. "Mongolia in Democracy, Civil Society and Movement." In *Routledge Handbook of Civil Society in Asia*, edited by Akihiro Ogawa, 95–109. New York: Routledge.

Burawoy, Michael, and Katherine Verdery. 1999. *Uncertain Transition: Ethnographies of Change in the Postsocialist World*. Lanham, MD: Rowman and Littlefield.

Burcher, Catalina, and Fernando Bértoa. 2018. "Political Finance in Mongolia." https://www.idea.int/sites/default/files/publications/political-finance-in-mongolia.pdf. Accessed February 26, 2021.

Burmaa, Radnaagiin. Personal Archive Documents.

———. 2008a. A Petition to the Constitutional Court of Mongolia. Odonchimed L., Ganhuyag Ts., Burmaa R., July 18, 2008.

———. 2008b. A Petition to the General Election Commission. July 21, 2008, by Burmaa Radnaa.

———. 2008c. Declaration of the Constitutional Court of Mongolia: A Hearing Concerning a Classification of Citizen Burmaa's Legal Case, which Has Been Rejected by All Courts. December 29, 2008.

———. 2009. Supreme Court of Mongolia Final Hearing for a Civil Case #188, April 14, 2009.

Burmaa, Radnaagiin (with Sumyagiin Oyuntuya and Avirmed Mönkhnaran). 2008. *The Parliamentary Election of 2008: Manual for Organizing Elections*. Booklet prepared by the Center. Ulaanbaatar, Mongolia: Voter Education Center.

———. 2012. *The Parliamentary Election of 2012: Manual for Organizing Elections*. Booklet prepared by the Center. Ulaanbaatar, Mongolia: Voter Education Center.

Burn, Nalini, and Oidoviin Oyuntsetseg. 2001. *Women in Mongolia: Mapping Progress under Transition*. Ulaanbaatar, Mongolia: United Nations Development Fund for Women.

Buyandelger, Manduhai. 2013. *Tragic Spirits: Shamanism, Memory, and Gender in Contemporary Mongolia*. Chicago: University of Chicago Press.

———. 2014. "Engineers and Shamans as Heralds of the New Mongolia." Vital Topics Forum Anthropology in and of MOOCs, guest editor Graham Jones. *American Anthropologist* 116, no. 4 (Dec. 2014): 829–38.

———. 2018. "Asocial Memories, 'Poisonous Knowledge', and Haunting in Mongolia: Asocial Memories." *Journal of the Royal Anthropological Institute* 25, no. 1. https://doi.org/10.1111/1467-9655.12963.

———. 2020. "Writing Oneself Out of the Oppression: Biographies of Reconciliation and Re-Collection." *New Literary Observer* [in Russian]. No. 161 (January 20): 199–218.

Buyandelgeriyn, Manduhai. 2008. "Post-post Transition Theories: Walking on Multiple Paths." *Annual Review of Anthropology* 37:235–50.

Cerwonka, Allaine. 2008. "Traveling Feminist Thought: Difference and Transculturation in Central and Eastern European Feminism." *Signs: Journal of Women in Culture and Society* 33 (4): 809–32.

Chaney, Joseph, and David Stanway. 2010. "Special Report—Mongolia's Fabled Mine Stirs Asian Frontier." *Reuters*, October 12, 2010. https://www.reuters.com/article/uk-special-report-mongolia -mine/special-report-mongolias-fabled-mine-stirs-asian-frontier-idUKLNE69B05T2010 1012. Accessed October 29, 2019.

Chari, Sharad, and Katherine Verdery. 2009. "Thinking between the Posts: Postcolonialism, Postsocialism, and Ethnography after the Cold War." *Comparative Studies in Society and History* 51 (1): 6–34.

Chimid, B. 2008. *Election Study Guide: System, Process, and Rights* [In Mongolian: Songuulid Suraltsahui: Togtoltsoo, Uil Yavts, Erhzui]. Ulaanbaatar, Mongolia: Admon Publishing.

Choi, Dale. 2010. "HDF to Receive $94 M from Royalties and Erdenet, $150 M from OT, to Spend $235 M on Human Development in 2010." *Independent Mongolian Metals & Mining Research.* November 23. http://uclalum.blogspot.co.uk/2009/11/hdf-to-receive-94-mfrom-roalties-and .html.

Chumley, Lily Hope. 2016. *Creativity Class: Art School and Culture Work in Postsocialist China.* Princeton, NJ: Princeton University Press.

Coles, Kimberly. 2004. "Election Day: The Construction of Democracy through Technique." *Cultural Anthropology* 19 (4): 551–80.

———. 2007. *Democratic Designs: International Intervention and Electoral Practices in Post-War Bosnia-Herzegovina.* Ann Arbor, MI: University of Michigan Press.

Collier, Jane. 2009. "From Mary to Modern Woman: The Material Basis of Marianismo and Its Transformation in a Spanish Village." *American Ethnologist* 13 (1): 100–107.

The Constitutions of Mongolia. 2009. Ulaanbaatar, Mongolia. Compiled by J. Amarsanaa.

Creed, Gerald W. 2011. *Masquerade and Postsocialism: Rituals and Cultural Dispossession in Bulgaria.* Bloomington, IN: Indiana University Press.

Dashdondov, Tserendorjiin. 2003. "Gloomy Thoughts on Festivities." In *This Is a Chronicle Executed with a Stylus in Hand with a Cluster of Words Urged and Their Meaning Nurtured,* 6–18. Ulaanbaatar, Mongolia. The Union of Mongolian Journalists.

Dashpurev, Danzankhorloo, and S. K. Soni. 1992. *Reign of Terror in Mongolia, 1920–1990.* New Delhi: South Asian Publishers.

De Certeau, Michel. 1984. *The Practice of Everyday Life.* Berkeley: University of California Press.

De Haan, Francisca. 2012. "The Women's International Democratic Federation (WIDF): History, Main Agenda, and Contributions, 1945–1991." In *Women and Social Movements (WASI),* edited by Thomas Dublin and Kathryn Kish Sklar. http://alexanderstreet.com/products /women-and-social-movements-international Online Archive. Accessed November 7, 2021.

Delaplache, Grégory. 2010. "Marshal Choibalsan's Second Funeral." In *Representing Power in Modern Inner Asia: Conventions, Alternatives and Oppositions,* edited by Isabelle Charleux, Grégory Delaplace, and Roberte Hamayon, 97–116. Bellingham, WA: Western Washington University, Center for East Asian Studies.

Delaplache, Grégory, Christopher Kaplonski, and David Sneath. 2008. "The End of Post-socialism? An Account of the 1st of July Riots in Ulaanbaatar, Mongolia." *Inner Asia* 10: 323–65.

De Lauretis, Teresa. 1987. *Technologies of Gender: Essays on Theory, Film, and Fiction.* Bloomington, IN: Indiana University Press.

Diaz, Holly D. 2019. "Centuries of Navigating Resistance and Change: Exploring the Persistence of Mongolian Women Leaders." PhD diss. Antioch University, Yellow Springs, OH.

Dunn, Elizabeth. 2008. "Postsocialist Spores: Disease, Bodies, and the State in the Republic of Georgia." *American Ethnologist* 35: 243–58. https://doi.org/10.1111/j.1548-1425.2008.00032.x.

Durkheim, Émile. 1995. *The Elementary Forms of Religious Life*. Translated and with an Introduction by Karen E. Fields. New York: The Free Press. First published in 1912.

Edmonds, Alexander. 2010. *Pretty Modern: Beauty, Sex, and Plastic Surgery in Brazil*. Durham, NC: Duke University Press.

Elfimov, Alexei. 2003. *Russian Intellectual Culture in Transition: The Future in the Past*. Münster, Germany: Lit Verlag.

Ellis-Petersen, Hanna. 2018. "Malaysia to Reopen Inquiry into Murder of Mongolian Model." *The Guardian*. June 22. https://www.theguardian.com/world/2018/jun/22/malaysia-altantuya-re open-investigation-mongolian-model-murder. Accessed November 7, 2021.

Empson, Rebecca. 2020. *Subjective Lives and Economic Transformations in Mongolia: Life in the Gap*. London: UCL Press.

Empson, Rebecca, and Lauren Bonilla. 2019. "Introduction: Temporary Possession." Theorizing the Contemporary, *Fieldsights*, March 29. Editors' Forum. *Cultural Anthropology*. https://culanth.org/fieldsights/introduction-temporary-possession.

Erdene, L. 2008. "The Weakening of the Democratic Party." In *Mongolyn Ünen* [Mongolian Truth]. April 11, no. 70 (21044).

Eudin, Xenia Joukoff, and Harold H. Fisher. 1957. *Soviet Russia and the West, 1920–1927: A Documentary Survey*. Stanford, CA: Stanford University Press.

Fisher, Melissa S. 2012. *Wall Street Women*. Durham, NC: Duke University Press.

Fitzpatrick, Sheila, ed. 1978. *Cultural Revolution in Russia, 1928–1931*. Bloomington, IN: Indiana University Press.

———. 1979. *Education and Social Mobility in the Soviet Union, 1921–1932*. Cambridge: Cambridge University Press.

Foucault, Michel. 1977. *Discipline and Punish*. New York: Vintage Books.

———. 1988. "Technologies of the Self." In *Technologies of the Self: A Seminar with Michel Foucault*, edited by Luther H. Martin, Huck Gutman, and Patrick H. Hutton, 16–49. Amherst, MA: University of Massachusetts Press.

Fox, Elizabeth. 2017. "The Price of an Election: Split Hopes and Political Ambivalence in the Ger District of Ulaanbaatar." *Emerging Subjects* (blog), July 13. https://blogs.ucl.ac.uk/mongolian -economy/2017/07/13/the-price-an-election-split-hopes-and-political-ambivalence-in-the -ger-districts-of-ulaanbaatar/. Accessed October 30, 2019.

———. 2016. "The Road to Power." *Emerging Subjects* (blog), August 24. https://blogs.ucl.ac.uk /mongolian-economy/2016/08/24/the-road-to-power/. Accessed March 15, 2021.

Freeman, Carla. 2014. *Entrepreneurial Selves: Neoliberal Respectability and the Making of a Caribbean Middle Class*. Durham, NC: Duke University Press.

Friedland, Robert. 2005. "Nothing Like It on Planet Earth: Robert Friedland's Tour d' Tolgoi." Keynote Address presented at the BMO Nesbitt Burns Global Resources Conferences, Tampa, Florida. http://www.resourceinvestor.com/pebble.asp?relid=9010.

Friedman, Milton. 2001. *Free to Choose*. In Mongolian [Khuv, zaĭaagan songokh n']. Ulaanbaatar, Mongolia: "Monsudar" Khevleliin: "Altan Taria" khuv'aat Kompani.

Funk, Nanette, and Magda Mueller. 1993. *Gender Politics and Post-Communism: Reflections from Eastern Europe and the Former Soviet Union*. London: Routledge.

Gal, Susan, and Gail Kligman. 2000. *The Politics of Gender after Socialism: A Comparative-Historical Essay*. Princeton NJ: Princeton University Press.

Gaidar, Arkady. 1973 [original publication, 1940]. *Timur and His Squad* [Timur i yego komanda]. Moscow: Progress Publishers.

Ganhuyag, Dashtsevegiin. 2019. "Mongolians Have Not Participated in the Global Division of Labor for 30 Years." *Sudlaach Ganaa* (blog). May 29. https://ganaa.mn/2019/05/29/nbnby wywitisghs/. Accessed March 14, 2021.

Gerelsuren, N., and D. Altai. 2008. *Mongolian Women's Organization: Chronicles 1924–2008*. Ulaanbaatar, Mongolia: Urlah Erdem Publishing Company.

Gerelsuren, N., and J. Erdenechimeg. 2014. *On Tsagin Dursamj* [Reminiscence of the Years]. Vols. 1–3. Ulaanbaatar, Mongolia: Mönkhiin Üseg.

Gessen, Masha. 1997. *Dead Again: The Russian Intelligentsia after Communism*. New York: Verso.

Ghodsee, Kristen. 2012. "Rethinking State Socialist Mass Women's Organizations: The Committee of the Bulgarian Women's Movement and the United Nations Decade for Women, 1975–1985." *Journal of Women's History* (24) 4: 49–73.

———. 2014. "Pressuring the Politburo: The Committee of the Bulgarian Women's Movement and State Socialist Feminism." *Slavic Review* 73 (3): 538–62.

———. 2019. *Second World, Second Sex: Socialist Women's Activism and Global Solidarity During the Cold War*. Durham, NC: Duke University Press.

Ginsburg, Faye. 1989. *Contested Lives: The Abortion Debate in an American Community*. Berkeley: University of California Press.

Good, Mary-Jo Del Vecchio. 1999. "Foreword." In *Hermeneutics and Honor: Negotiating Female "Public" Space in Islamic/ate Societies*, edited by Asma Afsaruddin. Cambridge, MA: Harvard University Press.

Government of Mongolia, National Committee for Gender Equality. 2011. "Women's Participation in Decision-Making: Research on the Populace's Opinion." [Part One of the Research]. Document can be requested from the National Committee on Gender Equality, Government Bldg. 11, Room 611, 612. Desk Study Brochure.

———. 2012. "Women's Participation in Political Leadership: Research on the Populace's Opinion." [Part Two of the Research]. Ulaanbaatar, Mongolia: Soyombo Printing [In Mongolian].

Greenberg, Jessica. 2006. "Noć Reklamoždera: Democracy, Consumption, and the Contradictions of Representation in Post-Socialist Serbia." *PoLAR: Political and Legal Anthropology Review* 29 (2): 181–207.

Greenhouse, Carol. J. 1996. *A Moment's Notice*. Ithaca, NY: Cornell University Press.

Gruska, Ulriker, Christoph Dreyer, and Anne Renzenbrink. 2016. "Who Owns Media in Mongolia?" Press Institute of Mongolia and Reporters without Borders. https://rsf.org/en/news/who-owns-media-mongolia. Accessed April 4, 2021.

Hann, Chris. 2006. *Not the Horse We Wanted! Postsocialism, Neoliberalism and Eurasia*. Münster: LIT.

Hatcher, Pascale. 2014. *Regimes of Risk: The World Bank and the Transformation of Mining in Asia*. London: Palgrave Macmillan.

Heller, Nathan. 2017. "Is the Gig Economy Working?" *New Yorker*. May 15, 2017. https://www.newyorker.com/magazine/2017/05/15/is-the-gig-economy-working.

Herzfeld, Michael. 2000. "Uncanny Success: Some Closing Remarks." In *Elites: Choice, Leadership, and Succession*, edited by João de Pina-Cabral and Antónia Pedroso de Lima, 227–36. Oxford: Berg.

———. 2005. *Cultural Intimacy: Social Poetics in the Nation-State*. New York: Routledge.

———. 2015. "Heritage and Corruption: The Two Faces of the Nation-State." *International Journal of Heritage Studies* 21:531–44. Online 2014, https://doi.org/10.1080/13527258.2014.948486.

———. 2018. "Corruption as Political Incest: Temporalities of Sin and Redemption." In *Reconnecting State and Kinship*, edited by Tatjana Thelen and Erdmute Alber, 39–60. Philadelphia: University of Pennsylvania Press.

Hladík, Radim. 2011. "A Theory's Travelogue: Post-Colonial Theory in Post-Socialist Space." *Theory of Science* 33 (4): 561–90.

Højer, Lars. 2019. *The Anti-Social Contract: Injurious Talk and Dangerous Exchanges in Northern Mongolia*. New York: Berghahn.

Højer, Lars, and Morten Pedersen. 2019. *Urban Hunters: Dealing and Dreaming in Times of Transition*. New Haven, CT: Yale University Press.

Huat, Chua Beng. 2007. *Elections as Popular Culture in Asia*. London: Routledge.

Humphrey, Caroline. 1993. "Women and Ideology in Hierarchical Societies in East Asia." In *Persons and Powers of Women in Diverse Cultures*, edited by S. Ardener, 173–92. New York: Berg.

———. 2002. *The Unmaking of Soviet Life: Everyday Economies after Socialism*. Ithaca, NY: Cornell University Press.

———. 2008. "Reassembling Individual Subjects: Events and Decisions in Troubled Times." *Anthropological Theory* 8 (4): 357–80.

Interparliamentary Union. 1973. Mongolia. http://www.ipu.org/parlinee/reports/arc/MONGOLIA _1973_E.PDF.

———. 1977. Mongolia. http://www.ipu.org/parline-e/reports/arc/MONGOLIA_1977_E.PDF.

Ismailbekova, Aksana. 2017. *Blood Ties and the Native Son: Poetics of Patronage in Kyrgyzstan*. Bloomington, IN: Indiana University Press.

Jacob, Pearly. 2012. "Mongolia: Can New Electoral Law Help Women Enter Parliament?" In Eurasianet (online news outlet), June 27, 2012. https://eurasianet.org/. https://www.eurasiareview.com/29062012-mongolia-new-electoral-law-aims-to-help-women-enter-parliament/. Accessed October 31, 2019.

Jaggar, Alison. 1994. *Living with Contradictions: Controversies in Feminist Social Ethics*. Boulder, CO: Westview Press.

Jain, Kajri. 2007. *Gods in the Bazaar: The Economies of Indian Calendar Art*. Durham, NC: Duke University Press.

Jamian, G. 2017. *The Life of Resisting and Succumbing*. [In Mongolian.] Ulaanbaatar, Mongolia: Impresscolor Press.

Kanaaneh, Rhoda Ann. 2002. *Birthing the Nation: Strategies of Palestinian Women in Israel*. Berkeley. University of California Press.

Kaplonski, Chris. 2004. *Truth, History and Politics in Mongolia: Memory of Heroes*. New York: Routledge.

———. 2014. *The Lama Question: Violence, Sovereignty and Exception in Early Socialism in Mongolia*. Honolulu, HI: University of Hawaii Press.

Kligman, Gail. 1998. *The Politics of Duplicity: Controlling Reproduction in Ceausescu's Romania*. Berkeley: University of California Press.

Klima, Michal. 2019. *Informal Politics in Post-Communist Europe: Political Parties, Clientelism and State Capture*. London: Routledge.

Klumbyte, Neringa. 2014. "Of Power and Laughter: Carnivalesque Politics and Moral Citizenship in Lithuania." *American Ethnologist* 41 (3): 473–90.

Knapp, Michael, Anja Flach, and Ercan Ayboğa. 2016. *Revolution in Rojava: Democratic Autonomy and Women's Liberation in the Syrian Kurdistan*. London: Pluto Press.

Kohl-Garrity, Elisa. 2019. "The Weight of Respect: Khündlekh Yos—Frames of Reference, Governmental Agendas and Ethical Formations in Modern Mongolia." PhD diss. University of Halle-Wittenberg, Halle, Germany.

Kohn, Michael. 2013. "Mongolia Loan May Help Tavan Tolgoi Exit Chalco Deal, CEO Says." Bloomberg.com. January 24. http://www.bloomberg.com/news/articles/2013-01-24/mongolia-loan -may-help-tavan-tolgoi-exit-chalco-deal-ceo-says.

Kohn, Michael, and Yuriy Humber. 2013. "Mongolia Plans to Charge Rio's Oyu Tolgoi Interest on Tax." Bloomberg.com. February 28. https://www.bloomberg.com/news/articles/2013-02-28/mon golia-plans-to-charge-rio-s-oyu-tolgoi-interest-on-unpaid-tax. Accessed November 7, 2021.

Kracauer, Siegfried. 1995. *The Mass Ornament: Weimar Essays*. Cambridge, MA: Harvard University Press. First published 1963.

Krook, Mona Lena. 2009. *Quotas for Women in Politics: Gender and Candidate Selection Reform Worldwide*. New York: Oxford University Press.

Krook, Mona Lena, and Jacqui True. 2012. "Rethinking the Life Cycles of International Norms: The United Nations and the Global Promotion of Gender Equality." *European Journal of International Relations* 18 (1): 103–27.

Lawless, Jennifer, and Richard L. Fox. 2010. *It Still Takes a Candidate: Why Women Don't Run for Office*. Cambridge: Cambridge University Press.

Lazzarato, Maurizio. 2014. *Signs and Machines: Capitalism and the Production of Subjectivity*. New York: Semiotext(e).

Ledeneva, Alena V. 2006. *How Russia Really Works: The Informal Practices That Shaped Post-Soviet Politics and Business*. Ithaca, NY: Cornell University Press.

Lefort, Claude. 1988. *Democracy and Political Theory*. Cambridge, UK: Polity Press.

Leshkowich, Ann Marie. 2014. "Standardized Forms of Vietnamese Selfhood: An Ethnographic Genealogy of Documentation." *American Ethnologist* 41 (1): 143–62.

Leyenaar, Monique. 2004. *The Political Empowerment of Women: The Netherlands and Other Countries*. Boston/Leiden: Martinus Nijhoff Publishers.

Lhagva, G. 2015. "Neither Here Nor There." *Unuudur*, January 14, 2015. http://www.new.mn/News /Detail?news_code=29667.

Lhamsuren, B., ed. 1985. *Short History of the Mongolian People's Revolutionary Party* [Mongol Ardyn Khuvsgalt Namyn Tovch Tuuh]. Ulaanbaatar, Mongolia: State Publishing House. [In Mongolian.]

Lomnitz, L. A., Claudio Lomnitz Adler, and Ilya Adler. 1993. "The Function of the Form: Power Play and Ritual in the 1988 Mexican Presidential Campaign." In *Constructing Culture and Power in Latin America*, edited by Daniel H. Levine, 357–401. Ann Arbor, MI: University of Michigan Press.

Mahmood, Saba. 2005. *The Politics of Piety: The Islamic Revival and the Feminist Subject*. Princeton, NJ: Princeton University Press.

Mandel, Ruth, and Caroline Humphrey. 2002. *Markets and Moralities: Ethnographies of Postsocialism*. London: Bloomsbury Academic.

Manning, Paul. 2007. "Rose Colored Glasses? Color Revolutions and Cartoon Chaos in Postsocialist Georgia." *Cultural Anthropology* 22:171–213.

Marwick, Alice E. 2015. "Instafame: Luxury Selfies in the Attention Economy." *Public Culture* 27, no. 1 (Jan. 2015): 137–60.

Mauss, Marcel. 2006. *Techniques, Technology and Civilization*. New York: Berghahn Books.

MCC (Millennium Challenge Compact). 2008. "Making a Difference: 2008 Annual Report." https://pdf.usaid.gov/pdf_docs/PCAAB908.pdf. Accessed November 5, 2021.

McDowell, Linda. 1997. *Capital Culture: Gender at the Work in the City*. Malden, MA: Wiley-Blackwell Publishers.

McLeod, James R. 1999. "The Sociodrama of Presidential Politics: Rhetorics, Ritual and Power in the Era of Teledemocracy." *American Anthropologist* 101 (2): 359–73.

MEC LLC Research and Advisory. 2007. "Baseline Survey Women Participation in Electoral Process." As part of the "Support to Electoral Processes in Mongolia" Project of UNDP Mongolia, 2007. http://www.mec.mn/ or contact infor@mex.com. to request a copy of the report.

Miles, William. 1988. *Elections in Nigeria: A Grassroots Perspective*. Boulder, CO: Lynne Rienner.

Miller, Laura. 2006. *Beauty Up: Exploring Contemporary Japanese Body Aesthetics*. Berkeley: University of California Press.

Mitchell, W. J. T. 1984. "What Is an Image?" *New Literary History* 15, no. 3: 503–37. https://doi.org/10.2307/468718.

———. 2012. "Image, Space, Revolution: The Arts of Occupation." *Critical Inquiry* 39, no. 1: 8–32.

Mongolian People's Revolutionary Party (MPRP). Politburo Central Plenum Decree #338. December 22, 1966. "On the Promotion of Women to the Leadership Positions in Party, State, and Public Establishments." National Archives [MUÜTA], Ulaanbaatar, Mongolia, UTNONBBA, Kh-4, D-30, KhN-7, Kh., pages 337–42.

The Mongolian Women. 1964. Periodical, 1964, issue no. 3. Ulaanbaatar, Mongolia.

Mönkhchimeg, Davaasharav. 2018. "Mongolians Protest against Corruption as Temperature Plunges." *Reuters* (online newspaper). https://www.reuters.com/article/us-mongolia-politics/mongolians-protest-against-corruption-as-temperature-plunges-idUSKCN1OQ0RG. Accessed March 15, 2021.

Moore, Sally F., and Barbara Meyerhoff. 1977. *Secular Ritual*. Assen, Netherlands: Van Gorcum.

Munkh-Erdene, Lhamsuren. 2012. "Mongolia's Post-Socialist Transition: A Great Neoliberal Transformation." In *Mongolians after Socialism: Politics, Economy, Religion*, edited by Bruce M. Knauft and Richard Taupier, 61–66. Ulaanbaatar, Mongolia: Admon Publishing.

Namuun, A. 2019. "'Gifts of the Politicians' Exhibition Opens." *Ikon.mn* (online newspaper). May 14. In Mongolian. https://ikon.mn/n/1kob?fbclid=IwAR1P1KaqfaCsaDokA5QbUfGd kRJsge1TZ_ywyw5-o6YCQuUxHhGKqzchH2Q. Accessed November 5, 2021.

Naughton, Tracey, and Ondine Ullman. 2008. "Blue Sky Mining: Community and Mining in Omnogovi Aimag, Mongolia." Scoping Report. Ulaanbaatar, Mongolia: Pact Mongolia.

Nima, Dolgoryn. 2009. *The Life and Work of Pagamdulam, the Wife of Great Poet Natsagdorj*. Ulaanbaatar, Mongolia: Bembi San, LLC.

Nordby, Judith. 1988. "The Mongolian People's Republic, 1924–1928, and the Right Deviation." PhD diss., University of Leeds, Department of Chinese Studies.

Nugent, David, and Joan Vincent, eds. 2009. *A Companion to the Anthropology of Politics*. Oxford, UK, and Cambridge, MA: Blackwell Reference Online Collection. https://onlinelibrary.wiley.com/doi/book/10.1002/9780470693681.

Obeid, Michelle. 2011. "The 'Trials and Errors' of Politics: Municipal Elections at the Lebanese Border." *PoLAR: Political and Legal Anthropology Review* 34 (2): 251–67.

Odontuya, Turmunkh. 2016. "On Encouraging Mothers of Multiple Children through the Order of the Mother Glorious in Mongolia." In *Rethinking Representations of Asian Women*, edited by N. Igichi, 35–49. New York: Palgrave Macmillan.

Oleinik, Anton. 2012. "Institutional Exclusion as a Destabilizing Factor: The Mass Unrest of 1 July 2008 in Mongolia." *Central Asian Survey* 31, no. 2: 153–74. https://doi.org/10.1080/026 34937.2012.671994. Accessed March 12, 2021.

Ong, Aihwa. 2006. *Neoliberalism as Exception: Mutations in Citizenship and Sovereignty: Mutations in Citizenship and Sovereignty.* Durham, NC: Duke University Press.

Ong, Aihwa, and Stephen J. Collier, eds. 2004. *Global Assemblages: Technology, Politics, and Ethics as Anthropological Problems.* Malden, MA: Wiley-Blackwell.

Ong, Aihwa, and Michael G. Peletz, eds. 1995. *Bewitching Women, Pious Men: Gender and Body Politics in Southeast Asia.* Berkeley: University of California Press.

Ortner, Sherry B. 1974. "Is Female to Male as Nature Is to Culture?" In *Woman, Culture and Society,* edited by M. Rosaldo and L. Lamphere, 67–88. Stanford, CA: Stanford University Press.

———. 2001. "Specifying Agency: The Comaroffs and Their Critics." *Interventions* 3 (1): 76–84.

———. 2005. "Subjectivity and Cultural Critique." *Anthropological Theory* 5 (1): 31–52.

———. 2006. "Power and Projects: Reflections on Agency." In *Anthropology and Social Theory: Culture, Power, and the Acting Subject,* edited by Sherry Ortner, 129–53. Durham, NC: Duke University Press.

Oushakine, Serguei. 2004. "The Flexible and the Pliant: Disturbed Organisms of Soviet Modernity." *Cultural Anthropology* 19 (3): 392–428.

Oyungerel, Tsedevdamba. 2007a. *Notes on my Study in America.* Ulaanbaatar, Mongolia: Interpress.

———. 2007b. *Nomadic Dialogues.* Ulaanbaatar, Mongolia: Admon Publishing.

———. 2008. *The Green-Eyed Lama.* Ulaanbaatar, Mongolia: Admon Publishing.

Oyuntuya, Sumyagiin. 2013a. "Political Financing: Studies from 2008–2013." Powerpoint presentation. The Voter Education Center, Ulaanbaatar Mongolia. Personal communication with the author.

———. 2013b. "Women's Participation in Politics: Experiences and Lessons Gained." Powerpoint presentation. The Voter Education Center, Ulaanbaatar Mongolia. Personal communication with the author.

———. 2013c. "Some Issues on the Management of Electoral Financing: Mongolia." Report. The Voter Education Center, Ulaanbaatar, Mongolia. Personal communication with the author.

Paley, Julia. 2002. "Toward an Anthropology of Democracy." *Annual Review of Anthropology* 31: 469–96.

———. 2008. *Democracy: Anthropological Approaches.* Santa Fe, NM: SAR Press.

Parliament Archive. 2008. "2007 Fall Plenary Session Minutes." January 10, 2008, 10:30 a.m. Parliament Building, Parliament Library, Archive collections. Ulaanbaatar, Mongolia.

Paxson, Heather. 2004. *Making Modern Mothers: Ethics and Family Planning in Urban Greece.* Berkeley: University of California Press.

Pedersen, Morten A. 2011. *Not Quite Shamans: Spirit Worlds and Political Lives in Northern Mongolia.* Ithaca, NY: Cornell University Press.

Perlez, Jane. 2012. "From Mongolia, Clinton Takes a Jab at China." *New York Times,* July 9. http://www.nytimes.com/2012/07/10/world/asia/in-mongolia-clinton-offersmessage-to-china.html?_r=0.

Phillips, Sarah D. 2014. "The Women's Squad in Ukraine's Protests: Feminism, Nationalism, and Militarism on the Maidan." *American Ethnologist* 41:414–26.

Piliavsky, Anastasia, ed. 2014. *Patronage as Politics in South Asia.* Cambridge: Cambridge University Press.

Plueckhahn, Rebekah. 2020. *Shaping Urban Futures in Mongolia: Ulaanbaatar, Dynamic Ownership and Economic Flux.* London. University College London.

Prashad, Vijay. 2007. *The Darker Nations: A People's History of the Third World*. New York: The New Press.

Radchenko, Sergey, and Mendee Jargalsaikhan. 2017. "Mongolia in the 2016–17 Electoral Cycle: The Blessings of Patronage." *Asian Survey* 57, no. 6 (December 1): 1032–57. https://doi.org /10.1525/as.2017.57.6.1032.

Results of Parliamentary Elections in Mongolia. 2017. In the website of the General Election Commission of Mongolia, https://www.gec.gov.mn/. Accessed March 15, 2021.

Reuschemeyer, Marilyn, and Sharon L. Wolchik. 2009. *Women in Power in Post Communist Parliaments*. Bloomington, IN: Indiana University Press.

Ries, Nancy. 1997. *Russian Talk: Culture and Conversation during Perestroika*. Ithaca, NY: Cornell University Press.

Riles, Annelise. 2000. *The Network Inside Out*. Ann Arbor, MI: University of Michigan Press.

Rivkin-Fish, Michele. 2009. "Tracing Landscapes of the Past in Class Subjectivity: Practices of Memory and Distinction in Marketizing Russia." *American Ethnologist* 36 (1): 79–95.

Robinson, Bernadette, and A. Solongo. 2000. "The Gender Dimension of Economic Transition in Mongolia." In *The Mongolian Economy: A Manual of Applied Economics for a Country in Transition*, edited by F. Nixson, B. Suvd, P. Luvsandorj, and B. Walters, 231–55. Cheltenham, UK: Edward Elgar Publishing.

Rose, Nikolas. 1999. *Powers of Freedom: Reframing Political Thought*. Cambridge: Cambridge University Press.

Rossabi, Morris. 2005. *Modern Mongolia: From Khans to Commissars to Capitalists*. Berkeley: University of California Press.

Rupen, Robert A. 1956. "Cyben Žamcaranovič Žamcarano (1880?–1940)." *Harvard Journal of Asiatic Studies* 19 (June): 126–45.

———. 1979. *How Mongolia Is Really Ruled: A Political History of the Mongolian People's Republic, 1900–1978*. Stanford, CA: Hoover Institution Press.

Sablin, Ivan, Jargal Badagarov, and Irina Sodnomova. 2021. "Khural Democracy: Imperial Transformations and the Making of the First Mongolian Constitution, 1911–1924." In *Socialist and Post-Socialist Mongolia Nation, Identity, and Culture*, edited by Simon Wickhamsmith and Phillip P. Marzluf, chap. 2, 12–42. New York: Routledge.

Sabloff, Paula. 2013. *Does Everyone Want Democracy? Insights from Mongolia*. Walnut Creek, CA: Left Coast Press.

Sarantuya, Bjambaagijn. 2012. *Sorhugtani*. Ulaanbaatar, Mongolia: Admon.

Saruul-Erdene, Myagmariin. 2000. "An Internal Affairs' Chairman's Attempt to Connect with the USA or the Image of Khayankhirvaa Namjiliin." The Best Columnists of Mongolia (website), April 6, 2000. http://www.baabar.mn. April 6. Accessed March 27, 2021.

Schmillen, Achim, and Nina Weimann-Sandig. 2018. "Perceptions of Precariousness: A Qualitative Study of Constraints Underlying Gender Disparities in Mongolia's Labor Market." Washington: World Bank Group. A Study Report. https://openknowledge.worldbank.org/bitstream /handle/10986/29539/124451.pdf?sequence=4&isAllowed=y. Accessed November 7, 2021.

Schwenkel, Christina, and Ann Marie Leshkowich. 2012. "Guest Editors' Introduction: How Is Neoliberalism Good to Think Vietnam? How Is Vietnam Good to Think Neoliberalism?" *Positions: Asia Critique* 20 (2): 379–401.

Scott, Joan W. 2009. "Finding Critical History." In *Becoming Historians*, edited by James Banner and John Gillis, 26–53. Chicago: University of Chicago Press.

———. 2019. *Sex and Secularism*. Princeton, NJ: Princeton University Press.

———. 2018. "The Persistence of Gender Inequality: How Politics Construct Gender, and Gender Constructs Politics." *The Institute Letter* (Fall 2018): 8–10. Institute for Advanced Study. https://www.ias.edu/ideas/scott-gender-inequality. Accessed November 7, 2021.

———. 1981. "Politics and Professionalism: Women Historians in the 1980s." *Women's Studies Quarterly* 9 (3): 23–32.

———. 1991. "The Evidence of Experience." *Critical Inquiry* 17 (4): 773–97.

———. 1996. "Academic Freedom as an Ethical Practice." In *The Future of Academic Freedom*, edited by Louis Menand, 163–87. Chicago: University of Chicago Press.

Seale-Collazo, James. 2012. "Charisma, Liminality, and Freedom: Toward a Theory of the Everyday Extraordinary." *Anthropology of Consciousness* 23:175–91. https://doi.org/10.1111/j.1556 -3537.2012.01060.x. Accessed March 21, 2021.

Sengupta, Somini. 2015. "Most Nations Miss a Goal for Women in Leadership." *New York Times*, August 31. http://www.nytimes.com/2015/09/01/world/most-nations-miss-a-goal-for-women -in-leadership.html.

Shalin, Dmitri. 2012. "Intellectual Culture: The End of Russian Intelligentsia." http://digitalschol arship.unlv.edu/cgi/viewcontent.cgi?article=1005&context=russian_culture.

Shinkarev, L. 2006. *Tsedenbal and His Time: The Chronicles* [In Mongolian: Tsedenbal, Tuunii Tsag Uye: Barimtat Ögüülemj]. 2 vols. Vol. 2: 213–26. Ulaanbaatar, Mongolia: Monsudar.

Shirendev, Bazarin. 1969. *The History of Mongolian People's Republic*. Ulaanbaatar, Mongolia: State Publishing House.

Shlapentokh, Vladimir. 2014. *Soviet Intellectuals and Political Power: The Post-Stalin Era*. Princeton, NJ: Princeton University Press.

Shuudertsetseg, B. Chanrav. 2011. *Legendary Queen Anu*. Ulaanbaatar, Mongolia: Admon.

Siilegmaa, Tserenpiliin. 2004. *Siilegmaa of the Women's Committee*. Ulaanbaatar, Mongolia: Sogoo Khuur Publishing LLC.

Simon, Scott. 2010. "Negotiating Power: Elections and the Constitution of Indigenous Taiwan." *American Ethnologist* 37:726–40.

Smith, Marissa. 2020. "Power of the People's Parties and a Post-Soviet Parliament: Regional Infrastructural, Economic, and Ethnic Networks of Power in Contemporary Mongolia." Special Issue: Parliamentary Formations and Diversities in (Post-)Imperial Eurasia, edited by Ivan Sablin. *Journal of Eurasian Studies* 11(1–2): 1–10. https://doi.org/10.1177/1879366520916743.

———. 2018. "Mungu Idekh" [Eating Money]. In *Global Informality Project* (online encyclopedia). https://www.in-formality.com/wiki/index.php?title=Mungu_idekh_(Mongolia). Accessed November 5, 2021.

Sneath, David. 2006. "Transacting and Enacting: Corruption, Obligation and the Use of Monies in Mongolia." *Ethnos* 71 (no. 1): 89–112. https://doi.org/10.1080/00141840600603228.

———. 2010. "Political Mobilization and the Construction of Collective Identity in Mongolia." *Central Asian Survey* 29 (3): 251–67.

———. 2018. *Mongolia Remade: Post-socialist National Culture, Political Economy, and Cosmopolitics*. Amsterdam: Amsterdam University Press.

Sperling, Valerie. 1999. *Organizing Women in Contemporary Russia: Engendering Transition*. Cambridge: Cambridge University Press.

Spyer, Patricia, and Mary Margaret Steedly. 2013. "Introduction: Images That Move." In *Images That Move*, edited by Patricia Spyer and Mary Steedly, 3–41. Santa Fe, NM: SAR Press.

Stack, Carol. 1983. *All Our Kin*. New York: Basic Books.

Stacey, Judith. 1983. *Patriarch and Socialist Revolution in China.* Berkeley: University of California Press.

Steedly, Mary Margaret. 2000. "Modernity and the Memory Artist: The Work of Imagination in Highland Sumatra, 1947–1995." *Comparative Studies in Society and History* 42 (4): 811–46.

Stoler, Ann. 2009. *Along the Archival Grain: Epistemic Anxieties and Colonial Common Sense.* Princeton, NJ: Princeton University Press.

Strassler, Karen. 2020. *Demanding Images: Democracy, Mediation, and the Image-Event in Indonesia.* Durham, NC: Duke University Press.

Suren, N. 2008. "The Election Promises or Two Sides of a Coin." In *Mongolyn Ünen* [Mongolian Truth]. April 25, no. 080 (21054).

Tan, Netina. 2016. "Gender Reforms, Quotas and Women's Political Representation in Taiwan, South Korea, and Singapore." *Pacific Affairs* 89 (2): 84.

Tsenddoo, Byambajavyn. 2008. "Mongol Wife: Know Your Husband before Knowing the State" / "Mongol Gergii: Toroo Medie Gevel Eree Medeh." In *Olloo.mn.* http://archive.olloo.mn/News/91110.html. Accessed April 12, 2015.

Tsedengiin, Tsetsegjargal, Zhigzhidiin Boldbaatar, and D. Tumen. 2009. *Mongolyn emegteichuud XX zuund: Khuvisal, oorchlolt* [Mongolian Women in the Twentieth Century: Transformation and Changes]. Ulaanbaatar, Mongolia: Soembo Printing.

Tsogtgerel, B. 2008. "The Laments of Stolen Billboards." *Century News* [Zuunii Medee], June 20.

Tsolmon, Davaagyn. 1995. "An Historical Outline of Mongol-American Relations and American Studies in Mongolia." *American Studies International* 33, no. 2: 71–74. http://www.jstor.org/stable/41279346.

Tuya, Nyamosor. 2005. "Mongolia in 2004: Testing Politics and Economics." *Asian Survey* 45, no. 1: 67–70.

———. 2012. "What Is at Stake in Mongolia's Election." Brookings Institution. June 26. https://www.brookings.edu/opinions/what-is-at-stake-in-mongolias-election/.

Undarya, Tumursukh. 2009. "Arrested Democratization and Glimpses of Hope: Mongolia's Political Culture as Seen through the 2008 and 2009 Elections." In *Election and Democracy: Reflections on the Asian Experiences*, edited by the Korea Democracy Foundation, 137–65. Seoul: Korea Democracy Foundation.

———. 2018. "Interrogating Women's Activism in the Age of Neoliberal Democratization in Mongolia." PhD diss. Auckland University of Technology, Auckland, New Zealand.

United Nations. 1966. "1965 Seminar on the Participation of Women in Public Sphere." Ulan Bator, Mongolia, and United Nations, New York.

———. 1980. "Report of the World Conference of the United Nations Decade for Women: Equality, Development and Peace," Copenhagen, July 14–30. https://undocs.org/en/A/CONF.94/35. Accessed November 2, 2021.

———. 1986. "Report of the World Conference to Review and Appraise the Achievements of the United Nations Decade for Women: Equality, Development and Peace," Nairobi, July 15–26, 1985. https://www.un.org/en/conferences/women/nairobi1985. Accessed November 2, 2021.

———. 1996. "Report of the Fourth World Conference on Women," Beijing, September 4–15, 1995. https://www.un.org/womenwatch/daw/beijing/fwcwn.html. Accessed November 2, 2021.

———. 2020. "Report of the Commission on the Status of Women: Report on the Sixty Fourth Session." Economic and Social Council, United Nations. https://undocs.org/en/E/CN.6/2020/L.1. Accessed November 2, 2021.

Uranguya, Zhamsrangiin, and Batsukhiin Bayarsaihan, eds. 2004. *Jinhene dagaj yavah huuli' durem 1913–1918: Eh bichgiin sudalgaa* [The Essential Laws and Regulations to Follow]. Ulaanbaatar, Mongolia: Interpress.

Uyanga, Gantömöriin. 2017. "About MANAN." In Toim Medee mn. http://toimmedee.mn/index .php?view=article&type=item&val=5537&fbclid=IwARowVW1irHrUP1DolX8wNeeJb-S6 RfBaqtt3NQnQ6hSgnRrA_AKohIoVPeo. Accessed March 14, 2021.

Valdur, Mari. 2020. "Life and Abortion: The Post-Biopolitics of Reproductive Health in Ulaanbaatar, Mongolia." PhD diss. University of Helsinki, Finland.

Veblen, Thorstein. 2007. *The Theory of the Leisure Class.* Oxford: Oxford University Press.

Verdery, Katherine. 1991. *National Ideology under Socialism: Identity and Cultural Politics in Ceasescu's Romania.* Berkeley: University of California Press.

———. 1996. *What Was Socialism, and What Comes Next?* Princeton, NJ: Princeton University Press.

Vidart-Delgado, Maria L. 2017. "Cyborg Political Machines: Political Brokering and Modern Political Campaigning in Colombia." *Hau: Journal of Ethnographic Theory* 7 (2): 255–77. http:// dx.doi.org/10.14318/hau7.2.027.

Waters, Hedwig Amelia. 2016. "Erotic Capital as Societal Elevator: Pursuing Feminine Attractiveness in the Contemporary Mongolian Global(ising) Economy." *Sociologus* 66, no. 1 (2016): 25–51. http://www.jstor.org/stable/24755104.

Warner, Michael. 1992. "The Mass Public and the Mass Subject." In *Habermas and the Public Sphere,* edited by Craig Calhoun, 388. Cambridge, MA: MIT Press.

Weatherford, Jack. 2011. *The Secret History of the Mongol Queens: How the Daughters of Genghis Khan Rescued His Empire.* New York: Crown.

Werner, Cynthia. 2002. "Gifts, Bribes and Development in Post-Soviet Kazakhstan." In *Economic Development: An Anthropological Approach,* edited by Jeffrey Cohen and Norbert Dannhaeuser, 183–208. Walnut Creek, CA: Altamira.

Weston, Kath. 2002. *Gender in Real Time: Power and Transience in a Visual Age.* New York: Routledge.

Wickhamsmith, Simon. 2020. *Literature and Politics in Mongolia (1921–1948).* Amsterdam: Amsterdam University Press.

Wolf, Margery. 1960. *The House of Lim: A Study of a Chinese Farm Family.* Englewood Cliffs, NJ: Pearson.

Wood, Elizabeth. 1997. *The Baba and the Comrade: Gender and Politics in Revolutionary Russia.* Bloomington: Indiana University Press.

Woolf, Virginia. 2019. *A Room of One's Own.* London: Lector House. First published 1929.

Yang, Mayfair. 2018. "Millenarianism in the Soviet Union and Maoist China." In Immanent Frame: Secularism, Religion, and the Public Sphere (blog). November 23. https://tif.ssrc.org/2018 /11/23/millenarianism-in-the-soviet-union-and-maoist-china/ Accessed March 15, 2021.

Yurchak, Alexei. 2007. *Everything Was Forever until It Was No More.* Princeton, NJ: Princeton University Press.

———. 2015. "Bodies of Lenin: The Hidden Science of Communist Sovereignty." *Representations* 129 (Winter 2015): 116–57.

Zanaa, Jurmed. 2005. "The Concepts of Gender Equality and Their Application in Human Development." PhD diss., Mongolian National University, Ulaanbaatar, Mongolia.

Zubok, Vladislav. 2019. "Intelligentsia as a Liberal Concept in Soviet History, 1945–1991." In *Dimensions and Challenges of Russian Liberalism,* edited by R. Cucciolla, 45–62. Cham: Springer. https://doi.org/10.1007/978-3-030-05784-8_4.

Index